Schriften zum Religionsrecht

Edited by

Vol. 4

Christian Walter / Antje von Ungern-Sternberg (eds.)

Transformation of Church and State Relations in Great Britain and Germany

Nomos

Die Deutsche Nationalbibliothek lists this publication in the Deutsche Nationalbibliografie; detailed bibliographic data is available in the Internet at http://dnb.d-nb.de.

ISBN 978-3-8329-7862-4

1. Edition 2013

Transformation of Church and State Relations in Great Britain and Germany – Introduction

Christian Walter and *Antje von Ungern-Sternberg*

Western societies face the challenge of religious diversity. Religion has not disappeared from the public sphere as the secularisation thesis predicted. Instead, the immigration of non-Christian religions to Europe, in particular, but also the growing religious diversification within Christian denominations and an increasing number of atheists, agnostics and unconcerned change the religious setup of Western societies and raise the question whether traditional church and state relations will remain unaffected. These relations have developed within Christian societies and legal orders based on Christian culture. Thus, even if traditional church and state relations cover a variety of different models ranging from strict separation to cooperation or establishment, all are influenced by a Christian perspective and by Christian forms of organisation. Are these church and state relations suitable for non-Christian communities? In this regard, namely Muslim immigrants introduce previously unknown forms of organisations and religious practices into Western societies which might challenge the traditional forms of church and state relations.

How do different legal orders respond to the challenge of religious diversification? In Germany, for instance, many of the ensuing questions are dealt with by the right to freedom of religion and the principle of non-discrimination. Which answer fits for an established church like the Church of England? Religious tolerance possesses a well-established tradition in Great Britain; but how can a state with an established church remain strictly neutral in questions of religion? The Scandinavian countries which look back at a similar tradition of state churches and which, unlike Great Britain, have at least partly begun a process of disestablishment might be able to add answers of their own to these questions. Furthermore, the analysis of church and state relations in a narrow institutional sense does not exhaust the topic. In fact, this institutional perspective must be complemented by an individual perspective of the religious adherent who is confronted with (possibly conflicting) demands of his or her religious community and those of the secular legal order. Besides, conflicts may equally arise between the adherent and his or her religious community. Is freedom of religion, in this context, the principal and most apt legal instrument for reconciling conflicting interests or do other legal or non-legal approaches play a role, too?

The articles in this book try to respond to the above-mentioned questions by comparing the transformation of church and state relations in Great Britain and Germany. Both countries have developed special forms of cooperation with the Christian churches and are now confronted with religious diversification in general and growing Muslim and other immigrant minorities in particular. Furthermore, both states are obliged to respect legal requirements regarding freedom of religion, non-discrimination and religious neutrality. Some of those requirements constitute a common European standard based on the European Convention on Human Rights or European Union Law; others flow from national law and may vary accordingly. The comparative analysis of church and state relations presented in this volume, intends to reveal different legal instruments which accommodate religious diversity and to define the limits of particular forms of cooperation.

At the outset, two articles look at the experience that can be gathered from the historical development in Great Britain and in Scandinavia. *Augur Pearce* (Cardiff) explains, how the development of church and state Relations in England has been dominated by two questions. The first concerns the treatment of alternative religions – should be repressed, tolerated or valued – and was answered by a gradual progression from imposed uniformity to politically-prized diversity. The second concerns the explanation of public religion. Current answers still differ and refer either to the identity of church and society or to recognition and privilege. The Scandinavian experience is reflected by *Lars Friedner* (Uppsala) who shows that this region provides three models for legal systems of establishment: an earnest attempt at disestablishment (Sweden), a reform which nevertheless leaves intact the formal status of an established church (Norway), and the status quo ante (Denmark).

The following articles examine the legal protection of individuals in religious and secular courts. *Mark Hill* (Cardiff) and *Michael Germann* (Halle-Wittenberg) deal with legal protection in ecclesiastical and other religious courts. *Mark Hill* presents the British system which comprises ecclesiastical courts as well as Islamic (Shariah) Councils as a model which accommodates religious diversity and which also takes account of religious pluralism. *Michael Germann* shows that the German religious courts are founded on the constitutional guarantee of religious autonomy or self-determination of religious communities, but also points out that this form of religious autonomy might conflict with the right of an individual member of a religious community whose access to a secular court is denied.

The question of religious disputes in state courts is dealt with in more detail by *Lucy Vickers* (Oxford) and *Hinnerk Wißmann* (Bayreuth). Both articles focus on employment law, i.e. an area of law which clearly illustrates how the interests of a religious community and one of its members and employees might get into conflict, for example because the beliefs held or the life lead by the individual does no longer conform to the community's teachings. *Lucy Vickers* proposes to accommodate both interests by applying the flexible principle of proportionality. But she also stresses that religious freedom does not include the right to a job, which implies resolving some disputes in favour of the community's religious integrity. According to *Hinnerk Wißmann,* the German solution differs from the British situation by its material (rather than procedural) approach and by its larger protection of the religious community to the disadvantage of the individual employee. He therefore suggests that zones of jurisdictional immunity should be abolished and that religious communities should have to justify where, why, and to what extent religion requires special protection or support.

This national perspective is complemented by an analysis of international guarantees of the European Convention on Human Rights in the area of religious disputes provided by *Ian Leigh* (Durham) and *Katharina Pabel* (Linz). *Ian Leigh* shows how the growing collective dimension of religious liberty, gradually recognised by the European Court of Human Rights, increases the potential for conflict between it and individual human rights. He approves of the more recent balancing approach of the ECHR which allows taking into account the individual's right as well as Church autonomy. *Katharina Pabel* who also looks at the new case law by the European Court of Human Rights in *Obst*, *Schüth* and *Siebenhaar* is more critical of the Court's balancing exercise. She argues that the Court seems to weigh just one part of the two-part relationship, that is to say the individual applicant – thereby disregarding church autonomy but also the due reasoning of four national courts, including the constitutional court.

The question of Church autonomy and establishment in England is treated by *Peter Edge* (Oxford). He explains the current legal implications of establishment, i.e. formal involvement of the Church of England with key organs of the state which, however, should not be overstated, and State involvement in Church of England doctrine which has markedly declined. According to *Edge*, asymmetrical establishment may be possible in future, i.e. a one-sided state involvement in doctrinal disputes within religious communities in order to mould them more closely into conformity with state values. One example for this is the UK counter-terrorism strategy which also relies on the use of soft power to promote a form of Islam compatible with State goals.

In a final section, four articles are dedicated to aspects of status and organisation concerning religious communities. *Peter Cumper* (Leicester) and *Antje von Ungern-Sternberg* (Munich) analyse how religious communities participate in public life. *Peter Cumper*, after describing the privileges accorded to religious communities in Great Britain in the area of education, raises the question, whether they are still justified in an increasingly secular setting. He claims, furthermore, that there is no automatic correlation between faith and public morality and that philosophic convictions (environmentalism, pacifists, human rights activism) are worthy and legally entitled to enjoy similar privileges. *Antje von Ungern-Sternberg* compares the British and the German model of state-religion relations in schools and universities. She argues that both models have to correspond to the principle of non-discrimination and to neutrality which does not exclude, however, that pragmatic solutions accommodate the special needs of Muslim communities.

Julian Rivers (Bristol) and *Gernot Sydow* (Limburg/Freiburg) take a closer look at organisational questions of religious communities. *Julian Rivers* demonstrates that the British legal system solves many religious issues on a very specific basis as opposed to the German system which often links them to the (public) status of the religious community – a notion unknown in Great Britain. Furthermore, he draws our attention to a gain in formal recognition and collaboration between organized religions and the state on the one hand and a loss of autonomy on the part of organized religions on the other hand. The German model of a public legal status bundling several rights ("Körperschaft des öffentlichen Rechts") and its implications for the Muslim communities are highlighted by *Gernot Sydow*. He argues that Islamic communities will have to organise themselves according to the model of the Christian churches in order to obtain the status of a public religious community which, according to his analysis, might be problematic with regard to religious freedom.

What conclusions can be drawn from the book's comparative exercise? First of all, religious establishment, at least in western legal systems like Great Britain or Scandinavia, while still bearing witness to history and culture, seems to lose many practical implications and, in any event, is no obstacle to the accommodation of religious minorities. Second, one can perceive two overall tendencies in Great Britain and Germany alike: First, the increasing religious diversity is accommodated by the acknowledgement of rights and privileges, but also by various forms of cooperation. Second, the legal orders attempt to align, to a certain degree, secular and religious values by means of hard law, i.e. to impose certain minimum standards upon religious organisations, for example, in employment law, and by means of soft incentives aimed at the integration of Muslim communities, for example. Both developments seem to be a logical consequence of the process of religious diversification. Establishing exclusive relations with a religious community and granting a large degree of religious autonomy presuppose, after all, that state and church affiliation are more or less congruent and that the values embodied in both orders are more or less homogenous. Third, it is interesting to see that the relevant minimum requirements imposed upon religious communities and those to be respected by the state in favour of religious communities and adherents are based not only in national law, but increasingly on the European Convention and on European Union Law. Finally, some of the articles have also pointed at factual and legal impediments to religious accommodation. It is the lawyers' task to highlight these problems and to try to find feasible solutions.

The topics of this volume were presented and discussed at a conference held at the Westfälische Wilhelms University, Münster (Germany), on 1st – 2nd July 2010. We would like to express our gratitude to the Cluster of Excellence »Religion and Politics« of the University of Münster which provided the necessary financial and organisational means to host this conference. Special thanks also go to *Barbara Rox* (Münster) and the staff of the Chair of Public Law including International and European Law, Münster, for their help in organising the conference. We are very grateful that *Markus Vordermayer* as well as *Philip Nedelcu, Josef Schmid* and *Anna Perin* (München) assisted in preparing this edited volume.

München, October 2012

Christian Walter

Antje von Ungern-Sternberg

Contents

A. Historical Development

I. THE DEVELOPMENT OF CHURCH-STATE RELATIONS IN ENGLAND – Augur Pearce

1. Introduction

(a) Ecclesial state or established church?

Throughout the history of English law runs the distinction between public (national, official, »established«) and private (alternative, voluntary) religion. Since rulers of the Anglo-Saxon kingdoms accepted the Christian message brought by missionaries from Iona and Rome, England[1] has never lacked an »official« religion whose exponents play a role in government, whose practice is directly or indirectly facilitated by the proceeds of public levies, and whose core tenets the nation as a whole is declared to profess. But the private religion of the English has always been diverse – much more so, of course, since unbelief and non-Christian faiths have become significant demographic features – and the law has always faced the need to respond to this reality.

The English story has been dominated by two questions in particular. Is alternative religion to be repressed, tolerated or valued? And is the public religion to be explained in terms of identity with the society professing it, or merely recognition and privilege? The first question is easily answered: there has been a gradual progression from imposed uniformity to politically-prized diversity, with some controversy along the way. The second is more complex. There are strong views on both sides and legal phenomena not fully consistent with either analysis; yet the answer given to it will determine whether, in the context of the Church of England, one can meaningfully speak of »church-state relations« at all.

1 The focus of this paper is England in the strict sense, but the laws of England have extended to Wales since the passing of the Laws in Wales Act 1536; references to England therefore include Wales where the context permits. Since 1920, however, there has been very little structure of *public* religion in Wales, as Part VI will explain. This chapter is not concerned with Scots law, nor with any part of Ireland. In 1800 England was ecclesially united with Ireland, but this union was dissolved in 1870, leaving the United Kingdom united only for secular purposes, including the legal institutions serving private religion; although that understanding has arguably not been fully respected by either the Union's legislature or its highest court.

Today most commentators see the Church of England as a religious organisation distinct from a religiously-neutral »state«, having a finite membership and its own structures and rules which are capable of conflict with the »law of the land«; yet recognised and privileged by that law in a mutual relationship commonly described as »establishment«.[2] This view allows the English Church to benefit also, as »one church among many«, from the concessions made in recent centuries to organised alternative religion. Recent accounts commonly take this understanding as their starting-point.

But through most of its history since the Reformation, influential voices have explained and thought of the Church of England in a different way: namely, as a convenient label for the public ecclesiastical institutions of a Christian commonwealth or »ecclesial state« which knows only one law: »a compendious expression for the religious establishment of the realm considered in aggregate«.[3] This narrative will seek to do justice to that unfashionable but perfectly coherent view, although recognising that it was never universally held.

(b) The Brandenburg comparison

In the spirit of the Münster conference, the coverage here of the English position in each of the main post-Reformation periods will be followed by passages highlighting principal similarities and contrasts with the law of a representative German territory. Since the plethora of separately-governed German territories makes it impractical to compare them all, the focus will be on the Brandenburg March (or the wider unit to which this area belonged at the relevant time). Hence Part III will close by comparing England to Electoral Brandenburg; at the end of Part IV we shall consider the Brandenburg-Prussian monarchy in which the *Allgemeines Landrecht* of 1794 was enacted; the comparison in Part V will focus on the Prussian State under Friedrich Wilhelm III and his sons, including relevant Imperial legislation which applied in Prussia after 1870; and in Part VI a brief thought will be offered on the modern Germany of autonomous churches and fundamental rights to which Weimar Constitution and *Grundgesetz* both contribute.

2 The classic exposition of this view is that of Phillimore J. in *Marshall v. Graham* [1907] 2 KB 112, adopted by Lord Hope of Craighead in *Aston Cantlow (Parochial Church Council) v. Wallbank* [2004] 1 AC 546at para 61. The EComHR has described the Church of England as 'structurally a separate entity from the state', *Tyler v. United Kingdom* (1994) 77a DR 81.

3 *Town of Pawlet v. Clark* (1815) 13 U.S. (Cranch) 292, 325, Supreme Court of the United States.

2. The middle ages – 597-1532

A contribution to a comparative study of the law of religion in Britain and Germany need say little of the mediæval period, since conditions at the time in England and the Holy Roman Empire were very much the same. The public religion in both territories was a particular form of Christianity: Chalcedonian and episcopal but also »western«, acknowledging a leading role for the Bishop of Rome and a body of religious rules emanating most recently from papal decisions or councils under papal presidency. In German princely territories as in England, the clergy formed an estate of the realm, though this was more clearly expressed in German territorial Estates than in England, where only landholding senior clerics sat in parliament with the nobility, whilst the remainder focussed on more »spiritual« topics in separate convocations under the Archbishop of each province.[4] On both sides of the North Sea bishops and their representatives held court with a wide jurisdiction, and coercive sanctions were available to enforce rulings within their competence.[5] But the exact limits of that competence gave rise to continual tension. The continental Investiture Contest corresponded to the disputes between Henry II and Becket or between John and Langton, and the submission at Canossa found its echo at Runnymede. One important legacy to the future, as the English laity began to reassert itself, was the use of the »prerogative writs«, in particular *mandamus* and prohibition, as tools allowing the King's Bench to »patrol the boundaries« of the episcopal judges' remit.[6]

Alternative religion in the middle ages found little official sympathy. Jews were »in the nation but not of it«, tolerated for their financial expertise and services to the economy and *de facto* regulating their own community life, but largely ignored by the courts. Exposed to sporadic persecution, new restrictions eventually made life so impractical for England's Jews that they left the kingdom in a body at the close of the thirteenth century.[7] Dissent within Christianity was,

4 The inferior clergy withdrew from the House of Commons after it was agreed (c. 1340) that they would vote their taxes separately from laymen; this was thereafter done in the provincial assemblies which archbishops were already convoking. For a history of the convocations see Eric Kemp, *Counsel and Consent – Aspects of the Government of the Church as exemplified in the History of the English Provincial Synods*, London 1961.

5 The English ecclesiastical court hierarchy is said to date from a 1076 ordinance of William I; see Felix Makower, *Constitutional History and Constitution of the Church of England*, tr. 1895, Appendix 1.

6 S. A. de Smith, 'The Prerogative Writs' (1951) 11 CLJ 40, 48ff.

7 Aron Owen, 'United Kingdom Legislation concerning Jews', in *The Jewish Year Book*, 1999, records an edict of Edward I directing the Jews' banishment in that year; but the advice given to Lord Protector Oliver Cromwell in 1655 by Glyn CJ and Steel CB was that royal edicts of this nature did not create a lasting legal rule. See H.S.Q. Henriques, *The Jews and the English Law*, London 1908, 91.

if anything, even more hazardous: the episcopal courts punished heresy and schism, and the common law (augmented by statute between 1401 and 1558) allowed the Crown to burn heretics who proved obdurate or relapsed.[8]

3. Reformation to Revolution – 1532-1688

(a) Chronology of the Period

The Reformation of English religion took place in phases, and although it can also be studied in terms of popular religion or theological currents, its primary landmarks were legal ones, expounded and justified in one exceptionally influential ecclesiological work – Richard Hooker's *Lawes of Ecclesiasticall Politie.*

The constitutional framework for the Reformation was established by the battery of statutes passed in the middle years of Henry VIII's reign under the skilful management of Sir Thomas Cromwell, later Earl of Essex and the King's Vicegerent in Spirituals. These, together with some royal Injunctions and a programme of Visitation, addressed a few liturgical issues and ensured the availability of an English Bible translation[9]; but their chief importance was in how they addressed the authority question. Plenary authority in spiritual matters was – and properly always had been – located within the realm; it lay not with bishops and clergy, but with the whole community of the realm as represented in parliament; and the King enjoyed a very substantial ecclesiastical prerogative of his own.

Using the framework so defined, the regents for Edward VI, encouraged by the young King himself and with the co-operation of his father's appointee, Archbishop Thomas Cranmer, piloted through parliament two major revisions of the kingdom's official liturgy, the first and second Books of Common Prayer.[10] Themselves doctrinally weighty texts, these signalled a clear repudiation of many aspects of papal teaching. A new doctrinal statement in forty-two Articles also won the King's approval, but had achieved no practical legal effect by the time Edward's premature death ushered in the papalist reaction under his half-sister Mary I.

8 The statutory powers (particularly the 1401 statute *De haeretico comburendo*) were temporarily repealed in the reign of Edward VI but revived and liberally used under Mary I. The common law writ was used for the last time in 1612 and abolished by the Ecclesiastical Jurisdiction Act 1677.

9 Miles Coverdale's translation, the 'Great Bible', was required to be placed in parish churches by the second set of royal Injunctions (1538), anticipating its publication the following year.

10 Acts of Uniformity 1548 and 1551.

Mary too died childless, leaving it to Henry's remaining acknowledged offspring, Elizabeth I, to produce the religious settlement that would last until the Civil War (and in many respects to the present day). Though Mary's parliaments had repealed much of her father's and brother's legislation, most of Henry's was restored to force by the Act of Supremacy 1558, whilst a new Act of Uniformity[11] established a third version of the Edwardian Prayer Books. The question of alternative religion was also chiefly addressed in this reign. The Queen's reluctance to »make windows into men's souls«[12] left Englishmen freer to believe what they wished than they had been under the mediæval and Marian heresy jurisdiction, or would have been in Catholic countries under the Inquisition reorganised by Paul III in 1542; but there was little freedom to manifest that belief. Outward conformity, shown in attending official public worship and in refraining from alternative assemblies, was the order of the day. A revised set of doctrinal Articles was not, however, imposed on the lay population generally; merely upon the learned and preaching classes (through a system of subscription and assent by candidates for university matriculation or degrees, ordination or ecclesiastical preferment).

It was during Elizabeth's reign that Richard Hooker produced the eight volumes of his *Lawes*. Though a minister, not a lawyer, he enjoyed as Master of the Temple constant contact with the legal profession, whilst an uncongenial colleague gave him a clear insight into the Calvinist account of separate church government which he rejected as Crown and Parliament had done. The eighth volume, in particular, elaborated on the nature of the English Church, and on the interaction of monarch, parliament and clergy convocations in its governance. Though wholly consistent with the statutory framework of the 1530s, Book VIII postulated a greater role for parliament than the current Queen (who preferred to steer the kingdom's religious life through bishops of her choosing) would have favoured. It therefore appeared posthumously in 1648, in time to describe to good effect the public religious edifice of the »long eighteenth century«.[13]

After the English throne passed to the Scots royal House in 1603, the first Stuart monarchs interpreted the Elizabethan settlement in their own way. James I being too clever to provoke conflict on religious issues, the main developments

11 Act of Uniformity 1558.

12 A phrase attributed to her by Sir Francis Bacon; Peter Brimacombe, *All the Queen's Men – the World of Elizabeth I*, Stroud 2000.

13 The leading edition of Hooker's works is the Folger Library Edition, published 1977-93. Hooker began publication in 1593, but references here are all to Booke VIII of the *Lawes*, appearing posthumously in 1648. Page references are to the Folger edition of Book VIII. A leading work on Hooker himself is Robert Faulkner, *Richard Hooker and the Politics of a Christian England*, Berkeley CA 1982.

of his reign were publication of a further Bible translation[14] and a sharpening of sanctions against papal Catholicism. However the tension brewing since Elizabeth's reign – the question whether the King had a wider lawmaking power in spiritual matters than he enjoyed in other fields, and in particular whether he could impart such power to the episcopate or regulate religious practice through it – came to a head in the following reign, and was among the key issues over which Charles I fought – and lost – a Civil War against Parliament and its forces. Another interlude followed, comprising nine years during which the King was effectively unable to govern and another eleven after his death, spent by Charles II in exile whilst first the House of Commons, and later the Cromwell family, exercised *de facto* rule.

The exiled monarch's return brought recognition that no English government can be constitutional without the King[15], and generally speaking a return to the Elizabethan *status quo*; but also a much greater readiness than Elizabeth's legislators or judges had shown to defend parliament's rights in ecclesiastical lawmaking. The fourth and final revision of the Book of Common Prayer was approved in this period, imposing a form of assent that drove nearly 2000 ministers with their followings from official to alternative religion[16]; and fresh limits were set to the civil and political rights of religious dissenters, both papalist and protestant. But royal attempts to extend religious freedom further than parliament could accept were among the factors behind the »Glorious Revolution«: the invitation to James II's sister Mary and her husband William to enter England, upon which King James left the country and was held to have abandoned the throne.

(b) The Legislation of the 1530s

England's renunciation of papal obedience and the submission of the English clergy to the Crown effectively reversed the Johannine defeat at Runnymede. The promise of Magna Carta[17], *ecclesia anglicana libera sit*, was open to many interpretations; but if (as is likely) it meant that the bishops would be left to regu-

14 The 'Authorised' or 'King James' Version was completed in 1611 and replaced the 'Bishops' Bible', fruit of an Elizabethan project which had itself replaced the Great Bible in parish churches.

15 A range of judicial decisions (e.g. 5 St Tr 1025, per Bridgeman CJ) after the restoration recognised that ordinances made by the House of Commons, with or without the Lords, were no law lacking the King's assent.

16 Act of Uniformity 1662; this Act also made absolute the requirement of holy orders for ecclesiastical preferment or presidency at the Lord's Supper.

17 Issued in 1215 and regularly renewed, the edition now appearing on the statute book is Edward I's re-grant of 1297.

late without royal intervention all the spheres they considered as theirs, then it was impliedly repealed by the Acts of 1532-35.

These, along with the Act of Supremacy 1558 which restored most of them after the Marian interlude, were and are in every sense of the word constitutional statutes. They declared Christianity the common national faith.[18] They clarified the role of the kingdom's executive government in the religious field[19] and they relegated the purely clerical convocations to advisory and self-regulatory sidelines.[20] Episcopal courts were declared to operate »within the King's jurisdiction and authority«[21] and the laws governing Englishmen in both religious and other matters were identified as either »made within the realm« or adopted by the English, with royal sanction, »at their free liberty«.[22] The most important principle of all was not stated but implied in the passage of these Acts. The fact that enactments of the King in Parliament were successfully used to change the face of English religion placed the capstone on the developing doctrine of parliamentary legislative supremacy. The assembly representing the realm would henceforth be sovereign over the realm's spiritual affairs.

The breach with Rome and the emancipation of the laity were retrospective. Frequent contemporary references to papal and clerical »usurpation« of the King's prerogative[23] showed that the Parliament of the 1530s took the view that it was restoring what had *always* been the true constitutional position, though the middle ages had not perceived it. The legal orthodoxy of later years would be that the religious edifice already established in England had existed since well

18 Ecclesiastical Licences Act 1533 s.13.

19 Ecclesiastical Licences Act 1533, preamble (as to the dispensing power); Acts of Supremacy 1535 and 1558.

20 Submission of the Clergy Act 1533.

21 Ecclesiastical Appeals Act 1532, s.1 (extended to all ecclesiastical causes by Submission of the Clergy Act 1533 s.4).

22 See the appeal to 'divers sundry old authentic histories and chronicles' in Ecclesiastical Appeals Act 1532, preamble; the 'divers constitutions, ordinances and canons ... which *heretofore* have been enacted, and be thought ... much prejudicial to the King's prerogative royal' (Submission of the Clergy Act 1533) and the statement in Ecclesiastical Licences Act 1533, preamble, that 'your Grace's realm *has been* and is' (free from subjection to foreign laws).

23 e.g. Submission of the Clergy Act 1533 s.1. Insofar as the Tudor legislation was declaratory of the common law constitutional position, it has not lost its authority despite the wholesale removal of many provisions from the statute book by the Statute Law (Repeals) Act 1969. Lord Scarman's Law Commission consulted Michael Ramsey, the then Archbishop of Canterbury, on the repeal schedule: he was, unsurprisingly, happy to see much of the Tudor legislation removed from prominence, but glad to be able to retain Ecclesiastical Licences Act 1533 s.13.

before the Norman conquest[24] and been reformed, not established anew, under the later Tudors.

(c) The ecclesial State

If only one source of law bound Englishmen in their temporal and spiritual practice, did it follow that there was in fact only one entity to which they belonged and owed allegiance? The kingdom's inhabitants had been declared Christian by parliament: so was the English Church the kingdom by another name, or an entity distinct from it, merely recognised, supported and controlled »at arm's length« through the general law?

There was indeed some suggestion of distinction in the first major statute of Henry's reign, which equated »the English Church« with »the spiritualty« and called it *part* of the English body politic.[25] But that Act, passed whilst some possibility of a compromise with Rome remained, represented only a transitional stage in official thinking. It gave way to the later statutes' approach, by which lawmaking and executive responsibilities were the same in all aspects of national life, the spiritual included.[26] The oath required by the Act of Supremacy 1558[27] was significant, identifying the monarch as »Supreme Governor *of this realm* … as well in all spiritual or ecclesiastical things or causes, as temporal«: a telling acceptance that the realm could, and did, have spiritual concerns.

According to Hooker, the only reason for a church-state distinction would have been to preserve church government by the clergy – following the papal contention that jurisdiction *inspiritualibus* was the monopoly of the ordained.[28] That contention being rejected, there was no reason to except the ecclesiastical sphere from God's general committal of authority to princes, nor from the English convention that the prince's lawmaking would take place jointly with a par-

24 *Marshall v. Graham* (1907) 2 KB 112, 126.

25 Ecclesiastical Appeals Act 1532, preamble.

26 As well as the principle in the Ecclesiastical Licences Act 1533 that *prince and people* adopt laws, in the religious as in other spheres, the oath required by the Act of Supremacy 1558 was significant, identifying the monarch as 'Supreme Governor *of this realm* as well in all spiritual or ecclesiastical things or causes, as temporal': a telling acceptance that the realm could, and did, have spiritual concerns.

27 S.9.

28 Hooker, *Lawes* Book VIII, above, 323. Calvinists as well as Romanists made this claim, though the offices to which they ordained were different. But the Zwinglian strand of the Reformed tradition had experience of a magistracy altogether more sympathetic to the Gospel, and to this day has never dogmatically excluded state organs from wielding ecclesiastical authority; whilst Luther was prepared to accept a tacit delegation of authority from the congregation to the *praecipuum membrum ecclesiae*.

liament of lords and commons. Hooker concluded that, in the England of his time, church and kingdom were identical: two ways of looking at the same entity, an *ecclesial* state.[29] Public law, whether written or unwritten, was therefore an entirely appropriate vehicle to be used in establishing a system of local ministry, agencies of ecclesiastical oversight, a uniform public liturgy and »speciall articles for publique unities sake«[30] in the field of doctrine.

(d) Private initiative in conformity with the public religion

Apart from certain practices labelled superstitious, nothing in England's Reformation legislation set limits to the piety of individuals who accepted the official religious settlement. On the contrary, the law continued to encourage voluntary generosity benefiting the public, and there were many ways in which such generosity could bear fruit in the religious field, such as adornment of sacred buildings, foundations for religious learning or pensions for incapacitated ministers. In some situations one could only support the Establishment by surrendering control of an asset to public office-bearers, thus converting it from private to public property.[31] But usually the law kept private and official initiatives distinct, offering donors the chance to couple their own arrangements for long-term control with the advantages of charitable status.

Under Elizabeth I parliament sought to improve the regulation of charitable foundations; the resulting statute's preamble[32] referring to the »repair of churches« amongst a list of other purposes recognised as charitable was subsequently extrapolated by the courts into a general principle that the advancement of lawful religion for the public benefit was a distinct »head of charity«.[33] Other beneficial purposes (in particular education) might also be charitable whilst

29 Hooker, *Lawes*, Book VIII, above, 318 and 326: 'the care of religion being common unto all societies politique, such societies as do embrace the true religion have the name of the church given unto every of them...'; 'When we oppose the church therefore and the commonwealth in a Christian societie, we meane by the commonwealth that societie with relation unto all the publique affayres thereof, only the matter of true religion excepted; by the church the same societie with only reference unto the matter of true religion without any other affaires besides.' Put another way, it could be said that in the expression 'Church of England' the words 'Church' and 'England' stand grammatically in apposition to one another; cp. 'Kingdom of England'.

30 Hooker, *Lawes*, Book VIII, above, 390.

31 Land for a new parish church, for example, could only become such if the building were consecrated by the bishop, which in turn required conveyance of the land to the parish minister and brought the land under the supervision of the ecclesiastical court; 3 Co Inst 203, and see *Sedgwick v. Bourne* (1920) 2 KB 267.

32 Charitable Uses Act 1601.

33 *Special Commissioners of Income Tax v. Pemsel* (1891) AC 531.

stemming from a religious motive: one instance shortly before the Revolution was the growth of devotional and moral reformation societies following the restoration of Charles II.[34]

Charitable status allowed funds and land to be dedicated to a stated purpose in perpetuity (whereas private trusts were limited in duration, and non-charitable purpose trusts might not be enforceable at all). As *parens patriae* the King, acting through the Attorney-General, could bring proceedings to enforce trustees' loyalty to their trust even centuries after the original donor had died.

(e) Alternative religion – the penal laws

Religion alternative to the liturgies and structures established by law was, by its nature, private; its exercise was also in many cases criminal, taking place underground without recognition by the law. The Act of Uniformity 1548 punished ministers who obstinately used any »open prayer« not set forth in the Prayer Book, defining this as »prayer which is for other to come unto or hear, either in common churches or in private chapels or oratories, commonly called the service of the church«[35];but by 1580 there was also a blanket ban on saying or hearing mass anywhere[36], and in 1592 protestant recusants[37] were also forbidden to assemble »under colour or pretence of religion« in groups numbering five or more outside a domestic setting.[38]

The focus of new legislation was, however, on religious *practice*. Tacit alternative believers continued to exist and no attempt was made to challenge people to state what they believed on particular topics, unless they sought some office to which belief were legally relevant. The mediæval canonical offences of heresy and blasphemy survived the Elizabethan settlement, but the scope of heresy was drastically narrowed and it was only by open advocacy of heretical beliefs that a layperson might bring himself into danger.[39]

34 John Spurr, 'The Church, the Societies, and the Moral Revolution of 1688' in John Walsh, Colin Haydon & Stephen Taylor (eds.), *The Church of England 1689-1833 - From Toleration to Tractarianism*, Cambridge 1993, 131-32.

35 S.2.

36 Stat 23 Eliz I c.1.

37 The term recusant in Tudor statutes was not confined to Roman Catholics ('popish recusants'), but covered any persistent absentee from mandatory Sunday worship.

38 Stat 35 Eliz I c.1.

39 Act of Supremacy 1558 s.20 narrowed the scope of heresy as prosecuted before the Court of High Commission; Coke CJ commended a similar narrowing to other competent courts in *Case of Heresy* (1601) 12 Co Rep 56. The common law writ *De haeretico comburendo* was last issued in 1612, and abolished in 1677 by stat 29 Car II c.9.

This underlined the fact that the rationale behind the penal laws was at least as much political as religious. In the early decades of the Reformation there was a genuine belief that certain Catholic practices, superstitious or idolatrous, were calculated to lead souls astray or call down divine displeasure. But by his 1570 Bull *Regnans in Excelsis*, Pope Pius V incited his English supporters to treason against a Queen he considered illegitimate in every sense; and for a time Catholic attempts on the monarch's life were a reality, culminating in the notorious 1605 Gunpowder Plot. The Elizabethan liturgical settlement being held a moderate compromise which all subjects of goodwill should be able to accept, protestants rejecting it became stubborn resisters of authority. The post-Restoration laws obstructing (by qualifying oaths or a sacramental test) the access both of Catholics and of some dissenting protestants to public office[40] reflected at once a continuing anti-Catholic consensus and a conformist parliaments' revenge on the dissenting protestant victors of the Civil War.

Illegality, though, has never prevented people following strong convictions. Though England's Catholics dwindled to a small remnant in this period, divergent protestant opinions flourished, both within the religious Establishment (until deliberately excluded in 1662)[41] and in underground competition with it. Temporary Acts of Indemnity allowed tenure of office without the statutory tests, and more controversially, the later Stuarts' declarations of indulgence intermittently allowed open dissenting worship.[42] But the greatest contribution to organised dissenting identities was the era of the *de facto* republic, in which Presbyterianism gained some of its most influential formularies and Independents, Baptists and Quakers all reached consensus on the principles they held in common.[43]

Blasphemy was punished chiefly by the ordinary courts from the 17th century but abolished by Criminal Justice and Immigration Act 2008.

40 For example the requirement to receive communion according to the official liturgy, imposed for Crown officers by the Test Act 1672, and oaths denying Roman Catholic beliefs required from members of Parliament by 30 Car II st.2 (1678) as a balance to the anticipated accession of a Catholic prince to the throne.

41 Act of Uniformity 1662, s.2 required *ex animo* assent by ministers to everything contained in the Book of Common Prayer, which substantial numbers of more strongly protestant ministers, chiefly presbyterians, felt unable to give. A separated English presbyterianism, congregations following their ministers into nonconformity, dates from this time.

42 Charles II issued such a declaration in 1671-72; James II's similar action in 1687-88 was among the grievances which caused leading figures to offer the Crown to the Prince and Princess of Orange.

43 The 1646 Westminster Confession of Faith (Presbyterian) and the Independents' Savoy Declaration (1658) in response both flowed from the Assembly of Divines summoned by the Lords and Commons in 1642. In 1652 the first Quaker missionaries were sent out under the inspiration of George Fox, and 1677 saw adoption of the Second London Confession, one of the most important documents of the General Baptist tradition.

The courts could not, of course, enforce or establish trusts contrary to public policy or contracts for an illegal purpose. Dissenting groups' self-understanding as churches consequently won no legal recognition. A gift to support alternative religion was either void, or (if a general charitable intention could be discerned) might be diverted by the court to a charitable purpose quite different from what the donor had intended.[44] Even when alternative religion surfaced during a period of indulgence, therefore, it was not practical to vest meeting-houses or ministers' residences on declared religious trusts; nor could the courts even contemplate enforcing dissenters' religious rules (had the dissenters so wished). It is therefore premature to speak of church-state relations in this period, even in the context of alternative religion.

(f) The universality of the public religion

»There is not any man of the Church of England« declared Hooker, »but the same man is also a member of the commonwealth, nor any man a member of the commonwealth which is not also of the Church of England«.[45] Hooker was perfectly well aware that separatists were, as he wrote, meeting for worship and rejecting the law's religious settlement, whilst English Catholics denied parliament's religious competence and were in a few cases plotting violent countermeasures. He could still make his assertion, though, on the basis that dissent had no effect on membership. If the church were simply the kingdom considered in respect of its Christianity, one could no more opt out of the church than out of the kingdom. The law imposed religious duties upon all, and equally conferred religious rights which, insofar as dissenters wished to claim them, might not be denied.[46]

(g) Electoral Brandenburg – Territorial religious autonomy

The legal reformation of religion in Brandenburg began, as in England, as a bid for autonomy. Margrave-Elector Joachim II had resisted being tied to a confessional standard imposed from outside his borders. Saying to his clergy:

44 e.g. *A.-G. v. Baxter* (1684) 1 Vern 248 (purpose of a gift by will, to relieve the poverty of ministers deprived from their livings for refusal to make the statutory doctrinal subscription, void).

45 Hooker, *Lawes*, Book VIII, above, 319.

46 The universality of religious rights and duties will be considered in the following sections.

»I want no more to be tied to the Church of Wittenberg than I do to the Church of Rome. I say *Credo sanctam catholicam ecclesiam*, not *Romanam* or *Wittenbergensem*, and my church here in Berlin and Cölln is just as rightful a Christian church as that in Wittenberg«[47],

he echoed the 1532 claim that the English Church was

»for knowledge, integrity and sufficiency of number ... sufficient and meet of itself ..«

to regulate its own religious affairs.[48]

But unlike Joachim, Henry VIII and his parliament could make good this aspiration. Brandenburg was part of a wider political whole, but England was a sovereign nation dominating an offshore island; the first major statute of the Reformation era placed it on a par with the Holy Roman Empire itself.[49] Even though Joachim was not among the defeated princes, the protestant defeat at Mühlberg in 1547 signalled that lasting reformation in any German principality would depend upon some form of compromise on Imperial terms. But the destruction of the Catholic Armada in 1588 signalled England's ongoing ability to resist European pretensions.

(h) Electoral Brandenburg – Doctrinal basis of the public religion

Because of this, England was freer than Brandenburg to determine the theological basis of its ecclesiastical law: it could reform church government first, public doctrine later (and only for limited purposes).

Joachim initially secured the agreement of Brandenburg's lay territorial Estates to his 1540 *Kirchenordnung*, which began with a confessional document unique to the Hohenzollern dominions. But he set greater store by Imperial confirmation[50], and anyhow after Mühlberg the position changed. By adopting its long-term settlement of the religious question in 1555 the *Reichstag* claimed an overarching ecclesiastical authority. It »suspended« Catholic spiritual jurisdiction in the Empire's protestant territories[51] but restricted princely reform initia-

47 Quoted from H. Schmidt, *Kurze Einleitung zur brandenburgischen Kirchen- und Reformationshistorie* in Max Lehmann, 'Preußen und die katholische Kirche seit 1640 nach den Akten des Geheimen Staatsarchivs' in *Publikationen der preußischen Staatsarchive*, 1878, repr. Osnabrück 1965.

48 Ecclesiastical Appeals Act 1532, preamble.

49 'This realm of England is an Empire', Ecclesiastical Appeals Act 1532, preamble.

50 *Allgemeine Deutsche Bibliographie*, tit. Joachim II.

51 *Augsburger Religionsfriede*, 25.9.1555, Art 20; text in Ruth Kastner, ed., *Quellen zur Reformation 1517-55*, Darmstadt 1994, 523f.

tives to »the religion … of the Augsburg Confession«.[52] In effect, Joachim was allowed to retain protestant institutions only on conditions set by the Empire, and the principal condition was Lutheran orthodoxy. Hence, not only in Lutheran ecclesiology but constitutionally, a detailed doctrinal position would rank prior to Brandenburg's territorial ecclesiastical law. It is significant that Margrave John George's revised *Kirchenordnung* of 1572 commenced, not with his father's confessional document but by repeating the *Augustana* verbatim.

Henry and his parliament needed no such external approval to reform English religion. They did so as an act of God-given state sovereignty. The »very articles of the catholic faith of Christendom«, professed by parliament in the name of the whole community of the realm in 1533[53], were no more than the three ancient Creeds; and even these were to be interpreted exclusively within England since all external jurisdiction was denied. Far from being tied to a confessional identity, therefore, the only labels appropriate to the English Church were Christian and English.The country was never officially Lutheran, and although Calvinist thinking played a major role in the official liturgy for the Lord's Supper[54] it arrived too late to influence the religious constitution.

Hence the Articles of Religion approved by Edward VI in 1553 enjoyed nothing like the fundamental significance of the *Augustana.* They bound nobody for nine years. They were then revised, reduced in number and imposed on the clergy through a subscription requirement[55]; later the obligation to preach consistently with the Articles was confirmed (under penalty) by parliament[56] and they became a test of orthodoxy for those who aspired to leadership through the universities.[57] But many important laymen never subscribed to the Articles, and it was never possible to measure the validity of ecclesiastical law against them.

(i) Electoral Brandenburg – Vehicles of ecclesiastical oversight

The *Reichstag* suspended Catholic episcopal jurisdiction in 1555; but it did not alter the method of episcopal appointments, nor would the Empire have tamely

52 *Augsburger Religionsfriede*, above, Art 20.

53 Ecclesiastical Licences Act 1533, s.13.

54 See Colin Buchanan, *What did Cranmer think he was doing?* 2nd ed., Cambridge 1982.

55 The '38 Articles' of 1563 had the authority of the Queen and the convocations and so could never have bound the laity.

56 Ordination of Ministers Act 1571.

57 The requirement was imposed at Oxford in 1576 during Robert Earl of Leicester's Chancellorship. Cambridge complied more hesitantly in 1610 with the expressed wishes of James I. The University requirement was modified in later years and finally abolished for non-theologians by the Universities Tests Act 1871.

accepted the imprisonment or execution of Catholic bishops. The Margraves of Brandenburg could therefore neither deal firmly with recalcitrantincumbents nor have their own nominees consecrated to vacant sees. After a brief co-operation with reforming bishop Matthias von Jagow, it proved easier to leave episcopal sees vacant or filled with lay commendators. The new princely agency, the *Konsistorium*, became essential to fill the Hohenzollern need for oversight and ecclesiastical advice.[58] In England, where a compliant protestant bench of bishops could more easily be secured, there was no need for radical structural change; consequently Elizabeth I's equivalent agency (the High Commission in Causes Ecclesiastical), although operating in parallel with the diocesan structure and episcopal courts[59], never replaced them. In 1640 the High Commission became a permanent casualty of the rivalry between Crown and parliament, its abolition leaving diocesan episcopacy the unchallenged normal *locus* of first-instance executive and judicial authority.

(j) Electoral Brandenburg – limiting the princely prerogative

In one important respect, however, English monarchs were more constrained in religious affairs than the Margrave-Electors. Though less susceptible to external pressure, within the realm they had to co-operate with their parliaments in a way that the Hohenzollern found increasingly unnecessary. Joachim II had involved the lay Estates in the issue of his 1540 *Kirchenordnung*, but like Elizabeth I and Charles I was reluctant to involve a representative body more than absolutely necessary in matters of religion. By the reign of the Great Elector the Estates of Brandenburg were seriously losing influence, and in religious as in other matters the Margrave and his ministers were acquiring a free hand.

The opposite was happening in England. Elizabeth's personal stature and wise advisers had given her considerable personal influence over the character of the religious Establishment, but it was judicially established in the following reign that the monarch could not create new law without parliamentary agreement[60], and under the poorly-advised Charles the attempt to re-establish royal and episcopal control over religious affairs independently of parliament proved a recipe for disaster. The High Commission was abolished at the outset of the reaction

58 *Konsistorien* established at Cölln and Stendal (1543 and 1551) by Joachim II gave place to the more systematic provision of John George's 1572 *Konsistorialordnung*. The superintendents who supervised the life of parishes within each district were appointed through the *Konsistorium*, responsible to it, and ordained on its behalf.

59 The High Commission derived its permanent existence from the Act of Supremacy 1558, s.18.

60 *Case of Proclamations* (1611) 12 Co Rep 74.

against royal policy[61], and never reinstated. This freed the diocesan bishops from a rival judicial authority, though it also removed their chief support. It was anyhow clear to many after the Civil War, and to all after the Glorious Revolution, that ecclesiastical lawmaking was a matter neither for the King alone, nor for the bishops, but for the King in Parliament, representing the whole community of the realm.

4. The »long eighteenth century« – 1688-1828

(a) Prelude - The return of the Jews

English religious historians usually begin the »long eighteenth century« (the era in which alternative religion was tolerated although with no attempt at legal parity) at the Revolution. But the return of the Jews to England, an early potential challenge to Hooker's concept of the coterminous kingdom and church, took place slightly earlier.

Jewish refugees from Spanish persecution had arrived during the exile of Charles II, and were permitted to settle during both his and his brother's reigns. Soon after the Revolution, both Sephardi and Ashkenazi synagogues were recorded in the City of London. Steps were taken to prevent existing law being used against them[62], and individuals might benefit from concessions from a benevolent judge.[63] Their commercial expertise brought obvious benefits to the economy, their Iberian links brought useful intelligence, and their numbers were not such as to threaten the kingdom's Christian character.

The main reason why Hooker's reasoning was unaffected by this development was that Jews were not considered to be »men of the commonwealth«. The Christian oath necessary for naturalisation was impossible for them; even their children born in England were still considered part of a distinct »nation«. The legislature largely held back from overt recognition and so long as this was the case, charitable status did not cover Jewish purposes.[64]

61 Stat 16 Car I c.11 (1640).

62 An Order in Council of 13.11.1685 directing that the Attorney-General halt prosecutions for unlawful religious assembly was in line with the policy behind James II's Declarations of Indulgence; but not open to the same constitutional objections if the prerogative writ of *nolle prosequi* was used to halt each prosecution separately.

63 As early as *Barker v. Warren* (1677) 2 Mod Rep 271 a Saturday hearing was adjourned to accommodate a Jewish witness.

64 *Da Costa v. Da Paz* (1753) 2 Swans 532 n.

Yet this parliamentary »blind eye« in fact gave Jews greater practical liberty than most contemporary Christian dissenters enjoyed. The Clandestine Marriages Act 1753 requiring marriages to be solemnised in the parish church specifically excepted marriages between Jews according to their own custom. This avoided the test of wills which any attempt to force Jews into churches would have caused; but the Act was silent as to such unions' legal validity. In fact, though not the Christian marriage known to English law[65], they might carry property consequences because of the mutual understanding between Jews themselves.

Battei Din clearly became well-known and respected during this period. An ecclesiastical judge, to whom a question of Jewish marriage validity was referred by the Court of Chancery in just such a property dispute, decided it by the courts' usual technique for interpreting alternative religious doctrine – expert evidence supplemented by his own reading – but regretted that a competent *Beth Din* had not been asked to settle the question.[66]

(b) Chronology of the Period

The Prince and Princess of Orange accepted the vacant throne in February 1688[67] and reigned jointly as William III and Mary II. A new coronation oath, enshrined in an Act of Parliament, committed them *inter alia* to »maintaine the Laws of God, the true Profession of the Gospell and the protestant reformed religion established by law«.[68] At the same time they accepted a set of grievances and principles known as the Bill of Rights, subsequently enacted as a statute declaring England a »protestant kingdom« and excluding Catholic princes and the spouses of Catholics from the succession.[69]

Both during and after the reign of the Orange monarchs, the exiled Stuart pretenders remained a threat. The meeting of protestants for alternative worship was decriminalised in mid-1689 to create a broad front of support for the new régime.[70] Exemption from penalty was, however, subject to a number of conditions, only gradually relaxed: the conditions excluded Roman Catholics and a

65 A marriage tax was imposed upon Jewish couples by stat. 6 & 7 Gul III c.6, s.63 (1694), *as though* their union were a marriage by the laws of England. Such unions were validated retrospectively, however, by stat. 10 & 11 Vic c.58 (1847).

66 *Lindo v. Belisario* (1796) 1 Hag Con (App) 7.

67 1689 by the Gregorian Calendar already used on the Continent.

68 Coronation Oath Act 1688.

69 Bill of Rights 1689, s.1.

70 Toleration Act 1689, see below.

small group of separatist Protestant Episcopalians[71], perceived as the pretenders' likely allies, but also – on purely theological grounds – Unitarian protestants.

Mary II's sister Anne was perceived as hostile to alternative religion, though neither of the hostile measures of her reign[72] remained long on the statute book. The most significant development of the time was the agreement between England and Scotland that the Crown of both kingdoms would descend according to English law, and the monarch legislate for both territories with a single »Parliament of Great Britain«.[73] Until legislative alteration, however, each territory's law remained distinct. Further, it was a union for temporal purposes only, with safeguards in the treaty designed to ensure that the Union Parliament would not alter either Kingdom's religious settlement.[74] This study can and should therefore continue to focus upon England: it would be wrong to treat the United Kingdom as a country with a single basis for church-state relations, though the disappearance of an English legislature and appeals from England's courts to an Anglo-Scottish House of Lords have made it totally impossible to guarantee English public religion's distinctive features against change or interpretation influenced by Calvinist ecclesiology.

The Crown passed to the ducal House of Brunswick-Lüneburg in 1714, causing a second personal union (after that with Scotland from 1603 to 1707) in which the churches of the prince's territories remained wholly distinct. The accession of George I in Great Britain has traditionally been associated with the emergence of a first or »prime« minister who, though still dependent on the monarch's confidence, would lead the routine business of government on his own authority. Four Georges occupied the throne for the rest of our period, the future George IV serving as Regent from 1811 until his father's death.

Very broadly speaking, the »long eighteenth century« saw the western European Enlightenment work through into English religion. Weary of wars based on religious dogmatism, the educated classes welcomed a religion which reason could support: the abstract and miraculous retreated into the shadows, and stress was laid on the tangible good wrought by religion and its teachings. For public religion this meant an increasing equation of its goals with other concerns of government: the co-operation of ordinary and ecclesiastical courts made the unity of the law apparent as never before. As the convention grew that prime minis-

71 The so-called 'Nonjurors', led initially by ex-archbishop William Sancroft.

72 Occasional Conformity Act 1711 (tighter religious requirements for public office), repealed 1719; Schism Act 1714 (only conformists licensed by the bishop to teach), repealed 1718.

73 Union with Scotland Act 1706, Arts II and III.

74 Stat 6 Ann c.8 (1706); Union with Scotland Act 1706, Art XVIII.

ters must command parliamentary support, and that, having that support, they could expect the King to exercise the royal prerogative on their advice, there appeared no reason to treat the ecclesiastical supremacy any differently from prerogatives enjoyed in other fields.The stress laid on tangible benefits also boded well for alternative religion, since repression no longer seemed the right approach to mere differences of belief; restrictions and disabilities were therefore lifted as soon as the political considerations behind them ceased to apply.

The later part of the century also saw the start of the Industrial Revolution and a consequent population shift from country to town. As old traditions were lost, religiosity suffered: alternative religion was able to respond with new forms of mission more quickly than the public structure, meaning that conformity lost numbers to both dissent and non-belief. The evangelical movement was the English-speaking variant of European Pietism; it had an effect both within and without conformist ranks, and was equally suspect in the eyes of official religion and of »Old dissent«. It spawned the Methodist movement, organised from 1787 as a new dissenting tradition.

The French Revolution took the cult of Reason to extremes, spreading atheist ideas around the Continent but also provoking a strong reaction. By 1789 the Jacobite threat had disappeared, and with it England's Jacobite episcopalians. The need for Irish officers in the wars with France, and sympathy generated by treatment of clergy in the revolutionary »Terror«, now disposed England's governing classes to Catholic emancipation, and toleration of alternative religious assemblies was extended to the Catholic mass.[75]

(c) The Coronation Oath, the Bill of Rights and the principle of parliamentary consent

The constitutional significance of the Tudor statutory preambles was equalled by that of the two statutes enshrining the terms on which William and Mary took the throne. The new Coronation Oath, drafted in parliament and accepted by all subsequently crowned monarchs, impliedly confirmed the 1533 identification of England as a Christian nation. The duty to maintain the Laws of God and true profession of the Gospel assigned at least a religious goal, or arguably a binding limit, to all discretionary exercise of the royal prerogative (although it could not prevent royal assent being given to later legislation, given the principle that any statute can repeal its predecessors by implication).

75 Roman Catholic Relief Act 1791.

It had been stated at a much earlier date[76] that laws binding Englishmen required the consent of the governed. The Bill of Rights reiterated this as regards the Crown – »the execution of laws by regal authority without consent of parliament is illegal«[77] – and the aspirations of Elizabeth I and the Stuarts to regulate religious affairs alone were finally a thing of the past. But the same logic was also now applied to rules made for the lay population by the clergy. The ecclesiastical courts at last accepted (as the judges of Westminster Hall had done before them[78]) the Reformation parliament's declaration that Englishmen were bound only by laws »made within the realm« or adopted into English custom »at their free liberty«; in other words that the Continent's canonical rules needed adoption into the common law if they were to have any binding force within the realm.[79] Post-reformation clerical canons were also held incapable of imposing any new burden on laypeople, who were not represented in the convocations.[80]

Compared with these points, the exclusion of Catholics from the succession, on the ground that »it hath been found by experience that it is inconsistent with the safety and welfare of this Protestant kingdom to be governed by a popish prince, or by any king or queen marrying a papist«[81], carried less long-term significance for the nation's religious life. The personal influence of the monarch – let alone his spouse – on law and government was in decline from this moment. The risk that loyalty to papal teaching might outweigh respect for the law of the land or for the popular will was quite genuine; but measures to counteract it needed to be directed toward elected politicians ratherthan at the Crown.[82] Argu-

76 As regards external rules by Ecclesiastical Licences Act 1533, preamble; as regards royal edicts in e.g. *Case of Proclamations* (1611) 12 Co Rep 74.

77 Bill of Rights 1689, preamble.

78 *Edes v. Bishop of Oxford* (1667) Vaughan 18.

79 Sir Frederic Maitland showed in *Roman Canon Law in the Church of England*, London 1898, that mediæval bishops' courts had administered the western canon law as though it applied in England *proprio vigore*. Richard Helmholz, *Roman Canon Law in Reformation England*, Cambridge 1990, has shown that this approach continued until the Revolution; but there is no evidence of it continuing thereafter. The test to determine whether or not a canonical principle had been adopted was later laid down in *Bishop of Exeter v. Marshall* (1867) LR 3 HL 17; and the categorisation of adopted canon law as a part of English common law was confirmed by Lord Blackburn in *Mackonochie v. Lord Penzance* (1881) 6 App Cas 424, 446.

80 *Middleton v. Crofts* (1736) 2 Atk 650.

81 Bill of Rights 1688, s.1.

82 The exclusionary provision of the Bill of Rights was repeated in other statutes and backed up by a declaration and a sacramental test for acceding monarchs. The requirement to 'join in communion with the Church of England' (Act of Settlement 1700 s.3) was satisfied by the convinced Lutheran George I, who remained *summus episcopus* of his Hanoverian *Landeskirche* but had no qualms about receiving the Lord's Supper by the English official rite: it need not therefore be understood in the common modern sense of 'communion', denoting a relationship with an organised religious body. The polemical decla-

ably the most significant aspect of the exclusionary provision was that a »protestant kingdom« implies a Christian one; further proof of the continuity of England's constitutional religious identity.

(d) The Toleration Act 1689

Toleration of a relatively broad spectrum of protestant dissent was the only option left to William III's government, after parliament rejected alterations to the Prayer Book and other ecclesiastical law which might have allowed a narrower group of dissenters to conform once more to the public religion.[83] The Act of 1689 nevertheless opened a number of issues of what would later be called church-state relations, and rewards consideration in detail.

(aa) Individual alternative religion

The Act's primary focus was not on religious groups or denominations but on individuals, »Their Majesties« protestant subjects dissenting from the Church of England'. Dissenters subscribing certain oaths and declarations before magistrates were exempted from the requirement to attend official public worship and the penalties for taking part in an alternative religious assembly, provided this took place with open doors in a registered location.[84]Dissent itself was a mental state, never defined, and could be in reference to any aspect of the public religion; meeting-house registration and qualifying oaths were therefore the most important conditions imposed.

(bb) Alternative congregations and their preachers

The Act of course recognised that there would be »congregations or assemblies for religious worship«, and though it prescribed no structure for these it spoke of persons »belonging« to a congregation.[85] It also recognised that congregations might have their own »preachers or teachers«. Such a »preacher or teacher«,

ration required in 1688 was replaced by a moderate wording in the Accession Declaration Act 1910, but the King must still 'solemnly and sincerely in the presence of God profess, testify and declare that I am a faithful Protestant'.

83 See John Spurr, 'The Church of England, Comprehension and the Toleration Act of 1689' (1989) 104 *English Historical Review* 927.

84 Toleration Act 1689, ss. 1, 3, 4, 16.

85 Toleration Act 1689, ss. 11, 13, 16.

along with others in or pretending to holy orders,might officiate in a congregation or preach at a religious meeting, provided his relative orthodoxy was proved by subscription to most (35½) of the 39 Articles of Religion to which the official clergy were committed.[86]

(cc) Religious societies

Beyond the individual congregation or meeting, the Act made no reference to the collective organisation of alternative believers. It was far from recognising alternative »churches«, and gave no dissenting body legal personality as such. Provided their venue was registered and all participants »qualified«, congregations could lawfully assemble *ad hoc* with no permanent structure at all. But the decriminalisation of their activity made it possible, for the first time, for co-religionists to use the existing vehicles of private law to secure their religious arrangements. One such vehicle was the contract of association: if a group submitted to a body of rules imposing mutual obligations, and the purpose of the rules was no longer contrary to public policy, then *prima facie* a contract came into being under which, in appropriate cases, the rules could be enforced. At a later date such rules would provide for the oversight of local congregations by organs with a wider geographical remit, such as presbyterian synods, Roman Catholic bishops, the various Methodist Conferences and the United Synagogue.[87]

(dd) Alternative religious trusts

An initially more important vehicle was the charitable trust. We have already noted that private initiatives advancing lawful religion for the public benefit enjoyed the law's favour, expressed in the various privileges accompanying charitable status. The Act's removal of penalties was sufficient to render alternative protestant activity lawful, given the the common law principle that »every citizen has a right to do what he likes, unless restrained by the common law … or by

86 Toleration Act 1689, s.6. If actually in holy orders, though, a preacher remained bound by the clerical canons and certain ministrations in his dissenting congregation could render him liable to ecclesiastical court proceedings: *R. v. Barnes ex p. Shore* (1846) 8 QB 640. Effective freedom for episcopally ordained clergy to change religion came only with the Clerical Disabilities Act 1870.

87 Decided cases relying on contractual reasoning date from relatively late in our period; a modern case exemplifying the principle is *Davies v. Presbyterian Church of Wales* (1986) 1 WLR 323. But the official title of the Quaker body, the Religious Society of Friends, perpetuates the 18th century terminology into the present day.

statute«[88]; so the trust in perpetuity became available to organised dissenting religion and made a dramatic difference to its long-term viability.[89] A small number of individuals could now hold assets – chapels, manses, training colleges, common and associated society funds – to advance religion in the tradition concerned, and pass them on to successors.

(ee) Privileges of alternative religion

In its need to rely on vehicles of private law, organised alternative religion was treated very similarly to organised secular activity: a Baptist congregation which considered itself a church was, in the eyes of the law, not very different from a Bridge club. Yet as early as 1689 some contrasts operating specifically in favour of religious individuals and groups could be seen. We may divide them into exemptions and positive benefits, although the concepts overlap.

Alternative believers were exempted by the Act *because of their religion* from attending official Sunday and festival worship, and from taking oaths if their scruples forbade it.[90] Their preachers were exempted *as such* from jury service and other burdensome public duties.[91] The advancement of their religious tenets was charitable and their meetings for worship were protected from disturbance by new criminal penalties.[92]

(e) Later developments affecting alternative religion

The passing of the Crown to the Hanoverians allowed the rise of alternative religion to respectability. Queen Anne, as already noted no friend of dissent, had extended her personal charity to support the clergy of the public Establishment; her successor initiated a grant to the main dissenting traditions.[93]

88 The principle has existed throughout English history but was encapsulated in this form in *A.-G. v. Guardian Newspapers Ltd (No 2)* (1988) 2 WLR 805, 869.
89 The 1684 decision in *A-G.v. Baxter*, above, was reversed in 1689 following the passing of the Act.
90 Toleration Act 1689, ss. 5, 10 prescribed alternatives for people (typically Quakers) so affected.
91 Toleration Act 1689, s.8.
92 Toleration Act 1689, s.15.
93 'Queen Anne's Bounty' was established out of royal revenues in 1703 to augment poorer benefices; George I established the *Regium Donum* for poor dissenting ministers in 1721. The capital supporting the Bounty was united with centralised benefice endowments in 1947; the *Regium Donum* ceased in 1857 after being declined by the dissenters themselves.

The lords spiritual having been able for centuries to convey the interests of established religion to government, a spokesman body of »protestant dissenting Ministers and deputies« became a new channel of communication from 1732.

Fresh legal exemptions were rare in the period, but Quakers were exempted from service under the Militia Act 1757.

In 1812 the »dissenting Deputies« achieved their greatest success of the period, colloquially called the »Little Toleration Act«, which replaced »qualification« of individual protestant dissenters by oaths, and of preachers by subscription to the Articles, by the simple registration of meeting-houses.[94]

Enlightenment thought was never sympathetic to the Chalcedonian doctrine of the Trinity, and even under William and Mary a statute (never invoked) sought to penalise outright denial.[95] But Unitarianism won a considerable following in the eighteenth century, and although meetings for Unitarian worship remained unlawful, its principles were adopted by a number of Independent, Presbyterian and General Baptist congregations. This became overt when the Doctrine of the Trinity Act 1813 finally extended toleration to Unitarianism. Resistance to the trend brought the internal divisions of private religion more often before the King's courts.

In 1817 the principle governing such proceedings was stated. Alternative religious tenets would never be enforced in their own right, but under the law of trusts, as terms upon which assets were enjoyed. The right to enjoy buildings or stipends flowed from the will of original contributors, who had (usually) expressly directed or signified by implication that their property should be used in support of the tenets of a particular religion. The courts would look into that religion, »not for the purpose of animadverting upon it« but to protect individuals' rights to determine the use made of their gifts.[96]

(f) The universality of the public religion

Nothing in the Toleration Act, nor in later developments affecting alternative religion, denied the Hookerian premise that church and commonwealth were one and the same. The law neither called dissenting societies »churches«, nor treated

94 Places of Religious Worship Act 1812.

95 Misleadingly titled the Blasphemy Act 1698, and repealed 1967.

96 *A-G. v. Pearson* (1817) 3 Mer 353,413. The principle that a material interest must be shown before the courts would intervene applied equally to claims based on a religious body's contract of association, and was reaffirmed by the House of Lords in *Forbes v. Eden* (1867) LR 1 Sc & Div 568.

their members as withdrawing from the one national Church. A tolerated Baptist or Methodist took advantage of a voluntary facility but lost neither his rights, nor most of his duties, in the public provision: much as today an individual resorting to private medicine retains his right to call upon the National Health Service and the duty to pay for it.

Several points in the Act of 1689 indicated that the religious welfare of dissenters continued to concern the ecclesial state as well as their own societies. The exclusion of Unitarians (who posed no political threat) and the preachers' »35½ Articles« showed that orthodoxy remained an issue for government.[97] The primary register of tolerated meeting-houses was maintained at the local ecclesiastical court.[98] A dissenter who »qualified« to attend alternative worship on Sunday was bound actually to do so, or to go to his parish church; he could not simply stay away.[99] And all the religious obligations of Englishmen apart from public worship – in particular submission to ecclesiastical jurisdiction and support of the public ministry by tithe – continued to bind regardless of dissent.[100]

The courts of Westminster Hall, now no longer at odds with episcopal judges over the applicable law, complemented them as organs of the ecclesial state. Stressing the importance of (Christian) religion to the fabric of society, the King's Bench had introduced a criminal information for blasphemy when the penalties open to the ecclesiastical courts were becoming an inadequate deterrent.[101] It continued, through the writ of prohibition, its supervisory jurisdiction over those courts and asserted its own competence to declare and interpret the canonical branch of the common law when help was unavailable[102]; equally acknowledging that episcopal judges might when necessary interpret and apply the indigenous common law.[103]

Judicial decisions, often later than the period under review but convenient to recite here, showed that religious rights and duties under the common law (including adopted canonical rules) continued to apply to all parishioners, regardless of the Toleration Act or possible dissent. Conformist and dissenter alike enjoyed enforceable rights to attend their parish church for worship, and to be bu-

97 Toleration Act 1689, ss. 6, 14.
98 Toleration Act 1689, s.16.
99 Toleration Act 1689, s.13.
100 Toleration Act 1689, s.4.
101 *R. v. Taylor* (1676) 1 Vent 293.
102 *Carter v. Crawley* (1680) T Raym 496.
103 *Shotter v. Friend* (1690) 2 Salk 547.

ried in its churchyard if there was space.[104] The parish minister could not refuse their children baptism, nor to solemnise their marriages.[105] If a cause concerning fabric or furnishings of the parish church came before the ecclesiastical court, all had standing to be heard as the local public whom the building served.[106] Whether the parish assembly known as the Vestry comprised all ratepayers or a select few[107], there was no distinction between conformists' and others' rights to participate. As well as tithe, however, all parishioners shared in the duty to maintain the nave of the parish church.[108] Episcopal judges adjudicated for them on marriage validity and matrimonial conduct, general morality and testamentary matters, albeit embodying the new ideal of judicial independence.[109] And bishops remained lords spiritual of parliament, contributing theological expertise to all branches of lawmaking.

Throughout the period fresh legislation showed that parliament remained conscious of its responsibility for the whole nation's religion, and used public religious institutions for wider societal goals. In 1753, in the interests of family agreement and to avoid clandestine unions, it required all marriages to be solemnised *in facie ecclesiae*, the parish church providing the venue and the Book of Common Prayer the rite.[110] In 1772 it provided for »religious duties according to the rites of the Church of England« in county gaols to be performed by clergymen appointed, removed, and with precise duties defined by magistrates assembled in Quarter Sessions.[111] In 1800, and as late as 1833, it restricted commercial transactions to allow for »due observance« of Sundays and Good Friday.[112] Spo-

104 *Cole v. Police Constable 443A* (1937) 1 KB 316; *Kemp v. Wickes* (1809) 3 Phil Ecc 264. As with many such rights, their formulation in a reported judgment came many years later.

105 *Argar v. Holdsworth* (1758) 2 Lee 515. The right to childrens' baptism was formulated as a ministerial duty in canon 68 of 1603-05.

106 *Batten v. Gedye* (1889) 41 Ch D 507.

107 A question depending on local custom.

108 Stat 59 Geo III c.134 (1819) allowed repair work to be funded after the event by levying a local rate over ten years.

109 *Jones v. Bp of Llandaff* (1693) 12 Mod Rep 47 established this for episcopally-nominated judges even before the Act of Settlement 1700 did so for royal appointments.

110 Clandestine Marriages Act 1753. Besides the case of Jews already noted, the Act contained an exception for Quakers. But although this freed a group whose rejection of liturgical worship was absolute from any possibility of penalty, it is doubtful whether it actually made Quaker marriage effectual in English law. For a full consideration of this issue see Rebecca Probert, *Marriage Law and Practice in the Long Eighteenth Century: A Reassessment*, Cambridge 2009.

111 13 Geo III c.58. It was significant that bishops had no role to play in relation to these chaplains before 1815, except that they had to be 'clergymen', i.e. episcopally ordained. There was thus a close parallel to the official ministry provided at this date in the colonies, army regiments, the Royal Navy, and the royal peculiars.

112 Banking Act 1800; Sunday Observance Act 1833 s.1.

radic grants from public revenues to support established religion continued until and including the Church Building Act 1831.[113]

In short, the toleration of alternatives made very little difference to the identity of church and kingdom in the minds of the governing classes. As the parliamentarian Edmund Burke asserted in 1772,

> »An alliance between Church and State in a Christian commonwealth is, in my opinion, an idle and a fanciful speculation. An alliance is between two things that are in their nature distinct and independent, such as between two sovereign states. But in a Christian commonwealth the Church and the State are one and the same thing, being different integral parts of the same whole.«[114]

(g) Brandenburg-Prussia – The harmonisation of a patchwork of laws of religion

The Hohenzollern rulers of Brandenburg extended their dominions by degrees throughout the seventeenth and eighteenth centuries. The eighteenth century closed with a significant landmark in the transition from disparate lordships to a unitary Prussian State, the promulgation of the *Allgemeines Landrecht für die Preußischen Staaten,* and in 1808 the territories became provinces, each with a regional government responsible to central Ministries in Berlin.

The religious complexion of the Hohenzollern dominions was extremely varied. The Brandenburg heartland itself was typical of the monoconfessional protestant principalities of the Empire after 1555: religion reformed on Lutheran lines, with Catholics conceded the right to live under a Catholic prince elsewhere. In the Duchy of Cleves and County of the March, Margrave John Sigismund inherited lands where »reformation from below« had been tolerated by a moderate Catholic ruler, allowing both Lutheran and Reformed congregations to develop their own presbyterian structure alongside a continuing Catholicism. The initially-proscribed reformed tradition penetrated the heartland first through the conversion of the princely House itself, and later through the influx of religious refugees, permitted the exercise of their own religion under agencies of princely oversight.[115] In the Duchy of Prussia, outside the Empire but

113 This was the last of a series of Acts 'for building and promoting the Building of additional Churches in populous Parishes'.

114 Speech in the House of Commons, 11.5.1792; from *Works of the Rt. Hon. Edmund Burke*, Boston, Mass., 1826 vol 5.

115 The Lutheran *Konsistorien* already considered were supplemented by princely agencies to oversee the Reformed tradition after Margrave John Sigismund's conversion in 1613. In confirming the presbyterian *Kirchenordnung* for Cleves and the March in 1662, the Great Elector reserved his own right to replace it. Commissioners appointed by princely

under Polish suzerainty, the Counter-Reformation made itself felt and Polish rights were only relinquished on condition of an external bishop's continuing jurisdiction over the Duchy's Catholic inhabitants. And in many other territories, particularly in their acquisitions under the Treaty of Osnabrück, the *Reichsdeputationshauptschluss*[116] and the resolutions of the Congress of Vienna, the Hohenzollern succeeded to the position of Catholic princes or indeed prince-bishops in almost wholly Catholic lands.

Two important differences marked the development of the English law of religion. First, no foreign power was ever in a position to dictate how England treated religious minorities within its borders. There was no equivalent of the Imperial law which constrained the Hohenzollern from the 1550s, nor did England ever conclude a treaty affecting its internal religious polity.[117] Secondly, although some aspects of the variety of religion in Brandenburg-Prussia were replicated in the law governing the ceded colonies of England's Empire[118], the colonial law of religion was never allowed to reflect back onto England's own religious law during its formative period. In considering the long eighteenth century, we see these differences much more clearly when considering Catholicism than protestantism.

(h) Brandenburg-Prussia – The legal position of Catholicism

External pressures compelled the law of all Hohenzollern territories to recognise religious division in a way English law did not. Both retained, beyond the Reformation, the official understanding that the Christian Church in every nation was one, universal and apostolic. But English law never knew the separation of the one Church into »religious parties« that was the characteristic approach of

Patent dated 4.5.1694, replaced in 1701 by the *Consistoire Supérieure*, heard appeals from Brandenburg's French Reformed consistories, whilst German Reformed oversight lay from 10.6.1713 with a *Kirchendirektorium*.

116 The 1803 conclusion of a commission of the *Reichstag*, recommending reallocation of the Empire's smaller and spiritual principalities to the greater temporal princes, by way of compensation for western lands annexed by France.

117 The Treaties of Union with Scotland and Ireland did not have this effect. The Irish union merged two ecclesial states into one for seventy years, but Ireland's official religion was already in all material respects identical to England's. By contrast the union with Scotland was for temporal purposes only, the English religious establishment (and the legal position of the Scots Kirk) intended to be unaffected by the creation of a common legislature.

118 England inherited a variety of religious polities by cession of territory from other European powers: amongst others, Presbyterianism in the former New Netherlands and the Cape Colony; Roman Catholicism in the former New France, Gibraltar and Malta; Lutheranism in Heligoland.

the Empire and its constituent territories, and was officially recognised throughout the Prussian monarchy in 1788.[119] England was a »protestant kingdom«[120], not a kingdom containing one or more protestant churches. England's Catholics were members of that kingdom, despite their (initially illegal) private religious practice. England's denial of an objective papal authority within its borders[121] found expression in public law and applied to spiritual jurisdiction no less than temporal, to Roman appointees as well as to the Pope himself; it was not relaxed when the Mass was tolerated in 1791.[122] All that changed with Catholic toleration was that Catholics were able to concede *amongst themselves* a binding status to Roman canon law and episcopal structures: organised English Catholicism was known to England's legal system only as the product of such private agreement and the subject-matter of Catholic trusts.[123]

The Brandenburg-Prussian picture was quite different. In the heartland Catholics enjoyed the *beneficium emigrandi* from 1555.[124] In Cleves and the March, they were guaranteed the free exercise of their religion.[125] In 1648 the Peace of Westphalia prescribed a graduated scale of religious rights for the inhabitants of territories newly allocated to Hohenzollern rule.[126] The Treaty releasing the Duchy of Prussia from Polish suzerainty left its Catholics under the oversight of the Bishop of neighbouring Ermland.[127] These steps towards a public law that recognised Catholics as an ecclesial group quite separate from protestants, and Catholic jurisdiction as something objective, stemming not merely from private agreement, each left their mark on the harmonised law of religion set out in the *Allgemeines Landrecht*.

119 Frederick William II's 1788 Edict on Religion, operative throughout the Monarchy, identified Catholicism as one of the three 'principal confessions'; Text in Walther Hubatsch, *Geschichte der Evangelischen Kirche Ostpreußens*, vol. 3, Göttingen 1968, 254.

120 Bill of Rights 1688, preamble.

121 Articles of Religion, Art. 37.

122 The Roman Catholic Relief Act 1791 lifted the penalties attached to Mass attendance by persons who declared that they 'profess(ed) the Roman Catholic religion'. The penalties themselves were repealed by the Religious Disabilities Act 1846.

123 See *Brown v. Curé et Marguilliers de L'Oeuvre et Fabrique de Notre Dame de Montréal*(1874) LR 6 PC 157 and *Buckley v. Daly* (1990) NIJB 8. Although Lower Canadian and Northern Irish decisions respectively, there is no reason to doubt their relevance in England when explaining Roman Catholic rules as applicable (or inapplicable) on a contractual basis. The rules of other religious denominations have been treated in the same way, e.g. *Davies v. Presbyterian Church of Wales* (1986) 1 WLR 323.

124 *Augsburger Religionsfriede*, 25.9.1555, Art. 24.

125 The Treaty of Xanten, 12.11.1614, divided the former lands of Duke William of Cleves between John Sigismund of Brandenburg and a rival Catholic claimant. In the Duchy of Cleves and County of the March, protocols to the treaty guaranteed continuation of the religious *status quo*.

126 Treaty of Osnabrück, 30.1.1648, Art. 5.

127 Treaty of Wehlau, 19.9.1657.

The *Landrecht*, therefore, identified »spiritual superiors« for the Monarchy's Catholic as well as its protestant inhabitants.[128] Although a royal lawcode, it set out qualifications for Catholic ordinands[129], legislative[130] and disciplinary[131] powers for the Catholic episcopate, required official sanction for alteration to Catholic *Parochien*[132] and imposed a Catholic tithe.[133] In England such matters would not have concerned the law; after toleration they would have been internal affairs of the voluntary societies which Catholics chose to form, cognisable by the courts only insofar as they affected material interests.[134] More significantly still, the *Landrecht* distinguished the role of spiritual superiors from »the rights of the State according to law over ecclesial communities« and identified a government department as the repository of such rights.[135]

(i) Brandenburg-Prussia – Institutional expression of a »State« role in relation to religion

Having once conceded that Catholics and protestants were discrete confessional groups, having their own rules yet both present in a single territory, the legal systems of the Hohenzollern could not follow Richard Hooker's identification of church and commonwealth under a single set of governing structures. This had implications for protestantism as well. It was clear that whereas England had a »Supreme Governor of this Realm … as well in spiritual or ecclesiastical causes as temporal«, the Prussian sovereign played a distinct role in the protestant religious establishment from that which he played in the State. The closest approach to an overarching princely supremacy over both *Religionsparteien* »in spirituals« was the edict of Frederick William the »Great Elector« that the Catholics of Cleves and the March should »take him for their only Ordinary«.[136] But as the

128 Preuß. ALR Tit. XI § 115.
129 Preuß. ALR Tit. XI § 60 ff.
130 Preuß. ALR Tit. XI § 45 ff.
131 E.g. Preuß. ALR Tit. XI § 125 (bishop empowered to imprison contumacious clergy for up to 4 weeks).
132 Preuß. ALR Tit. XI § 238 ff.
133 Preuß. ALR Tit. XI § 857 ff.
134 Parliament was, however, concerned to ensure that Catholic bishops did not, by adopting geographical see designations, act as though their appointments had public significance or challenge the official ministers of religious oversight: see Ecclesiastical Titles Act 1851.
135 Preuß.ALR Tit. XI § 113.
136 The Edict of 7.9.1661 also threatened drowning for publishing external prelates' decrees; Lehmann, *Katholische Kirche*, above, I, 64, and see Martin Lackner, *Die Kirchenpolitik des Grossen Kurfürsten*, Witten 1973. Except in its peremptory nature, this may be compared to the negotiations in 1805-07 aimed at securing a royal grant of jurisdiction to the

Monarchy moved towards a single law of religion, it followed not the Cleves precedent for Catholic oversight, but the route mapped in Prussia by the Treaty of Wehlau. Although, in the protestant context, the distinction between *jus in sacris* and *jus circa sacra* would not find full institutional expression until 1848, it was conceptually inevitable – and therefore a separate agency charged with *jus circa sacra* was required – as soon as a territory acknowledged a Catholic jurisdiction with a public authority not derived from the Crown.

Such an agency, the »Spiritual Department«, was recorded as early as 1736. In relation to official protestantism it could not yet be categorised purely as an organ of the »State« since it exercised the King's *jus in sacris* as the second instance of protestant oversight, above the *Konsistorien*.[137] Even at provincial level, the institutional division of roles distinguishing State rights from protestant oversight would be temporarily blurred as a by-product of the 1808 administrative overhaul[138]; but as soon as liberation from the French invader was complete that tendency began to be reversed. In time new autonomous protestant agencies would emerge from the provincial governments, and a central Ministry for Spiritual Affairs would operate with an increasingly autonomous section covering the protestant *ius in sacris*.[139]

Neither the early Spiritual Department, nor the later Ministry, could be considered a Berlin counterpart of the Home Office. England, of course, had no *Konsistorien*: as already explained, first-instance oversight was the task of the episcopate. There was also an intermediate tier of authority *in sacris* (the archbishops and provincial courts) and a stricter notion of the separation of powers, which meant that appeals which in Prussia would have gone to the Ministry were made in England to an independent Court of royal Delegates. But the King still

Roman Catholic Bishop of Quebec; see Moir, *Church and State in Canada, 1627-1867– Basic Documents*, Toronto 1967, 116, 127. But the petition drafted for Bishop Pierre Denaut (although not the Crown's draft Patent) made clear that primarily 'civil recognition' was sought.

137 Preuß. ALR Tit. XI § 145.

138 *Publikandum, die veränderte Verfassung der obersten Verwaltungsbehörden betreffend*, 16.12.1808; *Verordnung wegen verbesserter Einrichtung der Provinzial-, Polizei- u Finanzbehörden*, 26.12.1808. This legislation abolished the old Spiritual Department, protestant Konsistorien and higher agencies of oversight, leaving only 'Deputations for spiritual matters' within provincial governments and a 'Cult and Public Instruction' section within the central Interior Ministry. Combining protestant oversight with the care of 'State' interests in relation to both confessions, the new organs functioned with a mixed staff, leading confessionally-conscious protestants to question their ecclesial role.

139 The first step was the renaming of the *Regierungsdeputationen* as *Konsistorien: Verordnung wegen verbesserter Einrichtung der Provinzial-Behörden*, 30.4.1815. In 1817 a new Ministry of Spiritual Affairs took over the religious role of the *Innenministerium*, and in 1825 *Konsistorium* personnel and responsibilities became purely protestant.

had a broad personal prerogative in the ecclesiastical field, extending from his right of visitation to the filling of parochial benefices by lapse. As administration in Whitehall became more specialised, the Home Secretary did indeed become the principal Minister advising the monarch in such matters; but the prerogative concerned only the public religious establishment.

One could say that the Home Secretary, First Lord of the Treasury and Lord Chancellor[140] had each inherited some part of the role of the sixteenth-century Vicegerent in Spirituals, taking decisions for the church-nation (which made it important to exclude Catholics from the Lord Chancellorship after 1829).[141] The only organ of the State concerned in any way with organised Catholicism was the Court of Chancery, exercising the royal supervision of charitable trusts; and its concern was not to vet episcopal appointments or Catholic parish boundaries, but merely to see that Catholic property was applied in accordance with its donors' wishes.

5. The »displaced nineteenth century« – 1828-1920

(a) Chronology of the Period

The wars with revolutionary and Napoleonic France made it imperative for the affairs of England and Ireland to have a single directing voice. The two kingdoms were united in 1800, two ecclesial states becoming a United Church of England and Ireland, with both countries' bishops Lords of Parliament. Irish public religion had been reformed on English lines in Tudor times so there was no pressure to confine the union to temporal purposes like that with Scotland.[142]

Irish private religion remained overwhelmingly Catholic, however, and the oaths and tests excluding Catholics from Crown office and English parliamenta-

140 It was until recently a notorious constitutional characteristic that the office of Prime Minister did not exist in statute. But as First Lord of the Treasury he was responsible, alongside the Lord Chancellor, for advising the Crown on a number of ecclesiastical appointments. Since the Constitutional Reform Act 2005 the Prime Minister has added the Lord Chancellor's responsibilities to his own.

141 Roman Catholic Relief Act 1829, s.12. Today the Lord Chancellor (Tenure of Office and Discharge of Ecclesiastical Functions) Act 1974 permits a Catholic to be appointed Lord Chancellor but provides for another minister to be entrusted with any ecclesiastical functions of that office.

142 The ecclesial union only lasted for seventy years, and was ended by the Irish Church Act 1869: its long-term significance for England was the indirect effect described in the following paragraph.

ry seats[143] did not apply there. Equating the position of English and Irish Catholics was inevitable, yet unthinkable without first placing English protestant dissenters on an equal footing. The 1820s therefore saw the lifting of important religion-based civil and political disabilities[144]; shortly after which franchise reform made representation of religious dissent in parliament an achievable reality.[145]

In the century from the Great Reform Act to the First World War, pressure was brought to bear on the law from three directions. Dissenters traded on their new political influence to challenge rules and institutions that they still found burdensome. Government and parliament, still predominantly conformist, found it expedient to devote less time to public religious affairs, and delegated a range of decisions to individual bishops or to the Ecclesiastical Commissioners for England.[146] But they still sought to hold the balance between the ecclesial state and dissenting demands: making politically necessary concessions without expressly dividing the population along denominational lines, opening its formerly »blind eye« towards the Jewish population, extending to private religion some privileges which public religion had always enjoyed (though without adopting any general principle of parity), conferring novel privileges on religion regardless of its public or private character, and assigning some public functions of the official clergy or their representatives (in parallel or instead) to new religiously-neutral organs. Finally, a new movement of doctrinally conservative Conformists reacted against the liberalising effect this was having on the public religious Establishment, looking to episcopal authority as the basis for a finite Church of England with its own constitution and rules.

Episcopal authority over the public religion benefited not only from Tractarian thinking and new statutory powers. The century also saw bishops making new use of existing legal rights (such as visitation) and discretions: to confer or with-

143 Test Act 1672; stat 30 Car II st 2 (1678).

144 Stat 9 Geo IV c.17 (1828) replaced the sacramental test imposed by Test Act 1672 with an innocuous oath; Roman Catholic Relief Act 1829 admitted Catholics to parliament and most Crown offices.

145 Representation of the People Act 1832, extending voting rights to the wealthier middle classes.

146 The title of this body, incorporated on a permanent basis by the Ecclesiastical Commissioners Act 1836, recalled the royal style recognised in 1558. In adjusting ecclesiastical boundaries to reflect industrialisation (previously done by statute), and in administering the newly-centralised endowments of episcopal sees, cathedral canonries and parochial benefices, they served not merely 'the Church of England', but England itself in its ecclesiastical concerns. Their membership included bishops and members of the Commons, ensuring spokesmen available in each House to answer for their stewardship of public religious assets (see now Church Commissioners Measure 1947 s.12(2)). The King in Council was empowered to confirm their schemes.

hold holy orders, to endorse or halt disciplinary proceedings. Collectively, they became more visible when the provincial convocations resumed substantive business from 1854. In the 1860s they initiated the creation of a structure of voluntary bodies from parish to provincial level. With effect from 1920 when our next period begins, the apex of this structure would gain a new role in the legislative process: but only in England proper. In Wales, a longstanding campaign against the religious Establishment and its tithes by dissenters who portrayed it as the church of an alien English-speaking upper class had won support from the Liberal Party and become enmeshed with that Party's campaign to curb the legislative power of the House of Lords. As soon as the Lords' veto power was removed[147], the Liberals secured passage of legislation to end the religious Establishment in Wales and the ecclesiastical law that underpinned it.[148]

(b) Voluntary religion – registration, fiscal privileges, and marriage

The Elizabethan penal statutes affecting alternative worship were repealed in 1846.[149] Relying on the general freedom of action implicit in the common law, individuals could henceforth worship as they pleased without worrying about oaths of loyalty or registration. Registration appeared in a new guise, however, from 1855: no longer as a condition of lawful worship, but an optional route to two long-term privileges for places of religious worship.[150]

First there were fiscal privileges. Local taxation (the poor rate) had been reformed in 1833 and places of tolerated public religious worship were exempt.[151] This exemption was henceforth tied to registration under the 1855 Act. This supplemented the exemptions from national taxation already enjoyed through charitable status, which had taken on new importance with the regular imposition of income tax.[152]

Even more significant was the link between building registration and marriage. Quakers and Jews excepted, parish church solemnisation had been required for the validity of all marriages since 1753. This was perhaps the leading grievance perceived by the newly-powerful dissenting interest after the franchise

147 Parliament Act 1911.
148 Welsh Church Act 1914 ss.1 and 3(1). The effective date of the legislation was deferred to 1920 because of the War.
149 Religious Disabilities Act 1846 *The Jews and the English Law*, London 1908
150 Places of Worship Registration Act 1855.
151 Poor Rate Exemption Act 1833.
152 Income tax, first levied in 1798, became a permanent phenomenon after the Income Tax Act 1842.

reform, and the first to be remedied. The Marriage Act 1836 provided two new alternatives for couples wishing to marry. They could solemnise their union either in a registered building (a place of public dissenting worship) »according to such form and ceremony as the parties see fit to adopt«, or in a public register office where no religious rite would be used.

(c) Non-Christian religions and Non-religion

The nineteenth century saw England's Jews fully recognised as part of the legal community. The Marriage Act 1836 gave legal effect to ceremonies following Jewish custom and required synagogue secretaries to maintain official registers.[153] The secretaries' identity was certified by the Board of Deputies of British Jews (descended from a group permitted to greet George III on his accession in 1760), which acquired its first constitution at this time and later became an important liaison group with government.[154] From 1846 Jewish trusts and schools enjoyed the same legal status as those of protestant dissent.[155] In 1860 Jews were relieved from the oath »on the true faith of a Christian« which had excluded them from Parliament[156], and in 1878 provisions preventing women and children's factory employment on Sunday were modified in favour of Jewish proprietors who closed on Saturday instead.[157] The Army acquired Jewish chaplains in 1892.

It was tacitly assumed that the legitimacy of organised English Jewry would apply equally to other non-Christian faiths. Non-religious philosophies or worldviews, however, still fell short of fully equal treatment. The benefits of building registration under the 1855 Act were not open to them. Although »ethical societies« had existed for some time and formed a Union in 1896[158], principled non-believers could benefit only from the »opting-out« and non-religious alternatives available to all (including dissident believers). Denied use of the charitable trust, the »advancement of irreligion« had to make use of a juristic person, the registered company, in pursuing its goals.[159] There was one concession to the non-

153 S.2.
154 Board of Deputies of British Jews, <http://www.boardofdeputies.org.uk/live/content.php?Category_ID=14>, accessed October 2012.
155 Religious Disabilities Act 1846 s.2.
156 Jews Relief Act 1860.
157 Factory Act 1878, s.51.
158 This became the British Humanist Association in 1967: <http://www.humanism.org.uk/about/history>, accessed on 12.10.12.
159 In *Bowman v. Secular Society Ltd.* (1917) AC 406 the legality of such a company's anti-religious objects and hence its power to receive and hold property was confirmed. The

religious conscience made during the First World War: conscientious objection to military service, even without a religious basis, gave entitlement to exemption from conscription.[160] But local tribunals administering this Act showed themselves hostile to philosophical pacifism and successful claims to exemption were rare.[161]

(d) Continuing inequalities

Even by 1920, it remained clear in many ways that the law did not place private religious initiatives on a par with the public provision. In some cases parity might exist in practice but rest on two quite different theoretical bases: for example the rates from which registered places of worship were exempt were never in any case levied on public buildings such as the parish church.

The law allowing dissenters to marry by their own rites in their own buildings also distanced itself from private religious polity. It was by statute the bridal couple themselves who chose the rite in a registered building, not a religious office-bearer. Indirect pressure could be applied from the tradition in question, since the registered building could only be used with its owners' agreement. But that gave the initial decision to the building's trustees, holders of the only position known to the general law.[162] It was not even open to office-bearers designated by religious rules to seek a building's registration; that was for the trustees and twenty householders using it.

Wherever a public service remained in the hands of public ecclesiastical office-bearers, or provided on ecclesiastical land, that provision remained the norm, even if alternatives were approved. After 1880 anybody (even a Conformist) arranging a parish churchyard burial could opt out of the official liturgy accompanying it[163], and after 1888 anyone could decline use of the New Testament

non-charitable nature of non-religious philosophies, taken for granted in *Bowman*, was confirmed in *Re South Place Ethical Society* (1980) 3 All ER 918.

160 Military Service Act 1916.

161 Peace Pledge Union, *Conscientious Objection in Britain during the First World War*,<http://www.ppu.org.uk/learn/infodocs/cos/st_co_wwone.html> accessed on 30.10.2010.

162 Recognition of this fact later led to amendments under which the minister officiating in the building could (or, in the case of a Roman Catholic parish priest, had to) give consent in lieu of the trustees; see now Marriage Act 1949 s.44(1).

163 Parish churchyards were the primary burial facility for the whole population because of the parishioner's right of burial whenever space allowed (*Kemp v. Wickes*, above). Burial Laws Amendment Act 1880 permitted either silence, or a 'Christian and orderly religious service' chosen by the funeral's organisers. However as the ancient churchyards filled up, both commercial and public alternatives became available, each offering a choice be-

and Christian language in official and evidential oaths[164]; but in default of objection the funeral service would be used, or they would »swear by Almighty God«. The public religious provision was also usually available to everybody, whereas alternatives might be for a more restricted circle. A Jew who chose to marry in his parish church after banns might do so, but a Christian could not invoke the law's Jewish marriage provisions.

True parity was seen only where functions were removed from ecclesiastical organs altogether and transferred to new public authorities, or in novel statutory provisions. But although there had always been some public officers with no apparent connection to official worship,[165] deliberate creation of marriage registrars as a non-religious institution to meet the needs of a diverse population exposed the Home Secretary to angry criticism at the time.[166] The argument from efficiency prevailed in 1857, when the ecclesiastical courts ceded their testamentary and matrimonial jurisdiction to predecessors of today's High Court; and by 1899 all-purpose parish Vestries were replaced in their »temporal« role by new »civil« Parish Councils and Metropolitan Boroughs.[167] As for innovations, in 1861 England's closest approximation to a criminal code attached aggravated penalties to arson in, or theft from, a place of worship, regardless of that worship's character, and to assaults on all ministers in the execution of their duty.[168]

(e) Schools: a private religious initative

The advancement of education had always been a charitable purpose, but that in itself identified it as a private initiative. Even the public schools were only public in the sense that any pupil capable of winning a scholarship or paying fees could enter: children's education in England was not a State responsibility.However, religion was considered a vital part of any upbringing, and religious groups and

tween consecrated and unconsecrated land: Cemeteries Clauses Act 1847, Burial Act 1852.

164 Non-Christian oaths or, for non-believers, affirmation became available alternatives under the Oaths Act 1888.

165 Though not as many as one might think: the official liturgy still provides today for naval officers to lead worship, justices of the peace appointed gaol chaplains under the 1772 Act, and until the Municipal Corporations Act 1882, some town councils presented parish ministers to their livings.

166 Tractarian bishop Henry Philpotts called Lord John Russell's Act 'a disgrace to British legislation'; *The Times*, 13.10.1836.

167 Court of Probate Act 1857, Matrimonial Causes Act 1857; Local Government Act 1894, London Government Act 1899.

168 Malicious Damage Act 1861, s.1; Larceny Act 1916, s.24 (replacing an 1861 provision); Offences against the Person Act 1861, s.36.

individuals were regularly concerned with schooling. In 1808 a society for promoting the Education of the Poor took over the schools which a Quaker philanthropist had founded, and fearing this might give dissent a monopoly over cheap or free education, a group of Conformists founded a rival »National Society« for »Education of the Poor in the Principles of the Established Church« two years later.[169]

The »church schools« operated in connexion with these societies were not, in legal terms, *part* of any church. Their sites were acquired by local trustees, individual believers prepared to accept the relevant society's assistance and submit to rules designed to ensure consistent management and fidelity to religious principles. But even though parish ministers regularly accepted trusteeship (and bishops oversight) of »National« schools, this was by their individual choice: ecclesiastical law imposed no obligation to become involved. Such schools were never within the public religious establishment, but purely voluntary undertakings; and the »British« schools were separate charities from any dissenting chapel that might support them.

The first significance of the »National« Schools to this study, therefore, is that they accustomed the official clergy to regularly acting within a voluntary organisation, and Conformists to supporting it financially – a lesson that would bear fruit after 1860 as the Church of England began to develop a non-statutory support structure. But they are also early examples of religiously neutral treatment in the light of the 1832 franchise reform and the dissenting presence in Parliament. Both »National« and»British« schools shared in the government grants distributed from 1833 to assist in the newly-important task of »educating our masters«.

England never saw a general transfer of church schools to government. Many schools founded by believers remain held by successor trustees today: but the »partnership« with government begun with the receipt of grants from 1833 moved steadily towards a greater involvement of public authority. In 1862 it became a grant condition that schools allow withdrawal from religious instruction, thus making the school available to local children of other religious traditions or none.[170] In 1870 the system became statutory and School Boards opened schools

169 The body operating Joseph Lancaster's schools became the British and Foreign School Society in 1814, its Conformist rival is today the National Society for Promoting Religious Education.

170 The same right applies to the Christian worship and Christian-centred religious education required in today's government-provided 'community schools' under Education Act 1996, s.375(3) and School Standards and Framework Act 1997, Sch 20 para 3.

with no church connection where no church school existed.[171] Finally the Education Act 1902 replaced central grants to religious school trusts by comprehensive local taxation, funding free primary and secondary schools whether or not »provided by« local authorities, to whom the balance of control now shifted.

Religious instruction in church schools remained under the control of trustees or other representatives of the tradition in which the school was founded.[172] But the 1870 and 1902 provisions for the wholly State institutions (Board and »provided« schools respectively) showed the non-dogmatic bedrock of the English ecclesial state: instruction in such schools was to be Christian and derived from the Bible, but not distinctive of any religious catechism (including that of the Prayer Book).

(f) The Tractarian reaction

The way dissenting scruples were addressed had a liberalising effect on the public religion for those who still conformed to it. Conformists, like dissenters, retained all their religious rights, but found their religious duties significantly reduced. Even though they attended parish church worship, legal obligations to support the buildings and ministers that made this possible were disappearing. Those ministers themselves represented an increasingly broad range of theological positions, from evangelical pietism to an Enlightened and critical »modernism«. Observances once compulsory, from marriage in church to burial with the official rite, were becoming matters of choice; and the moral jurisdiction of the ecclesiastical courts was virtually obsolete.

This was welcome to the »broad church« of liberal protestant laymen. But a clergy-led reaction against this state of affairs, beginning in 1833 as the Oxford Movement to recall England from »national apostasy« to the doctrines of the Prayer Book, grew rapidly, and its supporters, the Tractarians[173], became the third force acting on the displaced nineteenth century's law of religion.

The Movement's pioneers saw England as their target. Their goal was to renew the public religion of the ecclesial state, purging it of modernism, relegating

171 Elementary Education Act 1870.

172 This made their funding out of local rates highly controversial with dissenting ratepayers. The Education (Local Authority Default) Act 1905 was passed to coerce dissenter-controlled authorities, but never invoked due to the fall of the government responsible for it.

173 They were so named after the *Tracts for the Times* in which the Movement's first leaders published their arguments; although for convenience we shall use the same term for their heirs well into the twentieth century.

dissent to the sidelines. Historic ecclesiastical funding should be left untouched, Crown prerogatives be used to defend the faith regardless of the views of a heterodox parliament.[174]But soon, realising that responsible governments and judges trained in the common law were unlikely to turn back the constitutional clock, Tractarians reached behind the Reformation to a mediæval concept of catholicity. Whilst invoking aspects of Hooker's writings, they departed radically from Hooker's identification of church and commonwealth and his location of authority in the whole church thus understood. In common with dissenters they proclaimed a church distinct from the nation; but one in which authority was committed by Christ to the apostles, transmitted to bishops through the tactile or »apostolic« succession, and shared with the rest of the ordained.

Legally-minded Tractarians appealed to the whole body of mediæval canon law, rather than just canonical rules adopted within the realm, and questioned the competence of laypeople to legislate or adjudicate in spiritual affairs.[175] Divergent views of authority would later culminate in defiance, then paralysis, of the ecclesiastical courts.[176] The provincial convocations resumed regular debate from 1854 with a strong Tractarian presence, and it was to them (rather than parliament) that the Movement's supporters deferred. Instead of speaking of English law establishing structures, ministry and rites, they spoke of these as facets of the pre-existent church: in their language the law »established« *the church itself*, in a technical sense referring to a relationship of privilege and control.

From small beginnings in the 1830s, Tractarianism had supporters in episcopate and judiciary by the turn of the century, and its understanding of »establishment« – a lay State, with a bias to Christianity, granting privileges to the pre-existent church which it considered the best teacher of the Christian faith – was

174 John Keble's 1833 sermon before the Assize judges in Oxford, which gave the Movement its name and is considered its historic starting-point, attacked legislation to redistribute the endowments of Irish sees. The Crown's appointment of suspected modernist John Hampden to the Regius Chair of Divinity at Oxford in 1836 was among the Tractarians' first battlegrounds.

175 E.g. Edward Wood, *The Regal Power of the Church, or the Fundamentals of the Canon Law – A Dissertation*, 1888, reprinted with an introduction by Eric Kemp, London 1948.

176 The Judicial Committee of the Privy Council had stood at the apex of the ecclesiastical court system since 1833. Dominated by common lawyers, this court heard a number of appeals concerning the liturgical practices of the clergy and the orthdoxy of their preaching between the 1840s and 1880s. Its critics considered it rigid in matters of ritual (where the law was statutory and clear, and Tractarians were usually the accused) but lax in matters of doctrine (where Tractarians were usually proceeding against Modernists, and the status of written formularies was disputed). Extreme Tractarians denied its competence, and that of the inferior courts bound to follow its precedents, in theologically sensitive questions; and there were several instances of ministers imprisoned for contempt until the bishops resolved to withhold the sanction required for new disciplinary proceedings.

formulated by a sympathetic judge in a well-known decision of 1907.[177] But there was also reaction, particularly in parliament, against the perceived proximity of Tractarian positions to Catholicism and the more extreme clergy's contempt of the courts; and though statutes of this period modified many rules consistent with the identity of church and kingdom, no legislation denied the ecclesial state's existence.

(g) The voluntary face of the Church of England

The cessation after 1831 of new parliamentary funding for public religion left ecclesiastical institutions reliant on historic assets, voluntary donations, and the continuing compulsory levies of church rate and tithe rentcharge.[178] These levies, however, ranked among the dissenters' grievances, and compulsory church rate (by which parishioners contributed to repair the nave of their parish church) was abolished in 1868.[179] In consequence, voluntary donation – a feature typical of dissent, but which public religion had always seen as properly supporting initiatives (such as the »National« Schools) *outside* its core activity – now became necessary to pay assistant ministers, maintain church fabric and finance projects at home and overseas.

This development coincided with the Tractarians' portrayal of the Church of England as a narrow episcopally-governed society with quite specific doctrines, but also with the realisation that in many overseas colonies, episcopal authority could rest *only* on consensual compact since bishops had no place in the colonial ecclesiastical law.[180] English bishops, as a result, began from the 1860s to encourage active conformists to work with clergy in voluntary collaborative bodies from parish to provincial levels.[181] The more influential laypeople were involved in decisions regarding the public religion, the greater interest they would take in

177 *Marshall v. Graham* (1907) 2 KB 112 (Phillimore J.).

178 The Tithe Act 1836 replaced tithes in kind by a fixed financial 'rentcharge' on burdened land; but the principle still remained that the whole population able to do so should support a public religious ministry.

179 Compulsory Church Rate Abolition Act 1868. Tithe rentcharge, however, did not simply cease, but was exchanged for a single large commutation payment to the Ecclesiastical Commissioners out of tax revenue under the Tithe Act 1936. Liable landowners then reimbursed the Treasury by annuity payments over 40 years.

180 *R. v. Eton College* (1857) 8 El & Bl 610 is considered the first, and the Privy Council judgment *In re Bishop of Natal* (1865) 3 Moo PC 115 the most momentous, of such rulings.

181 English bishops began to call diocesan conferences, and encouraged parish ministers to invite leading parishioners to parochial church councils, from the 1860s. The first provincial House of Laymen sat in conference with the existing clergy Convocation in 1885.

it and the readier they would be to fund it. Strictly Tractarian clergy had reservations about the lay element in this structure, but it enjoyed a wide base of support.

Though parish ministers and provincial convocations were recognised by public law, parochial church councils, the intermediate »conferences« and provincial lay Houses were not. No less than the circuit meetings of the Wesleyans, these rested on a compact between participants. Charitable trust funds were set up and premises donated to support religious activity under these voluntary bodies' control.[182] Thecreation of a »church electoral roll« in 1903 as the basis of a lay franchise gave the new structure a claim to be representative[183], but could not alter its voluntary character: the only authority behind the enrolment criteria was that of the convocations (which could not legislate for laity) and the existing voluntary lay Houses.

(h) Separation of Prussian protestant rules and structures from government agencies and the general law

Though the reigns of Frederick William III and his two sons were crucial in the history both of Prussian government and of the Old-Prussian[184] protestant *Landeskirche*, the changes that took place during these reigns in church-state relations built on foundations already laid. The position of Catholicism in the legal system had already ruled out an ecclesial state on the English model, and led to the creation of government organs concerned primarily with the *jus circa sacra*. From 1825, when State interestsat provincial level (including Catholic and school affairs) were detached from the responsibility of the *Konsistorien*[185], a

182 The 1868 Act itself assisted this process by providing (s.9) for incorporated church trustees in each parish, comprising the minister with nominees of the bishop and the patron. However wholly voluntary initiatives were usually preferred, even at the price of legal personality. For the 'Boards of Finance' serving the voluntary structures at diocesan and central levels, the option of a company limited by guarantee was popular: see Diocesan Boards of Finance Measure 1925.

183 The 'Rules for the Representation of the Laity' in 1903 styled the Convocations sitting with the Houses of Laymen the 'Representative Church Council'.

184 The term *altpreußisch* refers to the Prussian provinces in existence before 1866, and to the protestant religious establishment of those provinces later known as the *Landeskirche*. In an effort to win acceptance of Prussian rule within territories such as Hanover, annexed following the Austro-Prussian War, the protestant churches of those new provinces were not integrated into the victors' ecclesial structures (whose confessionally-United character they viewed with deep suspicion). After 1866, therefore, references here to 'Prussian' protestantism should be regarded as abbreviated references to old Prussian protestantism.

185 *Kabinettsorder* of 31.12.1825.

relatively clean pattern of authority could be seen. Catholic oversight vested in bishops and archbishops, protestant oversight in *Konsistorien* and the Berlin Ministry's protestant affairs section. Government interests were entrusted to the remaining departments of provincial governments and the Ministry.[186] When the protestant affairs section was renamed *Evangelischer Oberkirchenrat* and fully emancipated from the Ministry in 1850, that merely completed a separation pending since Waterloo.

The law itself followed the differentiation of institutions. By the time he granted a constitution to his people in December 1848, Frederick William IV was convinced of the majority's unfitness to take or influence ecclesiastical decisions. All recognised that the new *Landtag* could not take an ecclesiastical role with a considerable proportion of the potential electorate Catholic; but even those assigned by their baptismal setting to the protestant *Religionsparteien* included theological modernists and participants in the risings that had taken place all over Germany in March. These were not, in the King's view, suitable people to share in protestant church government. He was prepared to act with the *Landtag* in making law for the State, but did not wish it to intervene in his oversight of Prussian protestant religion, whether in person or through the agencies responsible to him.

Both Prussian constitutions thus provided that, »The legislative power shall be exercised in common by the King and by two Chambers«, but that »The Protestant and the Roman Catholic Church shall [each] like every other religious association, order and administer its affairs autonomously …«.[187]The constitutional convention in Frankfurt would in due course produce a draft containing similar wording (»every religious association shall order and administer its affairs autonomously but remain subject to the general laws of the State«);[188] but for the Prussian provision it was more important that the King wished to see a separation.

At the same time it was indicated by the Ministry in Berlin that the protestant church would continue to administer its affairs through the King as *summus episcopus*, and that, whilst the principle of acting with synods in the making of

186 Further changes were to come, for example the provincial governor (*Oberpräsident*) continued to chair the Konsistorium until 1845.

187 *Verfassungs-Urkunde für den Preußischen Staat*, 31.1.1850, Arts 15, 62. The 'revised' 1850 constitution agreed by the *Landtag* replaced a text issued by the King alone on 5.12.1848 following the collapse of the revolutionary movement for a united German constitution. These provisions are similar in both. The word 'each', not in the German text, is inserted to allow a grammatical English translation.

188 § 147(1) of the 'Paulskirchenverfassung' adopted in Frankfurt on 29.3.1849 but never given effect.

church rules was accepted, the proposal submitted in mid-1848 for protestant synods elected by all residents of each province categorised as protestant was unacceptable.[189]

It was thus critically significant for Prussia's »displaced nineteenth century« that it had not shared the outcome of England's civil war and Revolution. In England, where the ecclesial state was subject to an increasingly circumscribed monarch in a religiously diverse Parliament, but religious toleration had never divided the population legally into two or more churches, a separate church law and authority structure with public legal recognition was the pipe-dream of Tractarian activists: the price of legal autonomy was schism and, at best, private association status. But in Prussia, where the King alone exercised real State and protestant church authority before 1848 and was able to dictate the extent to which they would be shared thereafter, the emergent *Landeskirche* was able to develop a distinctive character without losing the official status that both it and Roman Catholic structures enjoyed.

(i) Stricter and narrower – the Prussian churches under the later Hohenzollern

We have noted how the »displaced nineteenth century« saw England's parishioners steadily relieved of ecclesiastical burdens and duties, whilst enforceable religious rights and their constitutional connection to the religious establishment were in no way diminished. No formal »opting-out of membership« was ever provided for because the disappearance of onerous duties made it unnecessary. The reaction against this liberalising trend was largely in the hands of the Tractarians but their notion of a narrowly-understood church, strict in both faith and morals, made little progress in the law until the period ended. Whilst Prussian protestantism metamorphosed during the century from *Kirchenwesen* to *Kirche*, not only in in literature and official terminology but in practical ways, the Church of England in 1919 still appeared in many ways to justify the American

189 This proposal stemmed from the Ministry of Spiritual Affairs under Count von Schwerin, appointed at the height of the March 1848 risings whilst the King felt bound to co-operate with the forces of radical reform. It promised the 'democratisation' of the protestant church which theological liberals imagined would have a broadening effect; but the King preferred the tests of orthodox belief and conduct represented by the congregational membership concept of the western provinces. A presbyterian *Kirchenordnung* for the West had been approved by Frederick William III in 1835; comparable structures for the East and then an overarching General Synod were created in 1873 and 1876.

justice who had called it »nothing more than a compendious expression for the religious establishment of the realm«.[190]

In Prussia royal support for the reaction against liberalism made all the difference: changes through the century in the protestant establishment tended towards a narrower and stricter body, with a defined membership and the right for those who disliked it to opt out. Catholicism, having an independent leadership from the start of the period, clashed seriously with the State on at least two occasions, when that leadership sought to impose a stricter discipline on its members than the government believed appropriate; but this tension was also ultimately resolved by a right to opt out of Catholic church membership with its obligations for those unable to accept the ultramontane approach.

Frederick William III admittedly had a higher view of State authority over the religious sphere than his sons. He imposed the common protestant liturgy, the chief tool in realising his dream of a Reformed-Lutheran Union, with little sympathy for the »Old Lutheran« dissidents, who suffered not only deprivation but in some cases banishment. He authorised imprisonment of both Roman Catholic archbishops in the first mixed marriages dispute, and confirmed only with misgivings the new presbyterian *Kirchenordnung* for the protestant congregations of the Rhine Province and Westphalia, seeing in synods dangerous parallels to secular one-man one-vote democracy.

Nevertheless each of these developments points up an English contrast. The view taken by the Roman hierarchy of marriages' validity never mattered so much in England. Catholic bishops were officers of a voluntary society, not »spiritual superiors« of a »principal confession«. Their rulings affected a lower proportion of the population and had no effect on legal status. The neutral context of the register office was available from 1836 for any protestant-Catholic couple wishing to marry.

The western *Kirchenordnung*, although perforce recognising the Prussian heartland's concept of the geographical parishioner (*Eingepfarrter*), preferred to concentrate on the duties and privileges of the congregation member or *Gemeindeglied*, leading the way to the finite membership of later Prussian church constitutions[191] and away from the religious rights by residence which every Englishman still enjoys.

190 *Town of Pawlet v. Clark* (1815) 13 US 292.

191 *Kirchenordnung für die evangelischen Gemeinden der Provinz Westfalen und der Rheinprovinz*, 5.3.1835, §§ 1-2; *Kirchengemeinde- und Synodalordnung 1876*; Walter Göbell, *Die rheinisch-westfälische Kirchenordnung von 5.3.1835 – ihre geschichtliche Entwicklung und ihr theologischer Gestalt*, Duisburg 1938, 225-27.

The Old Lutherans showed parallels in several respects with the Oxford Movement. They had different founding grievances: for the former, the royal appeal in 1817 for interchangeable ministry and intercommunion between Lutheran and Reformed, which was followed in the 1820s by imposed liturgical change; for the latter, the unwillingness of Crown and parliament after 1832 to halt the perceived drift of the national church toward religious modernism. Both, however, resisted by a call to rediscover historic formularies – the confessional documents or the Prayer Book. Liturgical rules became the cause for which clergy of both groups faced penalties undeterred, though fifty years separated the Prussian Union's liturgical *Agende* from the first proceedings against Tractarians expressing their concept of church and priesthood in high sacramental worship.[192] Voluntary churches formed in the English colonies, able to interpret the Prayer Book tradition with stricter dogma, stronger episcopal authority and longer-lived moral rigidity than the religious establishment at home, invite comparison with the Missouri Synod of North America, the best-known legacy of Prussia's Old Lutheran emigrants.

Yet the Old Lutheran question also marked the transition to a new reign in Prussia and the importance of royal opinion for the developing law. Whilst Parliament's distaste for Tractarian militancy delayed serious change in England until 1919, the Old Lutheran legal position improved drastically soon after Frederick William IV's accession in 1840.For our purposes the crucial aspect of the »General Concession« granted to the Old Lutherans was that, whilst able to separate from the protestant *Landeskirche* and form self-governing congregations, they were able to retain the public law prerogatives of »principal confessions« such as solemnisation of marriage.[193] The extension of such rights to smaller dissenting bodies *as such* went well beyond the private law status they would have enjoyed in England, where the nearest equivalent even after 1836 would have been a bridal couple solemnising their own marriage in a building placed at their disposal by trustees. Closer to the English position was that of less traditional Prussian religion such as that of the »Free Protestants«, whom the King discouraged. After 1847 these could leave the *Landeskirche* to form their own religious association, but they were not freed from financial obligations and might well

192 Suspended from his preferment in 1830 for refusing the new liturgical *Agende*, Silesian minister Johannes Scheibel ultimately chose exile along with numerous followers. Ritual prosecutions in England commenced with *Liddell v. Westerton* (1857) Moo Sp Rep 1, were expedited by the Public Worship Regulation Act 1874, and the first minister was committed for contempt in 1877.

193 *Generalkonzession für die von der Gemeinschaft der evangelischen Landeskirche sich getrennt haltenden Lutheraner*, 23.7.1845.

not enjoy marriage privileges, so the same edict provided the first arrangements for civil solemnisation.[194]

This leads us to one of the century's biggest Anglo-Prussian contrasts. The *Toleranzpatent* of 1847 was followed by a statute of 1873 allowing withdrawal from any church, by declaration before a judge after a period for reflection, with no requirement to join or form another and freedom from all financial dues.[195] Although intended as *Kulturkampf* legislation hostile to the Catholic hierarchy, this benefited non-believers and theological dissidents of all sorts, including those from the protestant establishment. The converse of the right to withdraw was the imposition of significant duties upon those who remained in *Landeskirche* congregations and could be assumed to be there by choice. In 1905 a general financial levy on members for *Landeskirche* purposes, going beyond earlier congregational powers, was authorised.[196] Church rules of the same year imposed a rigorous marriage discipline and punished (for example with exclusion from church offices including that of godparent) parents who failed to ensure their children's protestant baptism, instruction and confirmation.[197]

By then the financial liability even of regular worshippers in England's parish churches was almost reduced to voluntary donation alone[198]; and the convocations were bemoaning the lack of any effective discipline of the laity. When the general law relaxed marriage discipline it did so for everybody, and only the conscience of the individual parish minister could (sometimes) stand between the parishioner and a church wedding.[199] This meant no church withdrawal proce-

194 *Patent über die Bildung neuer Religionsgesellschaften*, 30.3.1847.

195 *Kirchenaustrittsgesetz* 14.5.1873.

196 *Kirchengesetz betreffend die Erhebung von Kirchensteuern in den Kirchengemeinden und Parochialverbänden der evangelischen Landeskirche der älteren Provinzen der Monarchie* 26.5.1905, with confirming State statute of 14.7.1905.

197 *Kirchengesetz betreffend die Trauungs-Ordnung* 27.7.1880; *Kirchengesetz betreffend die verletzung kirchlicher Pflichten in Bezug auf Taufe, Konfirmation und Trauung*, 30.7.1880.

198 Tithe rentcharge, levied on land and supporting the parish ministry, survived till commuted by the Tithe Act 1936. It must be said that voluntary donation worked passably as a system. Although twentieth century English churches never enjoyed the financial security which church tax until recently gave the larger German confessions, the Church of England could never have survived at all had worshippers not plugged the deficit from vanished public funding.

199 'There can be no duality in marriage', *per* Lord Ashbourne in *Thompson v. Dibdin* (1912) AC 533, so a marriage declared valid by the law of the land was equally lawful within the religious establishment, whatever the convocations might think. However parish ministers conscientiously unhappy about solemnising certain unions for reasons relating to divorce, affinity and later gender reassignment) had begun to benefit from statutory exemptions from their regular duty (first seen in the Matrimonial Causes Act 1857 and today typified by Matrimonial Causes Act 1965, s.8(2)).

dure was required: anyone reluctantly supporting the religious establishment could simply stop doing so. Even in alternative congregations, such as Jewish or Mormon, in which financial commitment was clearly spelt out, the freedom to resign implied in private contracts of association ensured public law did not have to intervene to allow believers a change of heart.

6. The mid- and late twentieth century – 1920-2000

(a) The fate of public religion in Wales

This survey's final period was ushered in by the Welsh Church Acts 1914-19 and the Church of England Assembly (Powers) Act 1919, both taking effect in 1920. In Wales the ecclesiastical law of the land ceased to have effect as law.[200] Those who wished to continue worshipping in the Prayer Book tradition within a protestant episcopal structure could of course do so, but this structure, like English nonconformity, would be held together by the private law vehicles of trust and contract. To enable the new »Church in Wales« to function immediately, the Act provided that the rules of English ecclesiastical law would bind its members »in the same manner as if they had mutually agreed to be so bound«, and be enforced in relation to property »as if such property had been expressly assured upon trust to be held on behalf of persons who should be so bound«.[201] The membership was however free to adapt the rules so inherited[202], and did so at once, adopting a constitution that had been prepared by a convention at Cardiff in 1917. This merged the institutions of the former religious Establishment such as bishops, parish ministers and churchwardens with the voluntary structures created for its support since the 1860s, surmounted by a new Governing Body.[203]

As a voluntary organisation the Church in Wales had no claim on public religious assets, and the endowments held by the Ecclesiastical Commissioners in respect of Welsh benefices and cathedrals were in part allocated to other public purposes. But the principality's church buildings and parsonages, with limited funds to maintain them, were made over to a corporation under the new church's

200 Welsh Church Act 1914, s.3(1).
201 Welsh Church Act 1914, s.3(2).
202 Welsh Church Act 1914, s.13(1).
203 See generally Philip Bell, *Disestablishment in Ireland and Wales*, London 1969.

control.[204] Its ministers succeeded to the right and duty to solemnise parishioners' marriages.[205]

(b) The two faces of the Church of England

Whilst public religion largely disappeared from Wales in 1920, the changes in England were in theory much less radical. Parliament simply recognised that some way of pre-digesting amendments to ecclesiastical law would enable it to perform its still-acknowledged task effectively.[206] The post-1860 voluntary structures became the key to this: a new organ at their head, the National (informally »Church«) Assembly, was empowered to submit legislative measures to parliament. The passage of such laws through the Houses was expedited by a simple resolution procedure in place of the customary three readings.[207]

In drafting the 1919 Act, care was taken to meet the Tractarian concern that the voluntary structures should not become creatures of parliament. The Church Assembly's membership and the rules governing the other structures and defining the lay electorate whom they would represent were therefore referred to, rather than actually contained, in the Act. Accordingly the voluntary structures remained voluntary[208], their funds the charitable funds of a private association[209], whilst the public religious establishment remained public. But after 1920 it be-

204 See, *inter alia*, Welsh Church Act 1914 ss.8 and 13(2), and Welsh Church (Temporalities) Act 1919.

205 Marriage law was, according to Welsh Church (Temporalities Act) 1919 s.6, unaffected by the Act of 1914; but that was difficult to see as realistic, given that the earlier Act abolished the law under which parish churches were consecrated and the clergy who licensed or solemnised marriage were appointed. However, appointees of the voluntary society stepped into the shoes of the former public officers without challenge and Welsh marriage arrangements were adapted to the changing geographical boundaries of Church in Wales ministry. In 1945 the representative corporation acquired most of the Welsh churchyards still used for burial, subject to burial rights similar to those which local residents enjoyed in England: Welsh Church (Burial Grounds) Act 1945, s.1.

206 For an account of the debates on the Church of England Assembly (Powers) Bill see David M. Thompson, 'The Politics of the Enabling Act of 1919' in *Church, Society and Politics*, ed. Derek Baker, Oxford 1975, 385.

207 Church of England Assembly (Powers) Act 1919. The procedure entailed consideration by a joint Committee of the two Houses, a report to each House by the Committee, an affirmative resolution in each House and the King's assent.

208 The private nature of the Assembly, rendering it unsuitable for review by the administrative law procedures of the day, was recognised in *R.. v. Legislative Committee of the Church Assembly, ex p. Haynes-Smith* (1928) 1 KB 411.

209 The Diocesan Boards of Finance Measure 1925, requiring that corporate bodies hold assets of the voluntary structure at diocesan level, relied upon limited companies, a typically private vehicle.

came increasingly difficult to tell the two faces of the Church of England apart. Parliament approved measures both to make changes to the voluntary structures[210] and to alter the church-kingdom's ecclesiastical law. Frequently these alterations took the form of transferring to the voluntary structures functions under public ecclesiastical law formerly exercised by churchwardens, vestries or patrons, or sharing the rights of parishioners with others on the church electoral roll.[211]

This blurring of the public-private boundary was accompanied by the final demise, in most minds, of the notion of the ecclesial state. Some politicians had habitually referred to the convocations as »the church« even before 1920; many more believed the Church Assembly to be the voice of the Church of England. Its constitution did indeed provide for it »to consider and express its opinion on any matter of religious or public interest«[212], and it was frequently taken to be speaking for »the church« when doing so. But the consequence was that very few still considered parliament to be that voice. Constitutionally only parliament, not the Assembly, could alter the ecclesiastical law of the land, whether by measures framed in the Assembly[213] or by traditional Bill procedure.[214] It was for parliament to decide whether the Assembly's proposals for public religion should have effect; yet there was outrage well beyond Tractarian circles when in the so-called Prayer Book crisis of 1927-28 the Commons rejected proposals relating to the official liturgy.

As the century progressed, Assembly-drafted measures came to replace large swathes of both the unwritten and the pre-1920 statute law regulating the public religion. Diocesan bishops, who had of course enjoyed important functions under the earlier law, but now added many new statutory powers to the influence they enjoyed through diocesan conference committees and as sources of ordination

210 Both the clerical and the lay composition of the Assembly were in fact altered by legislation very soon after it commenced business, and today (under its new designation 'the General Synod of the Church of England') it rests on the footing of the Synodical Government Measure 1969.

211 e.g. Parochial Church Councils (Powers) Measure 1921.

212 This provision is now in Synodical Government Measure 1969 Sch 2 para 6(b).

213 See *Church and State –Report of the Archbishops' Commission on the Relations between Church and State,* London 1935, vol 1, 34-35.

214 Easter Act 1928 and City of London (Guild Churches) Acts 1952-60 are examples of ecclesiastical legislation independent of the Church Assembly after 1920. The former provides for consultation with the convocations, but not with the Assembly, before the English date of Easter is changed. Mere inaction cannot found the 'long-standing constitutional convention that Parliament does not initiate legislation on such matters' alleged during parliamentary consideration of the Bishops (Consecration of Women) Bill on 21.3.2006 (Commons *Hansard* col 173).

and preferment. The Church of England became more episcopal than it had been since the Civil War.

The more the voluntary Church of England came to eclipse the religious Establishment of the realm, the more difficult it was for ordinary people to comprehend legal phenomena which recalled the ecclesial state. Why, it was asked, should the Crown control episcopal appointments?[215] Why should rules governing public liturgy or ministers' doctrinal commitment still pass through parliament?[216] Why – once a General Synod with lay members took over the convocations' canon-making power – should canons still bind only the clergy? Why should all parishioners enjoy a range of religious rights which Church of England organs had to respect? Why should ordinary judges outnumber bishops at the apex of the ecclesiastical judicial hierarchy?[217] Why should bishops', parish ministers' and ecclesiastical court decisions be open to review in the High Court when the internal decisions of ordinary religion were not?[218] Why should the High Court have a residual duty to enforce the ecclesiastical law when the rules of voluntary religion, in the absence of any material interest, were unenforceable?[219]

Several Archbishops' or Assembly Commissions sat during the century to consider »establishment« in the sense of a Church of England relationship at arm's length to a non-ecclesial state. The last of these commented in 1970:

> »Those who dislike Christianity naturally dislike laws which make it appear as if England is a Christian country. ... Some of our laws descend from a time when church and State were identical, when the church was believed to be society in its religious aspect. ... We

215 In 1976 Prime Minister James Callaghan indicated willingness to co-operate with a Synod-appointed nominations committee when advising on the future exercise of royal patronage; his successors have shown the same willingness and the committee's views have assumed increasing weight.

216 Most such decisions were delegated to the Synod to make by canon by the Church of England (Worship and Doctrine) Measure 1974.

217 This remains so in the most theologically sensitive cases, in which the final instance is a royal Commission of Review of three Supreme Court Justices and two bishops (Ecclesiastical Jurisdiction Measure 1963 s.11(4)); but such a Commission has never sat to date. Decision of the previous final court in doctrinal cases (the Judicial Committee of the Privy Council, which also had a lay judicial majority) caused a pattern of disobedience amongst Tractarian clergy which paralysed the system of ministerial discipline for three generations.

218 compare the mandatory order granted in *R. v. Bishop of Salisbury ex p. Kent* (1916) 1 KB 466, or the declaration contemplated in *R. v. Chancellor of the Chichester Consistory Court ex p. News Group Newspapers*, with the refusal of public law remedies in *R. v. Chief Rabbi ex p. Wachmann*; see n. 254 below.

219 compare the injunction granted in *Gill v. Davies* (1997) 5 Ecc LJ 131to protect an English diocesan bishop's monopoly of ordination with the refusal to review changes in the rules of a Scots dissenting body in *Forbes v. Eden* (1867) LR 1 Sc & Div 568.

used to doubt whether any of our laws today would suggest this to anyone. But we have been surprised to find that they do.

We want to make it clear that the Church of England is one church among several. So far as it is called a »national« church, it professes a mission to all the nation. … The Church of England does not suppose that it is an »expression of society«, the »religious aspect of society«. We had supposed that these were platitudes. We have found that with some they are not.«[220]

But hostile questions could be asked from another perspective as well. Many religious groups professed »a mission to the nation«; so did non-religious philosophies. If the Church of England were in essence no different from these – merely a section of the population united by particular beliefs – then why should its senior clerics share in the nation's lawmaking process, or governments defer to their views? Why should episcopal courts, alone amongst religious tribunals, be able to back up rulings by awards of costs or citation for contempt?[221] Above all, why should such a sectional interest retain sole use of buildings erected with parliamentary grants or repaired with centuries of compulsory levies, and of Treasury capital received in 1936 in lieu of parishioners' tithe?[222]

(c) Public religion and the law of marriage and gender

The 1936 Abdication crisis and the almost simultaneous passage of the Matrimonial Causes Act 1937 illustrated both the continuing influence of public religious office-bearers and the continuing religious responsibility of parliament itself. Remarriage following judicial divorce for adultery had been possible in England since the Matrimonial Causes Act 1857, and although parish ministers with a conscientious exemption to officiating could relinquish that duty[223] to others, the 1857 provision had in fact found majority episcopal support on the basis of the »Matthaean exception«. Like the Deceased Wife's Sister Marriage Act 1907, which removed certain impediments of affinity, it represented a decision of the ecclesial state, leaving no scope for a separate »Church of England law« which could create »duality in marriage«.[224]

220 *Church and State – Report of the Archbishops' Commission*, London 1970, 10.
221 Ecclesiastical Jurisdiction Measure 1963 s.81.
222 see n. 179 above.
223 The duty to officiate at the marriage of parishioners established in *Argar v. Holdsworth* (1758) 2 Lee 515 was confirmed in *R. v. Dibdin* (1910) P 47. The 1857 Act allowed an individual minister to decline to officiate but preserved the parishioner's right by allowing any willing minister to act in the parishioner's church.
224 *Thompson v. Dibdin* (1912) AC 533, 543, *per* Lord Ashbourne.

The lawfulness of remarriage after divorce did not make it respectable, as King Edward VIII found when he wished to marry an unpopular divorced American. But although Archbishop Cosmo Lang had enjoyed significant wielded whilst representing convocation views to the Baldwin government, several Commons speeches during the succeeding Matrimonial Causes Bill debates indicated members' belief that the recognition of hardship in the broadening of grounds for divorce represented a truer Christian position than the convocations' indissolubilism.[225]

The inter-war divorce debate foreshadowed the changed attitudes to sexual and gender ethics of the 1960s. New understandings of same-sex relations, women's political weight and hormonal contraception were all reflected in legislation on which the bishops had to vote, just after the well-publicised Hart-Devlin debate on the degree to which it was proper for any morality to influence the law.[226] Siding with Hart, an influential report to the Church Assembly[227] suggested the Church of England draw back from the endeavour to impose Christian discipline on society as a whole, and seek merely to discipline its own adherents. The Church Assembly's view was by now, in any event, patently not the only view of what Christian discipline required. Continental protestantism had allowed divorce and remarriage for centuries, women had been ordained to ministry in the Congregational churches since 1917[228], and a Quaker publication had contributed significantly to liberalising attitudes to same-sex relations.[229]

Hence, although an ecclesiastical measure imposed a stricter standard for ordination candidates[230], *Putting Asunder* facilitated passage of the Divorce Law Reform Act 1969, making irretrievable breakdown the basis for dissolution and

225 See the writer's paper 'The Christian Claims of the English Law of Marriage' in Adrian Thatcher (ed.), *Celebrating Christian Marriage*, Edinburgh 2002. In deference to the convocation standpoint, the new Act allowed reluctant ministers not only to stand back from a parishioner's second marriage, but to prevent its solemnisation in the parish church at all. This did not prevent the church marriage of divorcees living in parishes whose ministers took a broader view.

226 The Wolfenden Report recommending some decriminalisation of same-sex relations prompted the publication of H.L.A. Hart, *Law, Liberty and Morality* (1963) and Patrick, Lord Devlin, *The Enforcement of Morals* (1965). Matrimonial Causes Act 1963 reduced the importance of spouse collusion as a barrier to divorce; Sexual Offences Act 1967 decriminalised some same-sex relations between males; Abortion Act 1967 widened the grounds for lawful pregnancy termination; Sex Discrimination Act 1975 extended gender equality beyond pay to job selection and other aspects of employment.

227 *Putting Asunder: a Divorce Law for Contemporary Society*, London 1966.

228 *Reverence Constance Coltman 1889-1969*,Women and the Church 2004: <http://oldsite.womenandthechurch.org/celebrated_women/Constance%20Coltman.pdf>, accessed 12.10.12.

229 *Towards a Quaker View of Sex*, London 1963.

230 Clergy (Ordination and Miscellaneous Provisions) Measure 1964, s.9.

matrimonial »fault« a mere supporting »fact«. Although convocation resolutions in 1938 calling on clergy to refuse communion to those who remarried under the 1937 Act had lacked binding force (indeed been unlawful[231]), the extended »conscience clause« won for parish ministers in 1937 still enabled a »strict approach« to be taken to lay divorcees by ministers who saw fit to do so.[232]

In responding to new gender roles English public religion could still secure special legislative treatment. The General Synod wished in 1993 to permit women to be ordained priest whilst simultaneously allowing bishops and congregations to reject them. Existing religious exemptions from sex discrimination law would not have allowed this »piecemeal« approach, but the reforming measure accepted by parliament gave a new exemption exclusive to the Church of England.[233]

(d) Private religion – statute aiding ecumenism

For most organised Christianity in England and Wales, the mid-twentieth century was an era of decreasing numbers and increasing costs; but also one in which old controversies seemed less serious and separated groups sought to reunite. But, given the importance of the charitable trust to voluntary religion, reunion was difficult where assets had been given explicitly in order to advance one divergent view against another.[234] By compromising on their founders' principles, a group risked losing control of the assets those founders had given. A Scots reunion had fallen foul of this difficulty in a well-publicised House of Lords decision of 1904.[235] English churches, which had previously reunited with relative informality, felt after this that only the authority of parliament could cut through trust impediments.[236]

231 for the same reasons as the refusal of communion in *Thomson v. Dibdin*, above.

232 see note above; and see now Matrimonial Causes Act 1965 s.8. Most ministers in this position now follow guidance published by the General Synod House of Bishops in 2002.

233 Priests (Ordination of Women) Measure 1993, s.6.

234 This had become common practice after the Nonconformists' Chapels Act 1844 had provided for long usage to be accepted as evidence of trusts if there were no contradictory provision in a deed. Vesting ultimate control of property in a hierarchically superior officer or organ (e.g. trustees appointed by a Roman Catholic bishop) was the most effective insurance against local heterodoxy – in 1964 United Synagogue control over a dissident congregation's premises obliged it to withdraw, causing the beginning of the separate Masorti movement.

235 *General Assembly of the Free Church of Scotland v. Lord Overtoun* (1904) AC 515.

236 The first English statute of this type was the United Methodist Church Act 1907. The United Synagogue Act 1870, merging five Orthodox Jewish synagogues into a single structure, was not the result of a direct application to parliament but confirmed a Charity Commissioners' scheme.

Had any dissenting group been reconciled to the public Establishment in this period, an ecclesiastical Measure could have effected the necessary alteration of trusts. But dissenting groups on their own had to rely, like any other private body seeking parliament's assistance, on the so-called »private Bill« procedure.[237] After 1920 this was used notably to weld separated Methodist bodies into today's Methodist Church, and Congregational and Presbyterian bodies into the United Reformed Church.[238]

As a rule private religion valued its voluntary character and insisted on separate spheres of church and state, though conceding that property belonged in the state sphere. Care was taken to make clear that, even when an Act of Parliament facilitated the fusion of two bodies into one, the resultant body was not *created* by the Act. The governing organs of the uniting bodies would themselves resolve to form the united church; the facilitating Act would simply protect this step against legal challenge, and alter existing trusts of property into a trust for the united body.[239] The united body would thus share its predecessors' status as an unincorporated association. Other common uses of this procedure were to anticipate future gifts made without taking account of the union[240], to prescribe specific uses for particular types of asset[241], to incorporate a trustee body[242] or to identify and indemnify representative parties to litigation.[243]

Uniting bodies might also, however, use Acts of Parliament to entrench an agreed basis of doctrine or polity for the new church, to prevent the numerical strength of one tradition being used to reverse compromises won by smaller partners in the union discussions.[244] This did amount to a partial surrender of autonomy since, even if opinion in the united body shifted with time, doctrines confirmed by Parliament could not be altered without amending legislation, and the question whether an illegitimate change of doctrine had occurred became one for the courts to determine.[245]

237 Strictly speaking Acts passed following this procedure are styled not private but 'Local Acts'.
238 Methodist Church Union Act 1929; United Reformed Church Act 1972.
239 e.g. United Reformed Church Act 1972 ss.3 and 8-12. There is a parallel here to the way in which the 'voluntary face of the Church of England' preserved its independence by constituting the Church Assembly before the passing of the 1919 Act, which thus conferred powers on a pre-existent body.
240 e.g. United Reformed Church Act 1972 s.16.
241 e.g. United Reformed Church Act 1972 s.8(2) and Sch 2.
242 e.g. Methodist Church Act 1939. A Shi'a Muslim sect has also used private Bill procedure in this way: Dawat-e-Hadiyah (England) Act 1993.
243 e.g. United Reformed Church Act 1972 ss.25, 27(2).
244 Methodist Church Union Act 1929 s.8(2).
245 *Barker v. O'Gorman* (1971) Ch 215. The Methodist Church Act 1976 addressed the difficulty and avoided repeating the provision that had caused it.

On one occasion, not private but government legislation came to the aid of the Christian ecumenical movement. A public Act allowed temporary suspension of denominational trusts when two or more traditions agreed to use a particular building together. This allowed shared decision-making over the building's use, shared oversight. Because the Act covered buildings of the religious Establishment, it also modified ecclesiastical and marriage law; but it left denominational identities and organs untouched, and provided means to terminate any sharing agreement.[246]

(e) Private religion – the issue of ministerial discipline

The appointment, tenure, obligations and discipline of the ministers serving England's public religion were matters of public law[247], found in adopted canonical rules, clerical canons and statute. For equivalent rules and structures of voluntary religion to be enforced through the courts required reliance on private law: on the contract of association between the relevant society's members (to which its office-bearers were, of course, parties as members themselves), on the trusts of assets held to advance that tradition, or (rarely) on the use of controlling shares in a private company.[248] Such vehicles became channels through which the merely moral force of religious rules for those who accepted them was translated into an obligation the courts could recognise and enforce.

In some cases acceptance of particular rules was accompanied by an express disclaimer of contractual intention. If this disclaimer was clear to a new adherent (or office-bearer) and existing adherents, this could rule out enforcement on a contractual basis; though if representatives of the majority held property on trust to advance the religion concerned in their discretion, and chose to withdraw the benefit of that property from a colleague who »broke the rules«; this would still indirectly enforce the rule through the general law.[249]

246 Sharing of Church Buildings Act 1969.

247 *Diocese of Southwark v. Coker* (1998) ICR 140, 147.

248 The Church of Jesus Christ of Latter-Day Saints (Great Britain) is an unlimited company formed to further the work of its parent church through (*inter alia*) the provision of temples and meeting-houses. A Utah-registered corporation controlled by the Presiding Bishop in Salt Lake City is the sole shareholder. This would enable the church's American leadership to prevent a dissident office-bearer from ministering in its buildings (though no question of stipend arises since the church's English and Welsh office-bearers are all unpaid).

249 *Rogers v. Booth* (1937) 2 All ER 751. In *Koeller v. Coleg Elidyr (Camphill Communities Wales) Ltd.* (2005) EWCA Civ 856, trustees' discretionary power to control the occupation of residences enabled a religious community member to be evicted although the community ethos he was considered to have violated had no contractual force. These cas-

In most cases the mutual acceptance of obligations by adherents of a religious tradition *did* have contractual force: a new office-bearer was probably already party to a contract which made provision for his office and perhaps for an associated stipend or housing. Even if no new contract came into being on his admission to office[250], the constitution of the church might impose express procedural requirements for disciplinary removal from office, and/or contain an implied term that such removal would meet »natural justice« demands such as an independent and unbiassed judge.[251] The courts could enforce such rules as ancillary to the office-bearer's material rights. Recognising this around 2000, several churches created adjudicatory panels independent of the council or prelate which had normal oversight of a minister and by whose decision any proceedings would begin.[252]

It was rare, though, that a person deprived of office could prove either bias or a procedural flaw; and private law proceedings could also be slow and expensive. The Industrial Relations Act 1971 having introduced the right of employees not to be unfairly dismissed, and the Court of Appeal having in 1987 shown itself willing to review the decisions of certain privately-established bodies[253], both these avenues appeared to offer dismissed ministers more effective remedies. A spate of applications under both procedures marked the closing years of the century. Public law remedies were denied to private religion. Only the Church of England had the necessary »public element« to warrant the hard-

es were approved in *New Testament Church of God v. Stewart* (2007) EWCA Civ 1004, but Lawrence Collins LJ pointed out (at para 66) that a court might properly discern a contract from conduct if only one of the parties (the church) understood contractual intent to be lacking.

250 As was held to be the case in *President of the Methodist Conference v. Parfitt* (1984) ICR 176.

251 In *Davies v. Presbyterian Church of Wales* (1986) 1 WLR 323 Lord Templeman stated at 329 'The law will ensure that a pastor is not deprived of his salaried pastorate save in accordance with the provisions of the book of rules'. The natural justice point was considered in *R. v. Provincial Court of the Church in Wales ex p. Williams*, though it failed in that case since the applicant had accepted at ordination a system allowing his bishop both executive oversight and a penalty-determining function; (1998) EWHC Admin 998 at para 25.

252 e.g. the Assembly Commission which adjudicates in the name of the United Reformed Church General Assembly in disciplinary proceedings; the church constitution (Structure of the URC, para 2(6)(B), as in force October 2010) forbids the Assembly itself to intervene. Compare the Clergy Discipline Measure 2003, which provides for Bishop's Disciplinary Tribunals over whose composition and proceedings individual Church of England bishops have no control.

253 *R. v. Panel for Takeovers and Mergersex p. Datafin plc* (1987) QB 815.

pressed administrative courts reviewing disciplinary decisions regarding ministers.[254] But employment law seemed to offer the minister a slightly better chance.

A voluntary body's contract of association mentioned above was never considered a contract of service, even if it established or recognised religious offices. For much of their existence, employment tribunals had jurisdiction only where a contract of service existed, and the indefinite duration of appointments and extreme difficulty of identifying an »employer« led courts to deny repeatedly that the appointment of a minister created a contract of service.[255] But whereas this view had first relied upon the pre-existent office to which a minister of religion (whether public or voluntary) was appointed excluding any employment relationship[256], it was held in 1979 that an office and an employment contract might co-exist.[257] In any event, the new field of discrimination law added new grounds for intervention of an employment tribunal, and in that context it sufficed to show that a minister served under a contract »personally to execute work«.[258]

(f) Public and private religion – dialogue and partnership with government

In 1941 a number of Christian bodies formed the Churches' Main Committee to facilitate dialogue with government on legislation affecting their interests, and to monitor future legislative proposals. With the United Synagogue as an associate member, this was a broader, less specialised forum than the Dissenting Deputies or the Board of Deputies of British Jews[259]: but it proved useful monitoring de-

254 A series of cases following *R. v. Chief Rabbi ex p. Wachmann* (1992) 1 WLR 1036 established that no sufficient public interest exists where the respondent is merely an officer or tribunal of a voluntary religious society interpreting its rules, although public law remedies were once granted in such cases (*R. v Barker* (1762) 1 Bl W 352) and may be again (see Harry Lord Woolf, 'Judicial Review: A Possible Programme For Reform' (1992) PL 211): But the ecclesiastical courts of the land are another matter: *R. v. Dibdin* (1910) P 47, already cited, was a prohibition suit against an ecclesiastical judge by the accused minister; *R. v. Chancellor of the Chichester Consistory Court ex p. News Group Newspapers* (1991) *Times* 15 July also concerned the judge hearing a disciplinary case, though the applicants were a media group.

255 As in both *Parfitt* and *Davies*, above.

256 *Re National Insurance Act 1911 - Employment of Church of England Curates* (1912) 2 Ch 563.

257 *Barthope v. Exeter Diocesan Board of Finance* (1979) ICR 900, 904, approved in *Percy v. Church of Scotland Board of National Mission* (2005) UKHL 73, paras 21 and 26.

258 e.g. Sex Discrimination Act 1975, s.82(1); see *Percy v. Church of Scotland Board of National Mission*, above, para 13.

259 see n. 154 above.

velopments in tax, planning, health and safety, and many other branches of the law potentially impacting on religious groups generally.[260]

The willingness of government to deal with the Committee was symptomatic of a growing spirit of »partnership«. Co-operation was well-established in school education, and in 1944 the modern distinction between »county« (today »community«) and »voluntary« schools was introduced. The typical voluntary school was a state-maintained school run on land provided by a charitable (often religious) trust. According to the extent of the trust's financial commitment it might be »aided« or »controlled«, governors representing the religious interest having a greater say in aided schools.[261] Although Church of England and Roman Catholic trusts hosted the majority of religious voluntary schools, protestant dissent and Orthodox Judaism also took part. Religious education in county schools – those *not* run on religious trustees' land – was also a collaborative matter: education authorities put together advisory councils in which their own and teachers' nominees, with invited representatives of local religious and belief traditions, would compile an »agreed syllabus«. Reserved Church of England seats on these councils in England – not, of course, Wales – underlined that the official religion still enjoyed a special position.[262]

This triangular relationship between government, public and private religion was visible also in the consolidated prison legislation of 1952. Every prison was to have a chaplain, appointed by the Prison Commissioners (today the Ministry of Justice), but being a minister licensed by the local Church of England bishop.[263] »Prison ministers«, however, were to be appointed from other religious traditions whenever the number of inmates belonging to those traditions appeared to require it. For this purpose prison governors were to record a declaration of religion by every incoming prisoner. The chaplain could meet with any prisoner wishing it, but prison ministers could only meet declared members of their own tradition. Inmates belonging to religions not represented on the prison staff were to have opportunities to meet with willing »outside« ministers.[264]

(g) Private non-Christian religion

Such flexible provision was particularly important after the Second World War, as the religious makeup of the population began to undergo striking change.

260 The committee is now the Churches' Legislation Advisory Service.
261 Education Act 1944, Part II, esp. ss. 15, 24(2), 25, 28.
262 See now Education Act 1996 ss. 375, 390.
263 Prison Act 1952 ss. 7(1), 7(4), 9(2).
264 Prison Act 1952 s.10.

Within a few decades, migration from former Imperial possessions and within the European Communities, alongside reproductive trends, created a society much more diverse than that which had produced the inherited legal system. Islam, Sikhism and Hinduism became significant English and Welsh religions, building on the small communities that had sprung up in days of Empire around seaports, and spread into major conurbations. Muslims replaced Jews as the country's second-largest religious category. Like some protestant traditions, the newly-growing religions were conscious of a common identity but seldom expressed it structurally: self-financing independent congregations in a variety of legal guises were the norm.

The law allowed non-Christian faiths to worship and organise; charitable status was available for their purposes; mosques and temples could register under the Act of 1855. But for their stricter adherents, religion permeated every aspect of life, from banking to school sports, and laws built on earlier compromises between various shades of Christian and non-believer did not always accommodate this. The common law freedom to do anything not prohibited, together with »reasonable excuse« exceptions to some statutory offences[265], went some way towards a *de facto* liberty, and this was supplemented from time to time by specific concessions. Observant Muslims were fortunate, for example, that a concession made for Jews in the Slaughter of Animals Act 1933 would also let *halal* meat be produced. But the courts could not ignore the law simply because it created internal conflict for a religious believer; and sometimes it did.

Liberal construction of a statute passed after 1950 might be possible, though, on the premise that parliament would not have intended to place monarch and government in breach of their international commitments.[266] In that year Council of Europe members had adopted a Convention for the Protection of Human Rights and Fundamental Freedoms, with guarantees regarding holding and manifestation of religion or belief, free expression, free association and state education of children in accordance with parental convictions.[267] Though not directly justiciable in domestic courts, this could be applied (from 1966 on the direct application of a British resident) by supranational institutions, whose rulings could seriously embarrass government and award financial compensation. Distance and cost were among the reasons why the journey to Strasbourg was not undertaken more often.

265 e.g. Criminal Justice Act 1988 s.139(4) and 5(b) – knives carried for religious reasons.
266 *R. v. Home Secretary ex p. Brind* (1991) 1 A.C. 696.
267 ECHR Arts 9, 10, 11; Protocol 1 Art 2.

(h) Prussian religion under the Constitutions of 1919-20

England's last revolution took place in 1688. It was motivated largely by protestant fervour and followed immediately by legislation indicating the new régime's concern for true religion. The German revolution over two centuries later was bound to affect church-state relations differently. Many Germans in 1918, whether believers themselves or not, wished to see a clearer separation of roles. Catholics in particular, remembering the *Kulturkampf*, also wished for clear guarantees of church autonomy.Seven Articles of the *Reich* Constitution adopted at Weimar in August 1919, with separate provisions on education, reflected the compromise between religious and rival interests – on the one hand they guaranteed freedom of conscience, work-free religious festivals, forces and prison chaplaincy provision and protection of church property; on the other, a State-run school system (with religious education respecting confessional differences), commutation of State liabilities to the churches and no compulsory religious rituals.[268] The century-old provision of the German Confederation Charter which outlawed religion-based distinctions in civil and political rights[269] was carried forward into Article 136, though extended beyond the historic *Religionsparteien* to cover all creeds.

The most important provisions affecting organised religion appeared in Article 137. For Prussia these largely enshrined existing realities. There was to be no »State church« and religious bodies were to order their own affairs within the framework of the statutes applying to all: but we have seen that the notion of a church identified with the nation had long been impossible in the Hohenzollern dominions, and the Prussian constitution of 1848 had guaranteed church autonomy. The public legal personality of the major churches, the co-operation of State tax authorities in the levying of church members' contributions, military chaplaincy and State schooling had all existed in pre-revolutionary Prussia. The *Reichsverfassung* merely lifted them to a higher legal status, so that Prussia alone could no longer retreat from the principles involved. The parity between religious and non-religious philosophies promised in the Article[270] was new, and would probably not have pleased Frederick William IV.

Since the *Reich* constitution of 1870 and its immediate predecessors had not touched on religion at all, the Weimar constitution placed the first serious external limitation on Prussian religious policy since the days of the old Empire. When Prussia adopted its own republican constitution in November 1920 it had

268 WRV Arts 135-141; key schooling provisions in Arts 144 and 149.
269 *Deutsche Bundesakte*, 8.6.1815, Art 16.
270 WRV Art 137(7).

very little to add, except to elevate the statutory right to withdraw from a church to the status of a constitutional right.[271] A provision for three protestant Ministers in the Prussian government to exercise the King's role as protestant *summus episcopus* was expressed to be transitional, until the Landeskirchen should transfer the relevant functions to organs of their own.[272] The existence of synods, the *Evangelischer Oberkirchenrat* (and equivalent bodies in the newer Prussian provinces) made this possible, and new church leadership organs rapidly came into existence.

England, of course, avoided a twentieth century revolution, retained its monarchy, adopted no codified constitution and did not subject itself to external limitations in the religious field.[273]Religious freedom flowed from the individual freedom of action given by the common law[274], coupled with the repeal of the last penal laws in 1846. Alternatives to religious oaths had been universal since 1888.[275] Many aspects of the English religious constitution, however, would not and could never have been compatible to the Weimar provisions. Religious tests still existed, at least for the monarchy itself. Whether explained in terms of the ecclesial state or merely as a privileged community, the Church of England would have been considered a *Staatskirche* in Germany and ruled out any general guarantee of religious autonomy. Its older organs might enjoy legal personality, but alternative religious bodies had to operate behind trusts. Inequalities between religious and non-religious world-views remained. The legal calendar acknowledged religious festivals but there was no assurance of their future as days of rest, and indeed Whit (Pentecost) Monday would be replaced by a secular bank holiday in 1967. English State-funded schools presented a more varied picture than the German, with an act of worship in even the most secular but tangible religious control of the »voluntary aided« category.

Both the contrasts, and such similarities as there were, between substantive church-state relationships in England and Prussia thus remained largely unchanged following the 1918 Revolution, except of course for the disappearance of the Prussian King. The most important change was the constitutional anchoring in the German *Reich* of what had previously been ordinary, or at most Prussian constitutional, law. Older works on the English law of religion often begin by attempting to explain the Church of England, newer ones with Article 9 of the

271 *Verfassung des Freistaats Preußen* 30.11.1920, Art 76.

272 *Verfassung des Freistaats Preußen* 30.11.1920, Art. 82(1).

273 Although it joined the European Communities in 1972, Community law pledged to respect member States' internal church-State relations: Final Act of the Treaty of Amsterdam 1997. See now Treaty on the Functioning of the European Union, Art 17.

274 see n. 88 above.

275 see n. 164 above.

European Convention; but in Germany the constitutional provisions – as perpetuated (in the absence of agreement on new provisions) by Article 140 of the 1949 Basic Law – are today's natural starting-point.

The arm's-length relationship between Prussia and the churches dictated by the Weimar constitution enabled agreements on matters of mutual interest to be negotiated in a way that would have been impossible in respect of the Church of England, and consequently very difficult to imagine with other English religious groups. The Holy See's anomalous international legal personality would, theoretically, have allowed a concordat with the United Kingdom in respect of Catholicism in England and Wales; but no counterpart of the Prussian concordat of 1929 was ever concluded. Officially at least, the government in London had no interest in the factors giving the impetus for a new accord in Prussia – the geographical arrangement of Catholic oversight or the appointment of Catholic bishops. The doctrine that the King in Parliament cannot bind himself would have made it difficult to give guarantees to the papacy – much less to the Church Assembly or to English religious groups lacking the Pope's international position – that religious provisions of the current law would not, at some future date, be altered. What was true of the Prussian State-Church Treaty of 1931 remains true of the various accords that followed the restoration of arm's-length church-state relations in Germany after the fall of Hitler.

7. The new millennium – 2000-10

(a) Human rights »brought home«

The Human Rights Act 1998 made European Convention rights, interpreted with regard to Strasbourg jurisprudence, directly applicable by English domestic judges. Courts were charged to interpret legislation compatibly with the Convention whenever possible[276], to strike down incompatible delegated legislation or other acts of public authorities[277], to make no incompatible orders themselves (which restricted their enforcement of the common law)[278], and to declare the incompatibility of any primary legislation which they were unable to reconcile with Convention rights.[279]

276 s.3.
277 s.6(1).
278 s.6(1) in conjunction with (3)(a).
279 s.4. The sovereignty of parliament meant such incompatible legislation nevertheless remained in force unless and until amended.

Coming into force in 2000, the Act caused a significant increase in the legal community's alertness to issues of »religious freedom«, which was reflected in both literature and litigation. Particularly amongst non-Christian believers, a »right« to expect modified application of laws which restricted the manifestation of their beliefs was a novel, though often welcome, concept.

(b) Human rights and public religion

Although the Convention's *raison d'être* was arguably to protect human individuals, Art 9 secured collective activity rights – to manifest religion »alone or in common with others« – and it was held that an organised religious body could apply to vindicate rights in Strasbourg »in its own capacity as a representative of its members«.[280] Voluntary religion in England and Wales remained private, but was privileged by Art 9 above other forms of private activity; as had the associations pursuing it. It was therefore important to know whether the distinction between public and private religion, consistently maintained in almost all other branches of English law, applied also to the human rights field.

In most of Europe, including Scotland, the concept of public religion in the Hookerian sense had long since been swept away, if indeed it had ever existed[281]: exceptions might exist in some Scandinavian kingdoms and some Swiss cantons, but modern Roman Catholic ecclesiology excluded it from traditionally Catholic territories, and constitutional change in the aftermath of the French Revolution had drawn clear lines elsewhere between nations and their religious communities. A majority of the Strasbourg judges were therefore conditioned to think of a church as something essentially different from the nation; and neither the British government nor the English episcopate felt any interest in arguing otherwise.

So were organs of the Church of England »public authorities«, their functions »public«, within the meaning of the 1998 Act? Were they, consequently, obliged to respect Convention rights? Or was a distinction possible between organs of the post-1860 voluntary structure, representing those who had voluntarily accepted ordination or placed their names on the church electoral roll, and the pre-1860 religious establishment of the realm from which all could benefit?

280 *Church of Scientology v. Sweden* (1979) 16 DR 68, para 2.

281 Church Act 1567, s.6 (Scotland) in declaring Scots rejecting the 1560 Scots Confession to be 'na memberis of the said Kirk within this realme', made it impossible to argue for an identity of church and commonwealth such as that in which Hooker believed. Belief in the distinct governments of church and state was declared lawful, and laws directed to be construed consistently with it, by the Church of Scotland Act 1921.

Early in the new century, the issue was held to turn on whether such organs were »non-governmental« under Art 34 of the Convention. England's highest court, the Court of Appeal, considered many of the indicators considered in this narrative, and concluded they were »public«.[282] But a further appeal lay from there to an Anglo-Scottish court, the House of Lords. The Lords of Appeal found assistance from a Strasbourg decision whereby monasteries of the Greek Orthodox Church had been held »non-governmental« eight yearsbefore.[283] The European Court's emphasis in that case on the »spiritual« element of a church's role led the House to hold that the »spiritual« primary function of a parochial church council meant it could not be governmental.[284] Even the function (transferred from parish churchwardens) of enforcing repair liabilities attached to the office of rector was not, apparently, public.[285]

The distinction between the voluntary and public faces of the Church of England was not taken at either instance. It appears relevant to the question whether Crown and government are internationally answerable for the behaviour of church organs; since a voluntary group created by agreement within a small section of the population in the nineteenth and twentieth centuries is in a different position from institutions existing under rules popularly adopted into the common custom of the realm at the dawn of England's existence. But this question seems likely to stand in doubt until an organ of the ancient Establishment is alleged, at the suit of a well-informed victim, to have violated a Convention right.

(c) Equality law, civil partnership and the public services debate

As with alternative religion (conditionally tolerated in 1689), so with alternative sexuality (conditionally tolerated in 1967), decriminalisation prefaced a campaign for complete parity. The Labour government which took power in 1997 set about eliminating relics of discrimination in criminal, education and local government law, and willingly implemented a European Union framework directive[286] that required discrimination by employers on grounds of sexual orientation to be outlawed. In England and Wales the existing freedom from discrimination on the ground of married status was extended to protect the registered same-

282 *Parochial Church Council of the Parish of Aston Cantlow v. Wallbank* (2002) Ch 51.
283 *Holy Monasteries v. Greece* (1995) 20 EHRR 1.That church was of course a clergy-governed institution, never identified with the Hellenic Republic itself (the former Kingdom of the Hellenes which, for much of its existence, had been an Ottoman Turkish province).
284 *Parochial Church Council of the Parish of Aston Cantlow v. Wallbank* (2004) 1 AC 546.
285 Though see, in this regard, the persuasive dissent of Lord Scott at paras. 130-32.
286 Council Directive 2000/78/EC of 27.11.2000, Art 1.

sex union introduced under the title of »civil partnership«[287], and regulations under the Equality Act 2006 extended such protection to the supply of goods and services.

This trend was bound to lead to tension with the conservative wings of all religious traditions which regarded same-sex relations as sinful and felt bound to signal this both internally, and in their dealings with the outside world. Religious exemptions were negotiated to each extension of protection, creating a varied and sometimes confusing patchwork of law.[288] In turn those (believers and non-believers) committed to the ideal of parity resented the exemptions. Some also regretted the promise exacted from government by religious hierarchies that civil partnership would remain a distinct legal institution from marriage. In an early challenge to the exemptions, it was held that the lawmaker had faithfully implemented the 2000 directive, but only if the exemptions were construed narrowly and if the court or tribunal – not the religious group – assessed the need for a discriminatory requirement.[289]

The likelihood that discrimination law and religious freedom rights would be played against each other was always strong. Since discrimination law protects »the rights of others«, proportionality seemed likely to be the deciding factor in many cases. But the idea that religious groups providing public services might »play the religious freedom card« to discriminate in ways forbidden to other providers caused questions whether such groups should be entrusted by government with any task that a religiously neutral agent could perform.[290] To exclude them, however, ran counter to government's desire to see all parts of the »voluntary sector« co-operate in meeting society's needs and reducing its own service burden.[291]

287 Civil Partnership Act 2004 c. 33 s.251(2).

288 Whether consistency has been satisfactorily imposed by codification in the Equality Act 2010 remains to be seen.

289 *R. (Amicus) v. Secretary of State for Trade and Industry* (2004) IRLR 430.

290 British Humanist Association, *Quality and Equality – Human Rights, Public Services and Religious organisations*, 2007, and *Not So Mythical*, 2010: <http://www.humanism.org.uk/_uploads/documents/BHA-Public-Services-Report-Quality-and-Equality.pdf>, <http://www.humanism.org.uk/_uploads/documents/EnsuringalevelplayingfieldBHAResponse-FINAL.pdf>,both accessed 12.10.12.

291 Department for Communities and Local Government, Face to Face and Side by Side – A framework for Partnership in our multi-faith society, 2008, and Ensuring a Level Playing-field, 2010: <http://www.communities.gov.uk/documents/communities/pdf/898668.pdf>, <http://www.communities.gov.uk/documents/communities/pdf/15073411.pdf>, both accessed 12.10.12.

(d) Latest developments

Conscious of all these tensions, government intensified efforts to maintain a fruitful dialogue with religious interests, regardless of public or private character. New consultative fora and initiatives have appeared with some regularity from the turn of the century, some specific needs have been addressed[292] and the criminal law has once again offered special protection to religion.[293] Yet a reform of charity law in 2006 appeared to recognise that the public benefit of religion was not as obvious to the general public as it had once been; and an official guidance document raised the possibility that religion might sometimes be detrimental, rather than beneficial, to the public interest.[294]

(e) Conclusion

Prussia lost all meaning as a political unit in 1934 and was dissolved by the victorious Allies in 1947. The *Landeskirche* of the older provinces continued under a new name and is recalled today in the Union of Protestant Churches. The German *Länder* comprising its historic Brandenburg heartland today are far from enjoying the same freedom to regulate religious affairs as once asserted by Margrave Joachim II: the Federation's Basic Law with its incorporated Weimar provisions exercise a significant constraint.

England and Wales exist within the United Kingdom, whose parliament has entrusted significant legislative authority to European Union organs and incorporated European Convention rights into domestic law. The fundamental principle of personal religious liberty is thus common to both English and German jurisdictions, and in political reality neither would be wholly free to depart from that.

292 The Divorce (Religious Marriages) Act 2002 allowed courts to defer finalising divorce in order to put pressure on an unwilling husband to give his Orthodox Jewish wife the bill of divorcement, or *get*, that would free her to remarry according to the religious rules she observed. In 2005 the Ministry of Defence began to appoint 'civilian chaplains to the military' to meet the needs of the relatively small number of Muslim, Hindu, Buddhist and Jewish servicemen and women.

293 Increased penalties for religiously aggravated public order offences (Anti-Terrorism, Crime and Security Act *2001 s.39); new forms of 'hate crime' (*Racial and Religious Hatred Act 2006*)*.

294 Charity Commission, The Advancement of Religion for the Public Benefit, 2008; see also the underlying legal reasoning at <http://www.charity-commission.gov.uk/Library/guidance/lawrel1208.pdf> (accessed 12.10.12), especially 3.15-3.17. At the time of writing the Commission guidance in relation to public benefit awaits judicial consideration in the Upper Tribunal (Tax and Chancery); see <http://www.thirdsector.co.uk/news/Article/1031979/Attorney-General-refers-Charity-Commissions-public-benefit-guidance-courts/>, accessed 30.10.10.

Few believe now in the ecclesial state in the sense of Richard Hooker, and even those who do must admit that its legal expression has been drastically diluted.

Their disparate histories have nonetheless made the detailed consequences of that principle, the official place of religion in the constitution, and the topics of modern debate in this field markedly different on both sides of the North Sea. They seem likely to remain so for a long time to come.

II. TRANSFORMATION OF CHURCH RELATIONS – THE SCANDINAVIAN EXPERIENCE – Lars Friedner

To share the Scandinavian experience of the transformation of church-state relations, I must begin by describing what Scandinavia is like. Traditionally, Scandinavia is considered to comprise Denmark, Norway, and Sweden.[1] This definition is also what will be used in this report.[2]

In several respects, these three countries are very similar. A Swede can quite easily understand written and spoken Norwegian or Danish (and vice versa)[3]. We have had a common labour market for decades, meaning that no permission is required to move between the countries. Nor has any passport been needed for many years to travel between these countries.[4] On the other hand, the three countries have chosen differing solutions in foreign policy, supposedly due to different historical experiences; Denmark and Norway are members of the NATO[5], while Sweden is not, and Denmark and Sweden are members of the EU[6], while Norway is not.

The three countries have also chosen different solutions regarding church-state relations. Some people would seek to explain this fact by saying that the three countries are at different stages of development regarding these relations. Other people would feel strongly offended by such thoughts and suggest that the three countries adopt different approaches to the matter.

In the following paragraphs, I will first sketch the Swedish situation and then give some remarks about the two other countries.

1 *Nationalencyklopedin,* vol. 16, p. 505.

2 In some contexts you will find also Finland and Iceland included in Scandinavia. There is a special question concerning the Faroe Islands and Greenland, which in some senses are to be regarded as parts of Denmark, though in other senses are independent. In some respects, they also have their own regulation of church-state relations, but they are not covered by this report.

3 *Nationalencyklopedin,* vol. 4 p. 408, vol. 14, p. 285.

4 Protocol concerning the exemption of nationals of the Nordic countries from the obligation to have a passport or residence permit while resident in a Nordic country other than their own, 1952 – Sw. *Protokoll angående befrielse för nordiska medborgare från att under uppehåll i annat nordiskt land än hemlandet innehava pass och uppehållstillstånd*

5 <www.nato.int>.

6 <www.europa.eu>.

1. Sweden

By the turn of the millennium Sweden had changed its church-state relations quite radically.[7] In British literature, a frequently discussed question is whether a church is *established* or *disestablished.*[8] You could have different opinions on whether or not the *Church of Sweden*, the former state church, has become a *disestablished* church as a result of these decisions. I think you could find arguments for both of these views.[9]

Through the change of church-state relations, the *Church of Sweden* became a legal entity of its own and thus is no longer a part of the legal entity of the State, which it had been until then.[10] The parishes[11] ceased to be municipalities under public law[12]; instead, they – as well as the dioceses – became legal entities as parts of the *Church of Sweden.*[13]

The *Church of Sweden* became free to handle its own affairs. A symbolic aspect of this was the right to appoint the *Church's* bishops.

Some state-church features still remain. Some relate to the new legal solutions, where the Constitution expressly says that there is a *Church of Sweden.*[14] There is also a *Church of Sweden Act*[15],which contains 14 sections that provide the framework of the *Church's* structure. A special question relates to the King and the Royal family. No changes affecting them were made, neither in the Constitution nor in the Act of Succession. It is stated in the Instrument of Government of 1809 that the King shall always profess the pure evangelical faith, as adopted and explained in the unaltered Confession of Augsburg and in the Resolution of the Uppsala Meeting of the year 1593, and this is supplemented by the Act of Succession which provides that »... princes and princesses of the Royal

7 A decision in principle was taken by the Riksdag (Swedish Parliament) in 1995 (Government Bill 1995/96:80, 1995/96: Parliamentary Standing Commission on the Constitution KU12, Riksdag Communication 1995/96:84), followed by separate decisions concerning various aspects of the matter.

8 See e.g. Hill, Ecclesiastical Law (London 1995), p. 11.

9 From a German perspective, the cornerstone of the church-state relations is the phrase from the Constitution »*Es besteht keine Staatskirche*« (Weimar Constitution art. 137; Eng: There is no state church) – still, also in Germany you would find signs of *establishment*. The purpose of this report does not allow me to amplify on this discussion here.

10 Section 3, Church of Sweden Act (1998:1591) – Sw. *Lagen om Svenska kyrkan.*

11 As well as the associations of parishes.

12 Government Bill 1997/98:116, p. 48.

13 Section 3, Church of Sweden Act.

14 Chap. 8, Art. 6 Instrument of Government (i.e. the Swedish constitution – Sw. *Regeringsformen*).

15 Code of Swedish Statutes number SFS 1998:1591.

House shall be brought up in that same faith and within the Realm. Any member of the Royal Family not professing this faith shall be excluded from all rights of succession«.[16]

The Church Property was handed over to the *Church of Sweden*. This property largely consists of the church buildings (which are, of course, of substantial value to the *Church*, yet on the other hand also represent an economic burden), but also of foundations controlled by the *Church*. Some parts of the property were given to the *Church* with ownership rights, while other parts remained in the hands of foundations, though these in turn continue to be controlled by the *Church of Sweden*.[17]

The Swedish funeral system is based on the *Church of Sweden* taking care of the cemeteries. It is only by a decision of the Government that a local municipality can assume such responsibility instead. There are in fact only two such municipalities in Sweden, including the capital Stockholm.[18] In all other parts of Sweden the *Church of Sweden* has remained in charge.[19]

Before the year 2000, Sweden had a church tax system. In practice, this still is in effect. The members of the *Church of Sweden* pay their church levies through the tax system.[20]

Even before the year 2000, the church buildings of Sweden were regarded as cultural monuments. No church building erected before the year 1940[21] can be changed in any way without the consent of the cultural heritage authorities.[22] On the other hand, the State has granted compensation to the *Church* for the extra costs resulting from the cultural heritage protection of the church buildings.[23] This compensation now amounts to about EUR 50 million per year.[24]

16 14 p. temporary regulation of the Constitution, Art. 2 Instrument of Government of 1809 and Art. 4 Act of Succession – Sw. *Successionsordningen.*

17 Sections 9 and 10 Act on Inauguration of the Church of Sweden Act (1998:1592) – Sw. *Lag om införande av lagen om Svenska kyrkan.*

18 Official Government Report – SOU 1997:42 p. 54 f.

19 Chap. 2, Sect. 1 Burials Act (1990:1144) – Sw. *Begravningslagen.*

20 Sect. 7 Church of Sweden Act, Sect. 16 Religious Communities Act (1998:1593) – Sw. *Lag om trossamfund;* Act on Levies to a Registered Religious Community (1999:921) – Sw. *Lag om avgift till registrerat trossamfund*; also other religious communities than the *Church of Sweden* may utilise the tax system, see below.

21 Some newer church buildings are also under the protection of the cultural heritage authorities, Chap. 4, Sect. 4 Cultural Heritage Act (1988:950) – Sw. *Lagen om kulturminnen m.m.*

22 Chap. 4, Sect. 3 Cultural Heritage Act.

23 Chap. 4, Sect. 16 ibid.

24 Government Bill 2009/10:1, Area of Expenditure nr. 17, p. 98.

Disestablished or not, the *Church of Sweden* is no longer the state church. The loosening of the ropes that have tied the *Church* to the State has also had effects on the other religious communities in Sweden. As the *Church of Sweden* was given legal capacity of its own, a new form of legal subject was created: the *registered religious community*.[25] The *Church of Sweden* was the first religious community to become registered under these new provisions.[26] But the other Swedish religious communities were also invited to register.[27] Many of them did register[28], although registration does not carry any special privileges.[29] Another innovation was the possibility for religious communities other than the *Church of Sweden* to utilise the tax system for collecting their membership fees.[30] The provision states that the assistance in collection of membership fees may only be offered to a religious community that »contributes to the maintenance and strengthening of the fundamental values on which society is based« and that is »stable and has its own vitality«.[31] These provisions had the effect that only a limited number of religious communities have applied for and been granted the right to utilise the tax system.[32]

2. Norway

Norway has a Lutheran state-church, the *Church of Norway*, although for quite a long time there have been discussions about the question of changing state-church relations.[33]

In April 2008, all the major political parties in Norway signed an agreement which will be in effect until 2013 and »can only be changed if all the parties agree«. In June 2008, as a result of this agreement, the *Storting* (the Norwegian Parliament) decided on the principles of new state-church relations in Norway. The agreement – and the decision – states that bishops and deans will be appointed by the *Church* and that there will be changes in the electoral system concerning the national synod of the *Church* and the diocesan synods.[34, 35]

25 Sect. 5 Religious Community Act.
26 As a part of the new state-church relations, the registration of the *Church of Sweden* was decided by the Riksdag, Sect. 5 Religious Communities Act.
27 Sect. 7 Religious Communities Act.
28 For the current situation, see Edqvist *et al*, *Kyrkoordning för Svenska kyrkan med kommentarer och angränsande lagstiftning*, 3rd ed., Stockholm 2010, p. 784 f.
29 Except the possibility of using the tax system, see below.
30 Sect. 16 Religious Communities Act.
31 Ibid.
32 <www.skatteverket.se>.
33 <www.kirken.no>.
34 Ibid.

On the other hand, the agreement states that other possible changes will *not* be realised. The *Church of Norway* will not become an independent legal entity, but rather will legally remain a part of the State. The bishops and priests will continue to be employees of the State. The national and diocesan administration of the *Church* will continue to be state authorities. There will be no church tax or church levy. As before, the municipalities will pay the costs of the local parishes, and the State will pay for the national and diocesan levels. The same economic support that is granted the *Church of Norway* will be granted proportionally to other religious communities. Associations having convictions other than religious beliefs shall be granted economic support in the same way as churches and other religious communities.[36]

3. Denmark

The *Evangelical Lutheran Church of Denmark*[37] is a state church.[38] In contrast to Sweden and Norway - where changes in the state-church relations have been implemented or are under way - there have been very few such discussions in Denmark so far. In some circles in Denmark it would probably be considered offensive to raise the question of disestablishment. Of the three Scandinavian countries, the tightest links between state and church may be seen in Denmark. In principle, the *Evangelical Lutheran Church of Denmark* has no national structure but is governed entirely by state bodies.

The *Folketing* (the Danish Parliament) acts as synod of the *Church*, the Queen is the head of the *Church*, and the administration of the *Church* is run by the Government, which includes a Minister for Ecclesiastical Affairs who is supported by a ministry.[39] Because of these structural patterns, the conditions that would be necessary for change at present do not exist.

However, a national advisory council for economic matters was established in 2009, giving advice to the Minister for Ecclesiastical Affairs. The Council includes representatives from different parts of the *Church*. Those who are inclined

35 The members of the national synod and the diocesan synods today are elected indirectly; there will be changes so that church members are given more direct influence on the elections.

36 <www.kirken.no>.

37 Da. *Danske Folkekirke.*

38 <www.folkekirken.dk>.

39 There is a Minister (and a Ministry) of Culture and Church Affairs in Norway.

to do so might regard the Council as a first tiny embryo of a national church structure in Denmark.[40]

4. Conclusions

In the discussion concerning established and disestablished churches, the Scandinavian experience provides three examples. Norway, even after bringing into effect the changes in state-church relations that are currently pending, will still have an established church. In Denmark the *Evangelical Lutheran Church in Denmark* certainly continues to be established. The Swedish experience could show an earnest attempt at disestablishment, though the *Church of Sweden* still has some features of an established church.

40 There has also been for decades a national council for ecumenical matters, the *Council on International Relations of the Evangelical Lutheran Church in Denmark*; there is also a joint web-site for the *Church*, <www.folkekirken.dk>.

B. Interactions between Religious and Secular Law

III. LEGAL PROTECTION IN ECCLESIASTICAL COURTS – Mark Hill

1. Introduction

This short paper seeks to address the broad themes of this conference by way of a detailed practical consideration of Anglican and Muslim courts in the United Kingdom. The former have a very long history. Traditionally, Church of England Courts dealt with matters of probate, property and family although these jurisdictions were incrementally transferred to the civil jurisdiction during the nineteenth century. However, in point of fact, the same development had already taken place well before – for example, by around 1500 there had been a subtle transference of litigation from the church courts to the common law courts, not least because of the more attractive temporal remedies provided by them; this was the case in areas such as early actions for breach of what today we would classify as contract (with better secular remedies arising from the development of the action of *assumpsit* which contributed to the decline of the canonical suit of *fidei laesio*), as well as in the field of uses (the modern-day trust) with the expansion in the business of the Chancery and its provision of more material remedies in the event of breach than those available in the church courts.[1] Today sophisticated bodies of ecclesiastical courts continue, albeit that their subject matter relates solely to the internal Church of England matters, namely the control of sacred buildings and the discipline of clergy. Islamic courts and tribunals are considered next, however because their prominence in the United Kingdom is of more recent origin, and is less structured in national hierarchical terms, the description is not as detailed. This paper considers the role of religious courts as a mechanism of dispute resolution for the purposes of the Arbitration Act 1990, and concludes with a general discussion of pluralist legal systems.

1 However, whilst there were fundamental differences in the respective characters of canon law and the (royal) common law, as legal systems, the church courts and the royal courts shared a basic concern for large moral ideas shaped by the prevailing Christian religion – judicial decision-making in both commonly invoked notions of conscience, reason, and justice, and indeed parliamentary legislation itself often contained claims from, and rooted their substantive rules in, divine law: see N. Doe, *Fundamental Authority in Late Medieval English Law* (Cambridge University Press, 1990).

2. Church of England Courts

The origins of these courts owe much to the historical nature of Church of England as the established Church of the realm.[2] The Ecclesiastical Jurisdiction Measure 1963 simplified a system which had become both moribund and cumbersome, and this in turn has been revisited in several material particulars in the Clergy Discipline Measure 2003.

(a) Chancellors

The Ecclesiastical Jurisdiction Measure 1963 provides that for each diocese there is to be a court of the bishop thereof,[3] known as the consistory court, save in the diocese of Canterbury, where it is known as the commissary court.[4] Each court is presided over by a chancellor[5] (or commissary-general in that of the diocese of Canterbury),[6] who must be at least thirty years of age and either a person who has a seven year general qualification within the meaning of section 71 of the Courts and Legal Services Act 1990[7] or a person who holds or has held high judicial office, or the office of circuit judge.[8] The chancellor may be ordained or a layman, but if he is a layman, the bishop must satisfy himself that he is a communicant.[9] There is no express requirement that the person to be appointed chancellor have any experience of or expertise in the laws of the Church.[10] He or she is appointed by the bishop, who is obliged to consult the Lord Chancellor (Mi-

2 The jurisdiction of church courts in matters of probate, matrimonial affairs and defamation were transferred to the secular courts by the Court of Probate Act 1857, the Matrimonial Causes Act 1857 and the Ecclesiastical Courts Act 1855 respectively.

3 Ecclesiastical Jurisdiction Measure 1963, s 1(1).

4 Ibid s 1(1). Hereafter, save where the context otherwise provides, the expression 'consistory court' includes commissary court.

5 Ibid s 2(1). By virtue of his office, the chancellor is also the official principal of the bishop: ibid s 13(2). This is, at best, a vestigial office, since the majority of the powers formerly exercised by the official principal now vest in the chancellor: see ibid s 6.

6 Ibid s 2(1).

7 Ecclesiastical Jurisdiction Measure 1963, s 2(2), (amended by the Courts and Legal Services Act 1990, s 7(2), Sch 10 para 17). See also Canon G 2 para 2.

8 Ecclesiastical Jurisdiction Measure 1963, s 2(2),(amended by the Church of England (Miscellaneous Provisions) Measure 2006, s 7(2)); Canon G 2 para 2. The expression 'high judicial office' is defined as meaning that of Lord Chancellor or Judge of the High Court or Court of Appeal: s 66(1), applying the Appellate Jurisdiction Act 1876, s 25.

9 Ecclesiastical Jurisdiction Measure 1963, s 2(2); Canon G 2 para 2.

10 Formerly there was such a requirement under Canon 127 of the 1603 Canons (now revoked). Compare Canon G 4 para 2, which requires registrars to be 'learned in the ecclesiastical laws and the laws of the realm'.

nister of Justice) and the Dean of the Arches (Senior Appellate Judge) before making any such appointment.[11]

A chancellor's appointment ceases[12] upon his attaining the age at which a circuit judge is obliged to vacate office, currently seventy-two,[13] or upon his resignation or dismissal by the bishop consequent upon a resolution by the Upper House of Convocation that the chancellor is incapable of acting or unfit to act. The chancellor is required to take and subscribe the oath of allegiance (to the Queen) and the judicial oath and, if he is a layman, a declaration of assent.[14]

Though appointed by the bishop and adjudicating matters in the bishop's court, the chancellor (and, *ex hypothesi*, his deputy) are independent of the bishop.[15] This position reflects the separation of powers between the executive and the judiciary in the secular sphere although, as with many constitutional models, the analogy is far from perfect. In a characteristically robust judgment of Garth Moore Ch in *Re St Mary, Barnes*, it was stated:

> »the then petitioners [in an earlier matter, now seeking a further faculty] were foolish enough, for reasons best known to themselves, to crave the then bishop's judgment, and the then bishop . . . purported to deal with the case himself. Whether or not he was, by reason of this unusual patent [of the chancellor in the Diocese of Southwark] ever legally seised of the case, it was, on constitutional grounds, highly undesirable that he should try to deal with it, for to do so involved a breach of the constitutional principle of the separation of the functions of the legislature, the executive and the judiciary, and a return to the absolutism of the Middle Ages condemned in this country since at least the middle of the seventeenth century. He was, moreover, even if legally seised of the matter, simply not capable of the task of dealing with it, as the sequel clearly shows.«[16]

11 Ecclesiastical Jurisdiction Measure 1963, s 2(1A), (added by the Care of Churches and Ecclesiastical Jurisdiction Measure 1991, Sch 4 para 2(a)).

12 Although the appointment ceases, the chancellor may continue to act in any proceedings of which the court was already seized: ibid s 2(4)(c), added by the Ecclesiastical Judges and Legal Officers Measure 1976, s 1(1).

13 Ecclesiastical Jurisdiction Measure 1963, s 2(4), amended by the Care of Churches and Ecclesiastical Jurisdiction Measure 1991, Sch 4 para 2(c), read with the Courts Act 1971, s 17(1).

14 Ecclesiastical Jurisdiction Measure 1963, s 2(5), Sch 1 Pt I; Canon G 2 para 3.

15 See *Tyler v United Kingdom* (Application 21283/93), 5 April 1994, in which the European Commission on Human Rights declared inadmissible an application claiming that the consistory court breached Article 6 of the European Convention on Human Rights.

16 *Re St Mary, Barnes* [1982] 1 WLR 531 at 532G–H, [1982] 1 All ER 456 at 457, Southwark Cons Ct.

(b) Registrars

Although a provincial or diocesan registrar has no judicial powers,[17] his role is central to the smooth and effective running of the provincial and consistory courts. Each of the provinces of Canterbury and York is required to have a registrar, who performs specified statutory and other functions as provincial registrar and registrar of the provincial court in addition to those previously performed by the archbishop's legal secretary.[18] He is appointed by the archbishop of the province[19] and also acts as the archbishop's legal advisor.[20] He must have a general qualification within the meaning of section 71 of the Courts and Legal Services Act 1990, and must be learned in the ecclesiastical laws and the laws of the realm and be a communicant.[21]

The diocesan registrar is appointed by the bishop but, prior to making any such appointment, the bishop must consult the bishop's council and standing committee of the diocesan synod.[22] The appointee also acts as legal advisor to the bishop.[23] He takes the same oaths as the chancellor.[24] A registrar is required to resign at the age of seventy,[25] and his appointment may be terminated upon twelve months' written notice from the bishop.[26]

It is the responsibility of the registrar to ensure that the diocesan and provincial courts are convened as and when required, that the requisite notices are complied with and that the necessary fees are paid.

(c) Consistory courts

The consistory court no longer has a criminal jurisdiction under the Ecclesiastical Jurisdiction Measure 1963 for conduct offences concerning priests or deacons.

17 Save as may be delegated to him by the chancellor for the purposes of giving directions or holding a pre-trial review.

18 Ecclesiastical Judges and Legal Officers Measure 1976, s 3(1), (2). The office may be held by two persons jointly: ibid s 3(4).

19 Ibid s 3(3).

20 Ibid s 3(1).

21 Canon G 4 para 2.

22 Ibid s 4(3).

23 Ibid s 4(1).

24 Canon G 4 para 3.

25 Ecclesiastical Judges and Legal Officers Measure 1976, s 5(3).

26 Ibid s 5(6). This may only be done with the consent of the archbishop. Newsom suggests that it would be good practice to enter into a contract of employment to which the diocesan board of finance should be a party providing for a shorter notice period: GH and GL Newsom, *The Faculty Jurisdiction of the Church of England* (2nd edn, 1993) 20.

With effect from 1 January 2006, these matters have been the subject of an entirely new procedure under the Clergy Discipline Measure 2003. The consistory court has retained its first instance faculty jurisdiction, concerning church buildings and their contents.[27]

(d) Appellate courts

Appeals from the consistory court generally lie to the provincial court of appeal. In the province of Canterbury, this is the Court of Arches; in that of York, the Chancery Court of York. The former is presided over by the Dean of the Arches and the latter by the Auditor.[28] Both offices are required to be held by the same person.[29] In a faculty case, appeals are heard by the Court of Arches,[30] unless they concern doctrine, ritual or ceremonial (styled reserved matters), in which case the appeal is to the Court of Ecclesiastical Causes Reserved.[31]

Under the Clergy Discipline Measure 2003, an appeal lies to the Court of Arches[32] from a determination of a disciplinary tribunal in a case of clerical misconduct.[33] When exercising this jurisdiction, the Dean[34] sits with a further four judges; two are clergy and are appointed by the Prolocutor of the Lower House of the relevant province, and two are communicant laymen, appointed by the Chairman of the House of Laity after consultation with the Lord Chancellor, and possessing such judicial experience as the Lord Chancellor thinks appropriate.[35]

27 Ibid s 6(1)(b). Other areas of jurisdiction are set out in ibid s 6(1)(bb)–(e), but these are so rarely used as not to merit separate consideration.
28 Ecclesiastical Jurisdiction Measure 1963, s 3(2)(a).
29 The Dean of the Arches and Auditor is appointed by the Archbishops of Canterbury and York jointly, with the approval of the monarch: ibid s 3(2)(a).
30 Comprising, in this instance, the Dean of the Arches sitting with two diocesan chancellors designated by the Dean: Ecclesiastical Jurisdiction Measure 1963, s 47(1)(b).
31 Ibid s 10(1). The composition of the court is given at ibid s 5. As for determining to which tribunal the appeal lies and the appropriate procedure see Chapter 7.
32 Or the Chancery Court of York as appropriate.
33 Clergy Discipline Measure 2003, s 20(1). Likewise appeals lie to the appropriate provincial court from the Vicar General's court in misconduct cases concerning bishops or archbishops: ibid s 20(1).
34 Or auditor, as appropriate.
35 Clergy Discipline Measure 2003, s 20(2), incorporating by reference the Ecclesiastical Jurisdiction Measure 1963, s 3(2)(a)-(c).

(e) The Court of Faculties

Contrary to what its title may suggest, the Court of Faculties is not judicial in nature. It is the court of the Archbishop of Canterbury and has a vestigial jurisdiction in the exercise of legatine powers which belonged to the Archbishop at the time of the Reformation. Power to grant dispensations, inter alia, was vested in the Archbishop by virtue of the Ecclesiastical Licences Act 1533. The present-day work of the Court of Faculties is largely confined to the granting of special marriage licences, the registration and regulation of notaries public and the issuing of Lambeth degrees.

(f) Judicial review

By dint of its anomalous position as the established Church in England, the courts of the Church of England are subject to judicial review when acting ultra vires or in breach of natural justice.[36] The precise extent of the powers of the Administrative Court to review decisions of the consistory court is unclear.[37] The Provincial Court of the Church in Wales is not so liable.[38] Under the Human Rights Act 1998, all courts and tribunals are included as public authorities,[39] and thus it is unlawful for them to act in a way which is incompatible with a Convention right.[40] This includes not merely the right to a fair trial under Article 6 but also, for example, the right to respect for private and family life under Article 8, freedom of thought, conscience and religion under Article 9, freedom of expression under Article 10, and freedom of assembly and association under Article 11, all of which (and others besides) are justiciable in the court or tribunal.[41]

36 See *R v Chancellor of St Edmundsbury and Ipswich Diocese, ex parte White* [1948] 1 KB 195, [1947] 2 All ER 170, CA; *R v Chancellor of the Chichester Consistory Court, ex parte News Group Newspapers* [1992] COD 48; and *R v Exeter Consistory Court, ex parte Cornish* (1998) 5 Ecc LJ 212, CA.

37 See M Hill, 'Judicial Review of Ecclesiastical Courts' in N Doe, M Hill and R Ombres (eds), *English Canon Law* (Cardiff, 1998) 104–114. Note also J Laws 'A Judicial Perspective on the Sacred in Society' (2004) 7 *Ecc LJ* 317 at 323.

38 See *R v Provincial Court of the Church in Wales, ex parte Williams* (1998) 5 Ecc LJ 217.

39 Human Rights Act 1998, s 6(3)(a).

40 Ibid s 6(1).

41 See M Hill, 'The Impact for the Church of England of the Human Rights Act 1998' (2000) 5 *Ecc LJ* 431; and M Hill, 'A New Dawn for Freedom of Religion' in M Hill (ed), *Religious Liberty and Human Rights* (University of Wales Press, 2002) 1-13. Convention rights have been the subject of judicial comment in *Re Durrington Cemetery* [2001] Fam 333, [2000] 3 WLR 1322, Chichester Cons Ct, Hill Ch; and *Re Crawley Green Road Cemetery* [2001] Fam 308, St Albans Cons Ct, Bursell Ch, both of which are discussed in R Sandberg, 'Human Rights and Human Remains: The Impact of *Dödsbo v Sweden*'

3. Muslim Courts and Tribunals

It is less easy to provide a detailed discussion of the extent, structure and functioning of Islamic courts and tribunals, as they are more dispersed and less homogeneous in their nature. Sharia Councils exist in most mosques in which one or more Imams or other suitable individuals will determine disputes. The Muslim Arbitration Tribunal is a national organisation which provides arbitration facilities to which disputants may voluntarily submit. It is more fruitful to describe the Islamic position by reference to the subject matter of cases rather than the structure of the courts themselves.

(a) Marriage

Under Islamic law a marriage ceremony is performed by way of a *nikah*, which in essence is a contract between two parties. A *nikah* which is conducted abroad, and is recognised in that foreign country as a valid marriage, is generally recognised as a marriage under English law. An Islamic marriage conducted within the United Kingdom is not recognised as a marriage under English Law unless it is also registered as a civil marriage or takes place in a registered mosque. If neither of these applies then the parties are considered to be no more than cohabitees under English law.

By virtue of the Marriage Act 1949,[42] it is possible to have a marriage registered at the same time as performing a *nikah* in a mosque or religious building, as long as the venue is a registered building approved for the solemnisation of marriages. It is a requirement that the marriage is conducted either by a person authorised to conduct a civil ceremony or by a member of the community authorised to do so, and that the marriage does not conflict with the conditions for a valid marriage under English law. The Act requires certain declarations to be made for the marriage to be valid, derived from the procedure for a valid civil marriage. There are some significant differences between what constitutes a valid marriage under Islamic law and under English law. For example, it is not a requirement under Islamic law that the parties to a marriage must be over the age of 16, and a man in Islam can take up to four wives. Both these examples would invalidate a marriage under English law.[43] In order to solemnise a *nikah,* and

(2006) 8 *Ecc LJ* 453. Note also *Re Welford Road Cemetery, Leicester* [2007] 1 WLR 000, [2007] 1 All ER 426, Ct of Arches.

42 As amended by the Marriage (Registration of Buildings) Act 1990 and the Marriage Act 1994.

43 Matrimonial causes Act 1973, s. 11; s. 12.

have it recognised as a civil marriage, the Imam conducting the *nikah* would have to ensure that it does not contradict what is considered valid under English law. In practice it is thought that fewer than one of ten mosques in England occur in registered buildings for the purpose of conducting a *nikah*, obviating the necessity for the parties to have a civil ceremony separately.

(b) The Mahr

A mandatory requirement of a valid marriage under Islamic Law is the payment of a marriage gift (*mahr*) by the groom to the bride. This can either be payable immediately or deferred for payment at a later date in whole or in part. The *mahr* can take a tangible or intangible form although commonly it is a sum of money or gold jewellery and agreed by the parties beforehand. A deferred *mahr* is to be given at an agreed time future time. The *mahr* may become due upon a divorce given by the husband or upon his death or upon any other valid condition.

If there is a written record of the marriage contract then details of the *mahr* would normally be included within it as it is an essential element of the marriage contract; although an Islamic marriage is still valid without a *mahr* being declared, the wife being entitled to call for a *mahr,* the value of which is to be determined by an Islamic judge based upon certain conditions. If a dispute then arises as to the *mahr* it may be possible to apply contractual principles under English law to enforce the agreement in the civil courts.[44]

(c) Divorce

Where an Islamic marriage takes place in accordance with the Marriage Act 1949 in a mosque which is a registered building it is recognised under English law and therefore the same principles apply upon the breakdown of that marriage as to all other valid marriages under English law. Further advantage of the marriage being recognised under English law is that the children of the marriage are considered to be legitimate according to English law and the father acquires parental responsibility for them automatically. Moreover, upon the death of a spouse, the surviving spouse has a right of inheritance under the Rules of Intestacy.

44 For example, see *Shahnaz v Rizwan* [1964] 2 All ER 993 (enforcement of a deferred *mahr*).

A party to an Islamic marriage that was conducted abroad and is recognised as a valid marriage in that jurisdiction can apply for a declaration of validity of marriage and enforce matrimonial rights upon divorce but only where the parties are in a so-called potentially polygamous marriage which is in fact actually monogamous.[45] English law will not provide a divorce for the parties to a foreign actually polygamous marriage. However, where there is a polygamous marriage abroad between parties who are domiciled in that jurisdiction, and the law of that country permits polygamy, the marriage will be valid and recognised in England.[46]

A marriage under Islamic law is normally brought to an end either upon pronouncement of the *talaq* by the husband or by way of a *khula* obtained by the wife but there are also judicial methods by which an Islamic judge may bring a marriage to an end.[47] None of these methods legitimately dissolves a marriage under English law which may only be dissolved by a court decree from the civil family courts. Therefore, Muslims who also need to obtain a civil divorce have to do so as a separate process through the English courts. There are instances when a Muslim wife may petition for a civil divorce but due to the refusal of the husband to pronounce the *talaq* (or agree to a *khula*), she may find herself in a »limping marriage« – many Muslim women will not consider themselves free to remarry until they have obtained a divorce both under Islamic and English law. It is of course open to the wife to obtain a civil divorce and then seek the assistance of one of the various Islamic religious councils set up in the UK to obtain a *khula* terminating the Islamic marriage, but this will be a further process delaying the end of the marriage and the »freeing« of the wife. The husband will not be subject to the same constraints as under Islamic law he is free to marry up to four women at the same time.

The position of Muslim women can be compared in this respect to that of women of the Jewish community where a Jewish divorce document known as a

45 It is a marriage celebrated in a form which is polygamous under the law of the place of celebration because a party is entitled to take another spouse under that law but which is not actually polygamous at the time as neither party is already in a prior subsisting marriage, (Matrimonial Proceedings (Polygamous marriage) Act 1972 as replaced by the Matrimonial Causes Act 1973).

46 Foreign Marriage Act 1986. Also see D Hodson, *A Practical Guide to International Family Law*', (2008).

47 A *khula* is a divorce instigated by the wife whereby the parties agree that the husband will pronounce the divorce upon the wife providing the husband with a form of compensation or return the *mahr* given to her. It can be initiated by the wife through an Islamic religious council if necessary. A wife can also obtain an annulment of the marriage (*faskh*) through judicial methods by proving that her husband has behaved unreasonably and has not fulfilled his obligations towards her.

»get« is required for the dissolution of a Jewish marriage. A get has to be freely given and freely received and the Beth Din (Jewish religious courts) cannot compel a party to give or receive a get against their free will. This too can lead to a »limping marriage«. However, this problem was addressed through the Divorce (Religious Marriages) Act 2002,[48] making it possible for a party to the civil divorce proceedings to apply for an order that a decree of divorce shall not be made absolute until the English court has produced before it a declaration that both parties have taken the necessary steps to dissolve the marriage under Jewish law.[49] There is a power to extend this provision to other faiths, and therefore it is conceivable that »usages of the Muslims« could also be accommodated under the legislation.[50]

There are other considerations when looking at obtaining a civil and Islamic divorce within the same process, such as the timeframe for doing so – it is only possible to petition for divorce under English law one year after the date of the marriage (although there is no restriction on petitioning for judicial separation in the first year of marriage),[51] whereas there is no such requirement on bringing an Islamic marriage to an end. Moreover, under English law a petition for divorce can only be made and granted if the marriage has irretrievably broken down on one of the five grounds,[52] whereas there is no such requirement under Islamic law.

(d) Children

Islam appeals to the internal conscience of an individual upon the breakdown of a marriage and the parties are expected to reach a sensible and amicable arrangement in the best interests of any children of the marriage and in taking into consideration their welfare. In practice this is not always the case and often there are acrimonious child residence and contact disputes in the English courts upon marital breakdown. As far as general principles apply, the custody of the children is deemed more appropriate with their mother pre-adolescence, and girls with their mother and boys with their father after reaching puberty, although there is

48 The Act came into force in April 2003. Section 10 A, inserted in Matrimonial Causes Act 1973.

49 See S Faith and D Levine, *Getting Your Get*, (6th edition, 2008).

50 The provision under the Act applies to parties married in accordance with the »usages of the Jews« or »any other prescribed religious usages«. Under the Act »prescribed means prescribed in an order made by the Lord Chancellor and such an order...must be made by statutory instrument«, (sections 1(a) and 6(a)).

51 Matrimonial Causes Act 1973, s. 3; s. 17.

52 Matrimonial Causes Act 1973, s. 1.

some variation among the Islamic schools of law as to this. The wishes of the children after a certain age may also be taken into consideration.[53] Islamically, the father has a duty to maintain his daughter until she marries and his son until he is able to earn his own living.

One point of contention with respect to children matters is that if the children of the marriage are illegitimate under English law because their parents' marriage is not recognised under the law, and the father's name has not been recorded on the child's birth certificate, then he will not have parental responsibility for the child.

(e) Religious Councils

There are several independent Islamic (Shariah) Councils in England. In the context of family disputes they offer mediation and assist in negotiating matters between Muslim parties upon divorce. They also grant *khula* divorces terminating marriages where a husband refuses to give his wife the *talaq* and it is clear that the marriage is no longer subsisting. However, the role of the Shariah Councils is restricted in that they have no way of enforcing any decisions or agreements that are made. They are also not subject to codes of conduct or standards relating to the procedures before them.

Similarly, the Beth Din in the Jewish community assists the parties upon marital breakdown and administers religious Jewish divorces. It can also facilitate the negotiation of financial settlements which may be submitted to a family court for consideration.[54]

It is possible for parties to an Islamic marriage to have a written record of the marriage contract setting out what has been agreed, including details of the *mahr*, a condition that the husband not take further wives and what future arrangements for any children of the marriage should be. It can also be expressly agreed that in the event of a marital dispute the matter will be referred to a religious council or scholar. With respect to financial arrangements the parties may then come to an agreement between themselves which can be submitted to an English family court for consideration.

The religious councils do provide an important vehicle for alternative dispute resolution; however it can be said that they could be utilised more effectively if their decisions were accorded greater recognition under English law. A step in

53 The 'age of understanding' generally accepted as being aged 7.
54 See: *The Beth Din: Jewish Courts in the UK*, The Centre for Social Cohesion (2009).

this direction would require the training of religious scholars who would adjudicate between the parties and the establishing of a standard code of practice and procedural rules for the independent councils in line with tribunal standards that already exist.

4. A pluralist legal system?

The concept of legal pluralism is highly contested, attracting much debate and acrimony, and its definition often depends upon the background and ideological orientation of the author. There are a number of different ways in which countries around the world may be said already to have a pluralist legal system. In a Federal state, each individual state has its own legal system although they may be subject to areas of uniform federal law and a single overarching court authority. This is the case of the USA and Canada where common law and civil law systems exist side by side. It is also true of the UK which comprises the separate legal systems of England, Wales (until recently indistinguishable from the English legal system), Scotland and Northern Ireland, form all of which the ultimate appeal lies to the Supreme Court in London. In federal systems there are often complex legislative competencies at regional and state levels. The UK is also now part of a proto-federal European structure which means that it is also subject to European law and has accepted the ascendancy in some areas of the judicial decisions of European courts. Even within a state enclaves with separate legal rules may operate. Thus, in Canada the First Nations are recognised as having their own sphere of legal competence (restricted in criminal law to sentencing and in family law to provisions for non-Indians under the Indian Act) just as some Native Indian tribes do in the USA.

(a) Official or State pluralism

In some countries, different sources of legal rules are recognised within a legal system which sanctions or enforces them within its own jurisdiction. This normative state of affairs can be described as state legal pluralism or official legal pluralism. Many countries globally operate in this manner of legal pluralism even though that is not always acknowledged or appreciated. In Asia and Africa and, increasingly elsewhere, it is openly accepted that a number of parallel legal rules may operate within the state and be sanctioned by it. In particular, many of these states accept that, in the area of family law, ethnic or religious communities may operate their own rule systems with official legal effect. Thus marriage, divorce, inheritance, and other matters dealing with personal status are regulated by the rules of that particular community. In some states the state courts apply these different rule systems and in other states legal issues are dealt with within the community of people concerned whose decisions are accorded the force of law or are enforceable within the state system. In Egypt all the religious courts were abolished in 1955 so that the state courts now deal with all personal status issues even though the state recognises that a number of different religious legal systems may be applicable. Syria still maintains its religious courts for those communities (14 in number) which the state recognises and their decisions are enforceable in the state courts. Israel has no civil marriage or divorce, these being matters for religious institutions to determine.

Western states have generally unified and centralised their legal systems so as to remove the multiplicity of such courts. England still maintains religious courts for the Church of England but with a much circumscribed jurisdiction being limited mainly to areas of liturgy, clergy discipline and church property. Other European countries have abolished such courts completely. There has been however in recent years a realisation that the rules of minority ethnic and religious communities ought to receive state recognition particularly as exceptions to the application of certain state rules: for example, by accepting religious methods of animal slaughter or allowance for religious dress or by providing for special tax rules to promote religious types of contract. This is not necessarily making the state pluralistic but merely accepting that state law should accommodate as much as possible the desires of minorities to be governed according by their religious or cultural norms provided always that they are applied within the structures of state law.

(b) Non-state or non-official pluralism

This type of legal pluralism can be seen as a purely descriptive state of affairs in which more than one legal or cultural order operates within a given social field. In this definition, legal pluralism is seen simply as a statement about social reality in that people may be subject to or may follow more than one rule system, which is generally not given state recognition, but is adhered to for a mixture of religious and cultural reasons. It is a statement about how people act in their daily lives, and its focus is on the social field. This means that communities such as Jews or Muslims abide by practices which they accept as obligatory but which cannot or should not be enforced by the state. There may even be parallel or equivalent adjudicatory mechanisms which may be called »courts«. In the case of the Jewish community in the UK a number of such courts, known as Beth Din, have operated outside the official state system for many years and recently have been given some recognition as in the Divorce (Religious Marriages) Act 2002 where a High Court judge may refuse a divorce if one party is refusing to give the other a religious divorce. At the moment the Act is limited to Jewish divorces but there seems no good reason why it should not be extended further to religions such as Islam and Hinduism. These are some of the ways in which existing groups use optional legal mechanisms to allow them to regulate their lives in culturally or religiously acceptable ways. Further examples include optional arbitration mechanisms and the availability of immense flexibility in English law as regards the making of wills. The indirect recognition of these facilities by the state as in the enforcement of religious arbitration decisions, as long as they comply with the provisions of the Arbitration Act 1996, can also be seen as a type of official legal pluralism.

The example of Ontario in Canada is instructive as to the difficulty that a western secular state faces in according more official state recognition to the religious or cultural norms of minorities. The Hon Marion Boyd, who had been Attorney General of Ontario, was asked by the Government of the day to clarify the circumstances under which officially-recognised arbitration in family matters, specifically upon the break-up of marriage and in inheritance matters, could extend to a religiously based dispute resolution system. She was appointed when it became apparent that there was the prospect of a Muslim organisation seeking to use the existing mechanisms under the Arbitration Act of Ontario to obtain official endorsement of Muslim informal dispute resolution. Certain other religious communities were already using the mechanism under the Arbitration Act. Boyd prepared a report on the issues entitled »Dispute Resolution in Family Law: Protecting Choice, Promoting Inclusion« which was published in December 2004. Boyd's very well-informed and well-documented report recommended that such dispute resolution should be allowed, provided that certain safeguards to ensure the protection of the weaker parties were inserted through amending legislation.

It so happened that the ensuing amendments to the Ontario Family Law Act gave official sanction only to those arbitrations which were made in accordance with the law of a Canadian jurisdiction, effectively preventing recognition of arbitrations purporting to apply a religious set of norms. The amendment therefore largely ignored Boyd's recommendation to allow the continued use of such arbitrations with built-in safeguards. This does not mean that religious arbitrations have been made illegal in Canada; rather they simply have to continue to operate unofficially, without official imprimatur, and without the ability of a dissatisfied party being able to use any decision of such a tribunal in an official forum such as a state court. The report by Boyd was an attempt to address the question of how far the state should recognise and thereby control the results of applying religious law, not just whether to extend recognition to them in principle. In other words its remit could be encapsulated within the broader question: »How much further should Ontario law incorporate the normative rules and practices of minority ethnic and religious communities?« Because of the overall politicisation of the debate, which generated more heat than light, the question in fact answered by the amending legislation was »Should Ontario law accept any consequences of religiously based arbitrations?« to which the political answer given was clearly in the negative.

In February 2006, in a lecture perceived as highly controversial by the media, the Archbishop of Canterbury asked: »How should the existing legal systems in the UK incorporate the normative rules and practices of minority ethnic and religious communities, if at all?« But legal pluralism can already be seen operating to different degrees depending on whether one takes the perspective of state legal pluralism or non-official legal pluralism. Both perspectives appear to be adopted by the Under-Secretary of State for Justice in a parliamentary debate of 10 June 2009 which concerned the difficult position of a woman who could not obtain an Islamic religious divorce even though she was already divorced.

> »Sharia law is the code of personal religious law governing the conduct of Muslims, and Ms [X], and many others in this country, have chosen to live by it and wish to continue to do so. Sharia law is not part of the law of England and Wales and nor do the Government have any intention of changing that position. We believe that social cohesion is best served by people living together under one legal system, rather than a system of personal laws."

The Under-Secretary of State appears, on the one hand, to adopt a strong legal pluralist viewpoint when she accepts that the Sharia is a type of personal legal order, but then goes on to adopt a state-focused perspective when stating that such a system of personal law should not be accepted by the state. The tension is likely to be most acute when the state's executive is not confident that the principles enshrined in the state's laws and procedures are shared by the traditions within which alternative tribunals might be run. If the executive comes to fear, for instance, that the rights of women (as enshrined in UK law and the procedures of the UK courts) might not be protected in alternative tribunals, then the executive confronts a politically sensitive challenge: whether and how to regulate such tribunals closely. As the Archbishop of Canterbury said, »If any kind of plural jurisdiction is recognised, it would presumably have to be under the rubric that no 'supplementary' jurisdiction could have the power to deny access to the rights granted to other citizens or to punish its members for claiming those rights.« The practical question remains for the executive: how to ensure that this rubric is seen to be observed.

The application of certain areas of the Sharia are not to be feared and in fact do not seem to be so wholly different to the rules applied by the state. Acceptance of some norms and rules of religious law does not mean wholesale adoption of such a legal system. It merely seeks to find an accommodation between the secular state and the religious communities that live within the state. This duality is present in most states and is answered in different ways. France refuses to give any recognition to religious law and is considering a ban on the Islamic headscarf. Some states in the Middle East ban the full veil (the burqa or niqab) while English law often leaves it to the institutions discretion. English law has admitted the validity of some religious norms of certain religions for centuries (for example in the recognition of religious marriages) but acts unequally in preferring one religion over another in this regard (for historical but hardly supportable modern reasons).

The Archbishop recognised that unofficial legal pluralism would continue to operate in minority communities (that was what he said was inevitable) and sought to ask the question of how much of that unofficial law should be adopted by the state. Should the activities of the sharia councils or courts be brought within the aegis of the state? Should they be given any recognition at all? Would this compromise the willingness of the communities to use these institutions if for example the state was involved in the choosing of the religious judges? How far are legislators and judges to make rules which allow for a certain specified (although yet to be determined or clarified) official recognition of Muslim legal cultures? Is it right that the state should give official recognition to such institutions? If so, it then becomes a question of how much state legal pluralism we can handle, not whether we should or can do so.

THE GERMAN PERSPECTIVE - *Michael Germann*

1. Short Inventory: Ecclesiastical Courts in Germany

The term »ecclesiastical courts« in Germany refers mainly to those of the Roman Catholic Dioceses and those of the regional Protestant Churches.

(a) Courts of the Roman Catholic Dioceses

The Roman Catholic bishops exercise their judicial power as it has been conveyed to them by the Codex of 1983.[1] The German Roman Catholic Bishops' Conference, by virtue of a special mandate of the Apostolic See, has established special ecclesiastical courts for the settlement of disputes involving the employee representation committee or relating to the consensual regulation of the conditions of employment contracts.[2] In respect of other judicial matters within the Roman Catholic Church, its members, in Germany like in the whole Roman Catholic world, are under certain conditions referred to the tribunals within the Curia in Rome.

(b) Courts of the Protestant Churches

The regional Protestant Churches have established ecclesiastical courts in five branches.

Firstly, all of them nowadays provide legal protection in administrative courts, primarily in matters relating to legal conflicts among corporations and in matters relating to the employment of a pastor or an official.[3]

Secondly, some regional Protestant Churches add the competences of a constitutional court to these tasks.[4]

1 c. 391; 1419 ss. CIC.

2 Cf. »Kirchliche Arbeitsgerichtsordnung«, as determined by the plenum of the German Roman Catholic Bishops' Conference on 21 September 2004.

3 Cf. »Kirchengesetz über die Verwaltungsgerichtsbarkeit der Evangelischen Kirche in Deutschland« of 10 November 2010, in: Official Journal of the EKD, 2010, p. 330. This new ecclesiastical law is intended to replace a variety of previous legislation of the regional Protestant Churches. It is not yet comprehensive but exemplary for the existing laws on administrative courts. – Most of the legislation in force within the Protestant Churches can be found at <http://www.kirchenrecht-ekd.de/>.

4 For example, cf. »Kirchengerichtsgesetz der Evangelischen Kirche in Deutschland« of 5 November 2003, in: Official Journal of the EKD, 2003, p. 409, sections 25–27; or

Thirdly, disciplinary courts have jurisdiction over disciplinary actions concerning pastors and officials.[5]

Fourthly, there are courts for the settlement of disputes involving the employee representation committee or relating to the consensual regulation of the conditions of employment contracts.[6]

Fifthly, most of the regional Protestant Churches entrust special judicial bodies with cases where a pastor's teachings deviate unacceptably from the Protestant Church's denomination. These may crudely be labelled as »doctrine courts«.[7]

With the exception of doctrine courts, there are appellate courts for all of these jurisdictions.

The ecclesiastical courts of the Protestant Churches are made up of honorary judges. Most courts combine lawyers and theologians. They are usually elected by the synod. They enjoy independence from the bishop, the synod, and the administration.

The historical roots of these courts are short. Most of them have been established in the second half of the 20th century. From the 16th to the 19th century, the history of judicial institutions dealing with church matters resembles the history summarized by Mark Hill for the courts of the Anglican Church. While in England, the ecclesiastical courts persisted and kept some of their former competences, the corresponding institutions within the established Protestant churches in Germany vanished. But shortly before and some time after the Protestant

»Kirchengesetz über das Kirchliche Verfassungs- und Verwaltungsgericht« of the Protestant Church in Hesse and Nassau (EKHN), as promulgated on 1 August 1979, in: Official Journal of the EKHN, 1979, p. 119.

5 Cf. »Disziplinargesetz der Evangelischen Kirche in Deutschland« of 28 October 2009, in: Official Journal of the EKD, 2009, p. 316.

6 Cf. »Kirchengesetz über Mitarbeitervertretungen in der Evangelischen Kirche in Deutschland« as re-promulgated on 1 January 2004, in: Official Journal of the EKD, 2004, p. 7, and amended on 29 October 2009, in: Official Journal of the EKD, 2009, p. 349, sections 56–63; »Arbeitsrechtsregelungsgesetz der Evangelischen Kirche in Deutschland« of 10 November 1988, in: Official Journal of the EKD, 1988, p. 366, as amended on 6 November 2003, in: Official Journal of the EKD, 2003, p. 414, sections 12–14.

7 For example, cf. »Kirchengesetz über das Verfahren bei Lehrbeanstandungen« of the United Evangelical Lutheran Church of Germany (VELKD), as re-promulgated on 3 January 1983, in: Official Journal of the EKD, 1983, p. 99; »Ordnung des Verfahrens bei der Beanstandung der Lehre ordinierter Diener am Wort (Lehrbeanstandungsordnung)« of the (former) Evangelical Church of the Union (EKU) of 27 June 1963, in: Official Journal of the EKD, 1963, p. 476.

Churches' disestablishment in 1919, they begun the incremental development of the new ecclesiastical courts that exist today.[8]

(c) Courts of Smaller Christian Churches and Non-Christian religious communities

Smaller Christian churches and non-Christian religious communities do not have courts of their own to the same extent.

However, the Jewish communities operate »Beit Din« courts, which rule on matters of religious divorces, conversions and the like. Under the umbrella of the Central Council of the Jews in Germany, both the Orthodox and the General Rabbis' Conferences have each established a »Beit Din«.[9] The Central Council of the Jews in Germany itself has always provided an arbitral tribunal for settling disputes among its member communities. In addition, in December 2009, it established a »Superior Arbitral and Administrative Court« (»Oberes Schieds- und Verwaltungsgericht«) which is entrusted with preliminary proceedings and the settlement of disputes within the Council itself.[10]

The term »ecclesiastical« in its proper sense, just as the term »church«, apply, of course, only to Christian communities. As regards secular law, this makes no fundamental difference. To refer to all judicial institutions of any church or non-Christian religious communities as »ecclesiastical« courts is merely an abbreviation.

2. Constitutional Framework: the establishment and operation of ecclesiastical courts are acts of religious self-determination

Who decides on the establishment of ecclesiastical courts, on the matters in regard to which they are to provide legal protection, and on their procedure?

8 See *Ulrich Scheuner*, Grundfragen einer kirchlichen Verwaltungsgerichtsbarkeit, in: Zeitschrift für evangelisches Kirchenrecht (ZevKR) 6 (1957/58), p. 337–364 (337–341); also in: *idem*, Schriften zum Staatskirchenrecht, ed. Joseph Listl, 1973, p. 441–467; *Hartmut Maurer*, Die Verwaltungsgerichtsbarkeit der evangelischen Kirche, 1958, p. 11–32; *Karl Hansch*, Die Disziplinargerichtsbarkeit in der evangelischen Kirche, 1961; p. 3–56; *Friedrich Hermann Schoofs*, Geschichte und Gegenwartsgestalt der kirchlichen Gerichtsbarkeit der evangelischen Kirchen in Deutschland, Diss. jur. Köln 1963, p. 6–158.

9 See <http://www.zentralratdjuden.de/de/topic/266.html>; for more details on the orthodox Beit Din: <http://www.ordonline.de/index.php?option=com_content&view=article&id=77&Itemid=58>.

10 News on 16 December 2009 at <http://www.zentralratdjuden.de/de/article/2806.html>.

Since there is no state church but rather a separation of state and church in Germany, these questions are subject to the religious communities' constitutional right to self-determination under article 137, paragraph 3, of the Weimar Constitution, as incorporated into the Basic Law (Grundgesetz) by its article 140. The right to establish an ecclesiastical court and to determine its operation is granted to all religious communities, independent of their further legal status. In particular, it is not conditional on the legal status of a public law corporation that is made available by article 137, paragraph 5, of the Weimar Constitution. The legal status only affects the legal modalities of self-determination.

3. Legal Effects: religious autonomy as opposed to public power

The right to self-determination implies the ability to produce legal effects under secular law. Consequently, the findings of ecclesiastical courts must be recognized under secular law as relevant expressions of religious self-determination.[11] However, their legal relevance is subject to the limitations set by the state in the form of the secular »law that applies to all« (article 137, paragraph 3 of the Weimar Constitution). In particular, deciding whether and to what degree legal protection in ecclesiastical courts can contribute to the constitutionally ensured access to justice depends on their legal status under secular law.

(a) Ecclesiastical courts do not replace state courts

The most basic principles flow from the separation of state and church. Ecclesiastical courts neither are state courts, nor are they entrusted with public power to replace state courts in providing legal protection.

They are not able to satisfy the constitutional right to access to justice.

A dispute ruled by them does not become *res judicata.*

Their judgments do not take effect as enforcement orders.

The legal standards valid for state courts and their procedure do not apply to them. This is true, in particular, with respect to the fundamental rights of the Ba-

11 *Axel von Campenhausen / Heinrich de Wall*, Staatskirchenrecht. Eine systematische Darstellung des Religionsverfassungsrechts in Deutschland und Europa, 4th ed., 2006, p. 101 s., 312, 313–316; *Michael Germann*, Staatliche und kirchliche Gerichtsbarkeit, in: Recht in Kirche und Staat. Joseph Listl zum 75. Geburtstag, ed. Wilhelm Rees, 2004, p. 627–656 (650–655).

sic Law and of the European Convention on Human Rights. Thus, these standards impose no limitation on the religious communities' right to self-determination regarding their ecclesiastical courts.

(b) Foreign ecclesiastical courts may replace foreign state courts

The above is true for ecclesiastical courts operating in Germany. However, foreign ecclesiastical courts, when exercising public power under foreign law, can be ascribed to the foreign state judiciary. The judgment of a foreign state court will be recognized within the limits of public order (»ordre public«).[12]

This seems to correspond to what Mark Hill says about the recognition of Islamic marriages and divorces which were conducted abroad.

It can now be said that religious marriages conducted by the Church of England will be recognized in German lawin the same way as foreign Islamic marriages will be recognized in English law (and, of course, in German law, too).

(c) Ecclesiastical courts can be set up as arbitral courts but they usually are not

Returning to domestic ecclesiastical courts, they can be organized as arbitral tribunals pursuant to the provisions of the Code of Civil Procedure on arbitration procedure.[13]

The award of an arbitral tribunal »among the parties has the effect of a final and binding court judgment« (section 1055 of the Code of Civil Procedure). It can be appealed against only for certain reasons. The state court will not look at the equitability of the award, but only at the basic preconditions for a fair arbitration: at the arbitrability of the cause, at the validity and the scope of the arbitration agreement, at the correct composition of the arbitral tribunal, and, regarding the result of the arbitration, solely at its compliance with the public order (»ordre public«). Within these limits, ecclesiastical courts can, when set up as arbitral

12 Code of Civil Procedure (»Zivilprozeßordnung«, as re-promulgated on 5 December 2005, and amended later), section 328, subsection 1; Act on the Procedure in Family Matters and in Non-Contentious Matters (»Gesetz über das Verfahren in Familiensachen und in den Angelegenheiten der freiwilligen Gerichtsbarkeit« of 17 December 2008, as amended), section 109, subsection 1.

13 Code of Civil Procedure, 10th Book: sections 1025–1066.

tribunals, give judgment that effects the status of res judicata under state law. If so, upon request the state court will declare the award enforceable.

However, these legal effects require exact compliance with the model of arbitration provided by the Code of Civil Procedure. Since this model in many respects does not meet the demands of dispute settlement within religious communities, the arrangement of ecclesiastical courts as arbitral tribunals in that proper sense is rare.

(d) Ecclesiastical courts bring religious autonomy to bear in state courts

Finally, ecclesiastical courts can operate as an autonomous judiciary in the same ways as judicial bodies that associations establish by virtue of their statutes[14], as for instance sports associations do. Since religion is almost as serious a matter as sports, it is quite evident that the judgment of an ecclesiastical court deserves similar consideration to that of a sports court.

To what extent may the judgment of such an ecclesiastical court enjoy consideration? This question ties into a debate on legal protection against church acts in state courts.

Here, again, a strong similarity between Great Britain and Germany can be noted: »The precise extent of the powers of the Administrative Court to review decisions of the consistory court is unclear«, says Mark Hill.[15] That seems to be precisely the same in Germany.

Some scholars, most of them some fifty years ago, held that state courts should never grant legal protection against church acts.[16] They argued that church matters lay outside the reach of state authority. The courts adopted this argument and rejected all claims in church matters as being inadmissible.[17] Until

14 See *Dieter Reuter*, in: Münchener Kommentar zum Bürgerlichen Gesetzbuch, ed. Kurt Rebmann / Franz Jürgen Säcker / Roland Rixecker, 5th ed., vol. 1, 2006, § 25, no. 34–63.

15 See above, p. 80.

16 See by way of example *Konrad Hesse*, Der Rechtsschutz durch staatliche Gerichte im kirchlichen Bereich, 1956.

17 *Bundesverfassungsgericht* (BVerfG – German Federal Constitutional Court), judgment of 17 February 1965 – 1 BvR 732/64 –, in: official reports (»Entscheidungen des Bundesverfassungsgerichts« – BVerfGE), vol. 18, p. 385–388; *Bundesgerichtshof* (BGH – Federal Court of Justice), judgment of 18 February 1954 – III ZR 311/52 –, in: official reports (»Entscheidungen des Bundesgerichtshofs in Zivilsachen« – BGHZ), vol. 12, p. 321–327 (325); judgment of 16 March 1961 – III ZR 17/60 –, in: BGHZ 34, 372–375 (373 s.); judgment of 19 September 1966 – III ZR 199/64 –, in: BGHZ 46, 96–105 (99–103); judgment of 28 September 1967 – III ZR 45/66 –, in: ZevKR 14 (1968/69), p. 156–158;

today, a broad trend within the courts' practice continues to adhere to this reasoning. Recently, the Federal Constitutional Court (Bundesverfassungsgericht) has revealed its rehashed affection for denying legal protection against church acts.[18]

Some of those who feel uneasy with a gap in legal protection try to fill it with a »sufficient« legal protection in ecclesiastical courts. Provided that ecclesiastical courts are established and operating in a way that is equivalent to state courts, legal protection in state courts seems to be dispensable. After all, this idea suggests that ecclesiastical courts are able to replace state courts in order to grant legal protection against church acts and, by doing this, to implement the limitations which the secular »law that applies to all« imposes on the churches' right to self-determination. This idea urges the churches to shape their courts following the secular model. But most notably, it is at a loss for an explanation as to where the public power necessary to satisfy the right to access to justice, to turn a case into res judicata and even, if possible, to enforce their judgments should be drawn from.

Today, most scholars[19], followed by a considerable trend in some recent rulings[20], particularly in those of the Federal Court of Justice (Bundesgerichtshof)

Bundesverwaltungsgericht (BVerwG – Federal Administrative Court), judgment of 27 October 1966 – II C 98.64 –, in: official reports (»Entscheidungen des Bundesverwaltungsgerichts« – BVerwGE), vol. 25, p. 226–234 (229–234); judgment of 15 December 1967 – VI C 68.67 –, in: BVerwGE 28, 345–353 (347 s.); judgment of 25 October 1968 – VI C 1.65 –, in: BVerwGE 30, 326–344 (327 s.); judgment of 25 November 1982 – 2 C 21.78 –, in: BVerwGE 66, 241–251 (244 s.); judgment of 20 November 1992 – 7 B 48/92 –, in: Neue Zeitschrift für Verwaltungsrecht (NVwZ), 1993, p. 672; judgment of 28 April 1994 – 2 C 23.92 –, in: BVerwGE 95, 379–383; *Bundesarbeitsgericht* (BAG – Federal Labour Court), judgment of 11 March 1986 – 1 ABR 26/84 –, in: official reports (»Entscheidungen des Bundesarbeitsgerichts« – BAGE), vol. 51, p. 238–246 (244 s.); judgment of 7 February 1990 – 5 AZR 84/89 –, in: Neue Juristische Wochenschrift (NJW), 1990, p. 2082 s. (2083).

18 *BVerfG*, judgment of 9 December 2008 – 2 BvR 717/08 –.

19 See the comprehensive study by *Karl-Hermann Kästner*, Staatliche Justizhoheit und religiöse Freiheit. Über die Frage nach der staatlichen Kompetenz zur Rechtsschutzgewährung im Wirkungsbereich der Kirchen und Religionsgemeinschaften, 1991; as well as *von Campenhausen / de Wall*, Staatskirchenrecht (op. cit. supra, n. 11), p. 309–326; find more references with *Germann*, Staatliche und kirchliche Gerichtsbarkeit (op. cit. supra, n. 11); one of the few contemporary opponents is *Christian Hillgruber*, Das Selbstbestimmungsrecht der Kirchen und die Jurisdiktionsgewalt des Staates, in: Kirche und Religion im sozialen Rechtsstaat. Festschrift für Wolfgang Rüfner zum 70. Geburtstag, ed. Stefan Muckel, 2003, p. 297–316.

20 *BVerfG*, judgments of 18 September 1998, 2 BvR 1476/94, in: NJW 1999, p. 349 s., and 2 BvR 69/93, in: NJW 1999, p. 350; *BVerwG*, judgment of 28 February 2002 – 7 C 7.01 –, in: BVerwGE 116, 86–92; *BGH*, judgment of 11 February 2000 – V ZR 271/99 –, in: NJW 2000, p. 1555–1557; judgment of 28 March 2003 – V ZR 261/02 –, in: BGHZ 154,

prior to the most recent Federal Constitutional Court's fall-back[21], prefer to reserve final legal protection for state courts.

According to this view, state courts may never deny access to justice on the grounds that the claim touches an issue which is subject to the right to self-determination of a religious community. Instead, state courts have to decide the case on its merits, meaning that they recognize the church's act in question as an act of self-determination and analyse its compliance with the secular »law that applies to all«.

The right to self-determination on the one hand and the interests endorsed by the »law that applies to all« on the other hand have to be balanced. The complex operation of balancing these interests may be labelled, in short, as finding a »fair« adjustment.

At this stage, ecclesiastical courts can contribute. Their preceding rulings express their church's idea of self-determination and of its »fair« adjustment in a way tailored to the particular cause. The more the ecclesiastical court's procedure and reasoning meet the prerequisites for a »fair« adjustment, the less the state court will be able to question the ecclesiastical court's findings. Unless there are evident shortfalls, it will retrace and affirm them.

Furthermore, if a matter is brought to a state court before relief has been sought in a competent ecclesiastical court, the state court should stay the case or dismiss it for the time being in order to allow for prior ecclesiastical judgment.

In this way, legal protection in ecclesiastical courts has, to a certain extent and depending on its performance, a binding effect on legal protection in state courts.

306–315. However, stepping back, *BVerwG*, judgment of 30 October 2002 – 2 C 23.01 –, in: BVerwGE 117, 145–149; followed by some lower courts. Remarkably, the *Bundesverfassungsgericht* in the meantime had avoided the decision in a relevant case in its judgment of 27 January 2004 – 2 BvR 496/01 –, in: BVerfGE 111, 1–6, with a dissenting vote by judge *Lübbe-Wolff*, 7–10. These recent rulings are commented on by *Karl-Hermann Kästner*, Vergangenheit und Zukunft der Frage nach rechtsstaatlicher Judikatur in Kirchensachen, in: ZevKR 47 (2003), p. 301–311; *Hermann Weber*, Kontroverses zum Rechtsschutz durch staatliche Gerichte im kirchlichen Amtsrecht, in: NJW 2003, p. 2067–2070; *Michael Droege*, Neues zum »Quis judicabit?«, in: ZevKR 49 (2004), p. 763–771; *Hermann Weber*, Kirchlicher Rechtsschutz und staatliche Gerichtsbarkeit, in: ZevKR 49 (2004), p. 385–404; *Michael Germann*, Staatliche Verwaltungsgerichte vor der Aufgabe der Justizgewährung in religionsgemeinschaftlichen Angelegenheiten, in: ZevKR 51 (2006), p. 589–595.

21 See supra n. 18. This ruling has been commented on by *Michael Germann*, Die Nichtannahme einer Verfassungsbeschwerde gegen die Kirche: kein Grund zum Nachdenken über die Justizgewährung in kirchlichen Angelegenheiten, in: ZevKR 54 (2009), p. 108–114; *Hermann Weber*, Der Rechtsschutz im kirchlichen Amtsrecht: Unrühmliches Ende einer unendlichen Geschichte?, in: NJW 2009, p. 1179–1183.

However, no religious community is required to run a judiciary of its own following the secular model. Legal protection continues to be ensured by the state courts.

4. Pluralism

What about marriage? In Germany, marriage matters are reserved to the civil authorities and courts.[22] Ecclesiastical law on marriage and a possible jurisdiction by ecclesiastical courts on marriage matters in no way affects civil marriage.[23] Until a few years ago, any religious marriage ceremony was prohibited unless preceded by a valid civil marriage.[24] After this ban has been abolished, the most daring propositions considered allowing the churches to certify the civil marriage in the course of their services[25], maybe similar to the provisions of the UK Marriage Act of 1949 as referred to by Mark Hill. In Germany, however, even this timid attempt has met hardly any response, and both large Churches have declined.[26] All the more, legal pluralism in this matter is far out of sight.

Apart from this, the concept of religious self-determination within the limits of the »law that applies to all« offers a model for reconciling divergent ideas of living within one legal order, which is pointing at pluralism not of legal orders but of ways of life.

22 Civil Code (»Bürgerliches Gesetzbuch« – BGB), sections 1303 ss., especially section 1310, subsection 1, clause 1; section 1313, clause 1.

23 BGB, section 1588 states that any church duties with regard to the marriage remain unaffected.

24 Section 67 of the Law on Civil Status (»Personenstandsgesetz«) as promulgated on 8 August 1957, Federal Official Journal, part I, 1957, p. 1125, and amended, abrogated on 19 February 2007, Federal Official Journal, part I, 2007, p. 122, effective from 1 January 2009.

25 *Hans Michael Heinig*, Neuere Entwicklungen im Eherecht an der Schnittfläche von staatlicher und kirchlicher Rechtsordnung, in: ZevKR 55 (2010), S. 20–45 (41–45).

26 The EKD has published the opinion of an expert group advising not to celebrate wedding services without civil marriage and not to advocate the churches' right to certify civil marriage: Kirchenamt der EKD (ed.), Soll es künftig kirchlich geschlossene Ehen geben, die nicht zugleich Ehen im bürgerlichrechtlichen Sinne sind? Zum evangelischen Verständnis von Ehe und Eheschließung. Eine gutachtliche Äußerung, EKD-Texte 101, 2009 (accessible on <http://www.ekd.de/EKD-Texte/ekdtext_101.html>), p. 18–22. The Roman Catholic Bishops in Germany have confirmed that canon marriages normally should be preceded by civil marriage; exceptions need a particular authorisation which will be granted only if civil marriage cannot reasonably be expected: »Ordnung für kirchliche Trauungen bei fehlender Zivileheschließung«, e. g. in: Official Journal of the diocese of Magdeburg, 2008, No. 164 (<http://www.bistum-magdeburg.de/front_content.php?client=4&lang=5&idcat=1387&idart=2330>).

IV. RELIGIOUS DISPUTES REGARDING EMPLOYMENT IN GREAT BRITAIN - Lucy Vickers

1. Introduction

This paper considers the legal position in Great Britain regarding religious disputes between religious communities and those who work for them, in particular where disputes arise for reasons connected with conduct of an employed religious adherent which is incompatible with the teaching of the church. It assesses whether the courts have achieved a correct balance between protecting church autonomy, and protecting the rights of religious adherents who work for religious organisations. During the paper, contrasts are drawn between the position in Great Britain and Germany.

By way of background, it is important to set out the constitutional and legal context of the rules governing the relationship between law and religion in Great Britain. In the absence of a written constitution, and therefore no constitutionally guaranteed right to freedom of religion, as well as the presence of the established Church of England, it might be thought that there will be few rules limiting the rights of churches in Great Britain to determine employment issues. However this is not the case. First, constitutional conventions apply in the UK, and there is a well established tradition of religious neutrality in the courts, with an acceptance that in applying common law, courts must respect concepts such as religious freedom. This is underpinned by the UK's status as a signatory to the European Convention on Human Rights, which protects freedom of religion under Article 9, and since 1998 the Human Rights Act which requires UK laws to be interpreted, where possible, to comply with the ECHR.[1] Thus the absence of a written constitution does not mean that religious freedom remains unprotected in law; and the presence of an established church does not give the Church of England complete freedom to act towards its employees without legal restraint. However, these informal conventions operate in the background, so to speak, governing the thinking that develops the common law and the development of legislation, rather than operating as formal rules within the case law, and giving rise to formal individually enforceable rights, as is the case in Germany.

Having set out the background constitutional position, the ways in which religious disputes are determined will next be considered. This will involve looking briefly at the case law on the status of clergy in the Christian church, as well as the status of leaders of other religions. It will then consider the protection under

1 See further L Vickers, *Religious Freedom, Religious Discrimination and the Workplace*, (2008) Hart Publishing, Oxford, chapter 4.

the EU derived non-discrimination legislation, covering staff both in religious and secular employment.

2. Religious disputes between religious leaders and their religious communities:

The main form of employment protection available to employees in the UK is the law of Unfair Dismissal, currently governed by the Employment Rights Act 1996, but created in 1971. This provides that dismissal is unfair unless it is for one of a number of potentially fair reasons (conduct, capacity, redundancy, retirement, illegality, or the catch-all final category, »some other substantial reason justifying dismissal«).[2] If not for one of these reasons, the dismissal is unfair. Even where it is for one of these reasons, it must have been reasonable to dismiss in the circumstances, usually meaning that the dismissal must be procedurally fair.

However, this legal protection against unfair dismissal is not available to all workers, only those who are legally classified as »employees«, as opposed to those who are self-employed. This classification is a vexed issue for a range of workers, and can depend on issues such as the extent to which the employer exercises control over the day to day working of the employee, the level of mutual obligation to work and to provide work, as well as the intentions of the parties. The case law regarding the status of clergy has not always been consistent, but there is a general rule that clergy and other religious leaders are not recognised as »employees« for the purposes of dismissal law. There are some exceptions (e.g. *New Testament Church of God* v *Stewart*[3]), but these have tended to be fact specific, and the general rule remains that clergy are not employees. This has been most recently confirmed in *MacDonald* v *Free Presbyterian Church of Scotland.*[4]

Although most of the cases have applied to Christian clergy, the same rules are likely to apply to Imams and leaders of other faith groups. Given the reasoning in the cases showing that Christian ministers are not employed, it is likely that imams will not be employees either. With respect to Sikhs, *Santokh Singh* v *Guru Nanak Gurdwara*[5], priest at a Sikh temple was found not to be an employee.

2 Employment Rights Act 1996 S.98.
3 [2007] EWCA Civ 1004.
4 [2010] UKEAT 0034_09_1002.
5 [1990] ICR 309.

The denial of employee status to clergy and other religious leaders remains a highly contested issue within faith communities, with some clergy and some trade unions[6] very active in campaigning for employee status. The arguments in favour of granting employee status are based on the view that this will protect individuals from capricious decision making by church authorities or individual parishes; and there is certainly evidence of bad treatment of clergy which should be remedied.[7] The counter argument is based on the need to retain church autonomy, and to ensure the religious freedom of both the religious organisation and the clergy or religious leader, free from the interference of secular courts.

This counter argument certainly has strength, and thus far it is a view that is being reflected in courts' decisions. However, as will be seen in the discussion of discrimination protection, the subjection of the organisation to legal regulation does not necessarily remove all autonomy from the organisation, as long as the legal regulation applied is flexible enough to recognise the special religious aspects of the relationship being governed. For example, if unfair dismissal protection were to be granted to clergy or their equivalents, the test of fairness could take account of the religious context of the dismissal. A tribunal would not have to question the religious teaching involved, but could intervene when the employing organisation had failed to comply with its own rules. Such an approach would fit clearly within the current legislative framework, where all dismissals of employees have to be judged according to whether they are fair or unfair in the circumstances. The tribunal could therefore take into account the religious context in making this judgment.

3. Religious disputes and non-clergy employees of religious organisations:

The denial of employee status for clergy and other religious leaders will not apply to most other staff employed in a secular capacity by religious organisations. Thus administrative, catering or cleaning staff in religious organisations will be classified as employees. In addition staff of religious ethos organisations will be protected against unfair dismissal. Unlike the position in Germany, there are few large religious employers (with the exception of religious schools which are governed by separate legal provisions[8]). In particular nearly all health care provision

6 The union Unite (unitetheunion.org.uk) has a faith workers branch.
7 See for example <http://www.churchofengland.org/media-centre/news/2002/12/council_accepts_need_to_change_clergy_employment.aspx> (accessed 12/10/2012).
8 School Standards and Framework Act 1998. See L Vickers Religion and Belief Discrimination and the Employment of Teachers in Faith Schools (2009) 4 Religion and Human Rights 1-20.

is provided by the state. However, there is an increasing trend towards the provision of some public services by religious organisations,[9] and so this area of conflict between religious employers and their secular workers may increase in importance in the future.

In such cases, the unfair dismissal rules will apply. As referred to above, the test of whether a dismissal is fair or not will depend on whether there is a potentially fair reason for the dismissal (usually misconduct in this context), and whether the tribunal judges that dismissal was within a range of reasonable responses which a reasonable employer might make. The assessment should take account of the need to respect religious freedom because of the need to interpret laws to comply with the EHCR,[10] as well as taking into account all the circumstances, including the religious context of the employment. Thus, as with the position for clergy, the religious freedom of religious employers with regard to their secular workers is not significantly restricted despite being governed by the general law of unfair dismissal.

This approach complies with the current approach of the ECtHR when determining employment cases under the Convention. For example, in*Lombardi Vallauri v Italy*,[11] where a lecturer in a Catholic university was refused continuation of employment without being given reasons, the ECtHR found that the lack of reasons meant that his Article 6 rights (the right to a fair hearing) were infringed. The ECtHR did not try to interfere with the religious rules which the Church sought to apply, as these were clearly matters of religious doctrine with which the court could not interfere. However, the Court did intervene because of a lack of clarity about the processes by which the Church was applying its own rules.

As the position currently stands in Great Britain, clergy and religious leaders for other faiths are generally not protected against unfair dismissal. Instead they can lose their jobs without any system of legal redress. Although other employees are protected against unfair dismissal, the level of protection is not very high. This illustrates the less formal, but nonetheless reasonably effective, approach to the governance of religious affairs in Great Britain. In effect, although there is no

9 See, for example, Press Release, 11/1/07 by The Department for Work and Pensions, in which the Minister for Employment and Welfare Reform, Jim Murphy, said he wants to see a greater role for faith based groups in UK welfare delivery. Although there has been a change in government, there has been no clear change of policy, and the Coalition governments embrace of the idea of the 'big society' seems to envisage a clear role for the voluntary sector as service providers (July 19 2010 BBC News, <http://www.bbc.co.uk/news/uk-10680062> accessed 22/09/10) and this is likely to include religious organisations.

10 See Human Rights Act 1998 s. 3.

11 *Lombardi Vallauri v Italy*, Application 39128/05 (Court judgment 20 October 2009).

constitutional guarantee of collective and cooperative religious freedom to religious groups (as there is in Germany), religious groups are provided with freedom to determine their own employment relationships, and they remain free to hire and fire religious leaders on religious grounds, because of an absence of legal redress for those subjected to this treatment. For other staff, although there are some restrictions, they are all subject to judgments by tribunals which will be required to take into account the religious freedom elements of the case, as well as the general religious context of the employment. Thus legal protection for individuals is minimal, and the collective freedom of the religious employing group is maximised.

However, the implementation of the EU Equality Directive 2000/78 has led to some restrictions on the freedom of religious bodies to govern their employment relations, and these will be discussed below.

4. Protection against discrimination

The definition of protected workers under discrimination legislation is much wider, and does include clergy and other religious workers. The House of Lords case *Percy* v *Church of Scotland*[12] considered whether Miss Percy could claim sex discrimination under the SDA 1975 when she was dismissed from her post as Minister in the Church of Scotland following an affair with a married elder in her church. The definition of who is covered by sex discrimination legislation is much wider than that of the status of employee, (a person who is »contracted personally to do any work«) and is used in all the more recent discrimination legislation too. In *Percy* it was held that it covered clergy, and it is certainly the understanding that the new religion and belief and the sexual orientation employment protection covers this much wider category of »worker« too. This means that although not generally protected by unfair dismissal legislation, clergy and other religious leaders are covered by the prohibition on discrimination on grounds of sex, religion and belief, disability, sexual orientation and age. In Miss Percy's case, the court's concern was that the church had disciplined a woman's behaviour, while leaving undisciplined the same behaviour by a man, even though the church teaching about behaviour applied equally to men and women. The court did not question the rules being applied, but did question the fact that they had been applied differently to men and women.

It is clear from *Percy* that clergy and other staff of religious communities are protected by discrimination legislation in Great Britain. Moreover, Article 4 of

12 [2005] UKHL 73.

EU Directive which provides occupational requirements clearly envisages that the Directive will apply to churches. Thus it would seem that those EU member states who exempt clergy from the coverage of non-discrimination protection are in breach of the EU directive.

In the light of this, it may be that the position in Germany will need to be considered further. In German law exceptions to non-discrimination law exist for religious communities, to reflect the principle of the neutrality of the state and the autonomy of the Church. The autonomy of churches extends beyond the internal workings of the church to all institutions related to the church, as long as the institution has an inner relationship to the religious mission of the church. For Christian churches it has been accepted that charitable activities, such as running hospitals, are encompassed by the religion mission of the Christian faith.

Where discrimination laws do apply to churches and church-based organisations, they must be interpreted with due regard to the special status of churches and in a way that will not interfere with church autonomy. Thus, employment can be terminated if duties and obligations of loyalty are violated. For example, a doctor in a religious hospital could be dismissed if she leaves the church concerned or marries a divorced man if this contradicts the ethos of the church concerned.

These provisions are capable of being interpreted to comply with Article 4(2), although this may depend on the amount of discretion allowed to religious employers to determine whether their activities can be viewed as part of the mission of the church. The position in Germany is that the activity of running a hospital can be part of the mission of the Christian church. What is not clear is how German courts will decide cases where the dismissal for failure to meet requirements of loyalty to religious ethos also involve discrimination on other grounds, such as sex discrimination.

What, then, is the scope of the British non-discrimination protection? How does it address the position of disputes between religious communities and their adherent workers?

(a) The Equality Act 2010.[13]

The scope of the protection: The Equality Act 2010 replaces the 2003 Equality (Religion and Belief) Regulations, which implemented the Employment Directive 2000/78. Under the Equality Act, direct and indirect discrimination because of religion and belief are prohibited, as well as harassment and victimisation. Direct discrimination is defined as less favourable treatment »because of religion or belief« and would cover discipline and dismissal for religious reasons, as well as a refusal to employ, train, or promote staff on the basis of religion. The 2003 Regulations did not cover discrimination on grounds of the employer's religion. No such restriction appears in the Equality Act 2010, which merely states[14] that it does not matter if the discriminator shares the characteristic with the person discriminated against.Indirect discrimination covers the application of a provision, criterion or practice which is applied equally to those not of the same religion, but which puts persons of the religion in question at a disadvantage compared to others, and which cannot be shown to be a proportionate means of achieving a legitimate aim.

As with other grounds of discrimination, the regulations contain an exception where being of a particular religion is a genuine occupational requirement (GOR) of the job (Schedule 9 s1). It is fairly limited in scope, in that the requirement must be a defining aspect of the job. It is really limited to those employed in religious service, whose job involves teaching or promoting the religion, or being involved in religious observance. This enables churches to require that clergy be Christian, and mosques that Imams be Muslim, and is largely uncontentious.

What has been more contentious is the additional exception in Schedule 9 s 3, for organisations with an ethos based on religion and belief. This additional exception is also found in Article 4(2) of the parent Directive. It is a little wider than the general exception, in that the occupational requirement still has to be »genuine«, but in applying the exception the court will have regard to the religious ethos and to the nature or context of the workThis provision allows greater freedom to religious organisations to maintain their ethos by employing those of the same religion, even where the staff are not engaged in work whose nature is determined by the religion, such as Christian lawyers, and Muslim medical prac-

13 The Equality Act 2010 was given assent on 8 April 2010, and came into force in October 2010. Its provisions do not materially change the law on the issues discussed, and the case law discussed was brought under the Equality (Religion and Belief) Regulations 2003. This paper will, however, use the 2010 terminology.

14 In S. 24.

tices. It also covers workers for religious communities in roles which are not religious in nature, such as church gardeners or cleaners at a Mosque.

However, it should be borne in mind that under this exception the job does need to have religion as a *requirement* of the job, and it will be difficult to argue that *all* staff must share the religion. An understanding of the faith, and sympathy for its practice could be required, but it will be difficult to show that a shared faith is necessary for all jobs unless faith and its practice permeate the workplace, for example by the need for daily prayers. Moreover, even where the employment is of priests or imams, any occupational requirement relating to religious or belief must be proportionate, although in most cases of clergy or ministers of religion, they surely will be.

Applying the Equality Act 2010 to disputes between religious communities and their adherent workers: Discipline or dismissal of religious workers for matters relating to their faith, for example, for failing to live consistently with religious teaching, or for holding beliefs which are inconsistent with the mainstream religious teaching, will be covered by the Equality Act 2010.

With regard to clergy and other religious leaders, the requirement to hold the tenets of the religion are surely a genuine occupational requirement, and any discipline or dismissal for denying clear aspects of the faith are very likely to be proportionate. Given the need to uphold church autonomy and freedom of religion, it must be proportionate to allow religious communities to choose their leaders, and to impose on them requirements relating to belief. The freedom for religious communities to choose their clergy or leaders is certainly recognised within the case law of the ECHR,[15] and the Equality Act 2010 will be interpreted to comply. Similarly, where an employer can show that it has a religious ethos such that the broader GOR applies for those staff whose jobs are more loosely religious, a requirement to adhere to the basic tenets of the faith is likely to be proportionate. For example, in *Muhammed* v *The Leprosy Mission International,*[16] where Mr Muhammed, a Muslim, was not offered employment as a finance administrator at the Leprosy Mission, a Christian charity. The Leprosy Mission stated that one of the selection criteria for the job was to be a practising Christian, a requirement that Mr Muhammed clearly did not meet.[17] The Employment Tribunal held that the requirement was a genuine occupational requirement, in the context of that particular place employment, in which a Chris-

15 See for example, *Hasan and Chaush v Bulgaria* (2002) 34 EHRR 55 at para 62; and *Serif v Greece* (2001) 31 EHRR 20.

16 16 Dec 2009, ET/2303459/09.

17 The applicant, Mr Muhammed also failed to meet other criteria for the job, but the legal issue in the case concerned the scope of Regulation 7(3).

tian ethos permeated the daily life and activities of the workplace. For example, collective prayer and bible reading took place each working day, with all the staff in turn leading the worship, and where prayer was used to help resolve workplace disputes. Because of this context (as opposed to the nature of the work itself which was financial), the requirement on staff to be Christian was a genuine occupational requirement. It was proportionate to impose this GOR because otherwise the ethos of the organisation would have been entirely undermined, whereas Mr Muhammed would be able to find other financial work in other occupations.

It seems then that dismissals or discipline for failing to share the faith of an employing religious community are likely to be covered by the exception to the non-discrimination rules, although this does depend on the context of the employment, and the extent to which the religious beliefs are seen to be essential to the post.

For example, in the context of non religious-ethos employer and the stricter Schedule 9 s 1 GOR, an atheist teacher in a Catholic school was not offered an interview for the post of pastoral care teacher.[18] The Tribunal found that it was not essential to the post that the holder be Catholic, as the responsibilities of the job involved giving advice on a large number of issues only a few of which required knowledge of Catholic doctrine (and those could be assigned to a different teacher).

What is less clear is the extent to which discipline or dismissal for life-style choices with which the religious community may disagree will be protected under the Regulations. For example, private matters such as divorce or remarriage could be relevant as demonstrating good standing and loyalty to the religion. In such a case, the worker is disciplined not so much for failing to comply with a requirement to *be of a particular religion*, but for failing to comply with the teaching of the religion. It is arguable then that the GOR would not apply. However, it is also arguable that the individual has still been discriminated against because of religion, arguably not his or her religion, but because the employer, for religious reasons relating to the failure to comply with the religious teaching, has decided to dismiss or discipline. This could mean that dismissal or discipline by a religious community for failing to comply with lifestyle requirements will be unlawful religious discrimination, assuming that the Court would agree that this was action taken »because of religion«.

18 *Glasgow City Council v McNab* UKEAT/0037/06. The case is complicated by the existence of an agreement with the local education authority only to appoint Catholics to positions as 'guidance' teachers, and the interaction of that agreement with the Education (Scotland) Act 1980.

(b) Protection under other discrimination provisions

Even where the treatment of staff by religious communities may be lawful under the religion and belief provisions of the Equality Act 2010, such treatment may be discriminatory on other grounds, and thus protected under other legal provisions. For example, if a lifestyle requirement is enforced in relation to a female employee but not on a male employee then this may give rise to sex discrimination, as in *Percy v Church of Scotland*;[19] and where a decision to dismiss a member of staff is related to pregnancy, it will amount to sex discrimination. In *O'Neill v Governors of St Thomas More RCVA Upper School*[20] a teacher in a Catholic school became pregnant and was dismissed when it became known that the father of child was a priest. Her dismissal was found to be discriminatory on grounds of sex, because it was related to pregnancy. The employer's argument that the reason for dismissal was not the pregnancy, but the failure to comply with religious standards, was not accepted, because the pregnancy precipitated and permeated the decision to dismiss.

It is worth noting from cases such as *O'Neill* that, although lifestyle requirements will often be directed at men and women, they may, in practice, they have a greater impact on women, and so may involve direct or indirect sex discrimination. The presence of special protection for religious ethos organisations does not extend to the justification of discrimination on other grounds such as gender. Physiological differences and social differences can mean that lifestyle requirements can have particular impact on women. For example, it is often only with pregnancy that a breach of a requirement to abstain from sexual activity outside of marriage will become known to an employer, and discrimination against women who become pregnant will be pregnancy related, and therefore amount to sex discrimination.[21] Similar problems, where gender and religion interact, could arise if a religious employer refused to employ anyone who has had an abortion.

Religious communities may also discriminate against staff on other equality grounds. The ground which is most likely to arise is that of sexual orientation. For example, an employer who sets religious observance as a preference in making an appointment in order to maintain the religious ethos of the organisation may indirectly discriminate on grounds of sexual orientation where the religion in question is hostile to homosexuality. Any attempt to justify such treatment will need to meet the high standards required to justify sex or sexual orientation

19 *Percy v Church of Scotland Board of National Mission* [2005] UKHL 73.
20 [1996] IRLR 372.
21 See *Dekker v Stichting Vormingscentrum voor Jong Volwassenen* (VJV-Centrum) Plus [1990] ECR I-3941.

discrimination. It is rarely going to be proportionate to allow such indirect discrimination. The result is that where indirect discrimination results, the creation of religiously homogenous workplaces is not allowed.

There is one exception to this, which applies where the employment is for the purposes of an organised religion, contained in the Equality Act 2010 Schedule 9 s2. These provisions cover requirements relating to gender, marriage or sexual orientation imposed so as to comply with the doctrines of the religion, or (because of the nature of the employment and the context in which it is carried out), so as to avoid conflicting with the strongly-held religious convictions of a significant number of the religion's followers. In effect, discrimination against women is accepted where it is part of the belief system that such discrimination is necessary. For example this would apply to the Catholic Church where it is a doctrine of the religion that only single men can act as priests. The exception also allows churches or mosques to refuse to employ priests or imams on the basis of their sexual orientation.

These exceptions to sex and sexual orientation discrimination apply only to the appointment of religious personnel for the purposes of an organised religion. This refers to the appointment of clergy, or their equivalent for other religious groups. Concerns that this provision could cover a wide range of workers employed by religious organisations, such as teachers or nurses in religious foundations, were alleviated by the decision of the English High Court in the *Amicus* case,[22] which limited the words »for the purposes of an organised religion« to the appointment of religious leaders and teachers such as priests and imams.

The equivalent provision in the old Sexual Orientation Regulations was used in an Employment Tribunal case brought by a Christian youth worker who was denied employment as a diocesan Youth Officer because the Bishop did not believe his lifestyle would continue to be compatible with the church's teaching on homosexuality.[23] In accordance with the beliefs of a significant number of Christians about the appropriate lifestyle for a gay Christian, the Diocese required that the youth officer comply with a requirement to be celibate for the duration of the post. The youth office in question had stated that he would comply with this requirement, but the Bishop did not believe that he would. The Employment Tribunal held that the GOR relating to sexual orientation did apply to the post of youth worker, as the work involved teaching the doctrines of the faith. Had the work been limited to administration and management the GOR exception would not have applied. The Tribunal looked in a considerable amount of detail at

22 *R (on the application of Amicus – MSF and others) v Secretary of State for Trade and Industry and others* [2004] IRLR 430.

23 *Reaney v. Hereford Diocesan Board of Finance* Case No: 1602844/2006.

church teaching on sexuality in reaching this decision. It clearly did not just accept the arguments of the Diocese, but made extensive reference to church documents on the issue, to ensure that the Church was complying with its own teaching. The case is noteworthy in this regard, as it illustrates the fine borderline, which it is submitted was not crossed in this case, between challenging the implementation of a religious community's teaching as discriminatory, and challenging the teaching itself.

The applicant was, however, successful for a different reason, which was that the employer's belief that a GOR had not been met was said to be unreasonable. The test used was not whether the Bishop's conclusion was capable of being reasonable, or was »with a range of reasonable responses«,[24] but instead was objective and determined by the members of the Employment Tribunal. They considered in detail the reasoning of the Bishop in reaching his conclusion that the applicant did not meet the requirement to be celibate for the duration of the post and decided that the Bishop's belief on the matter was unreasonable. Thus, the gender and sexual orientation exception can apply to work involving religious teaching, but the *Reaney* case confirms that exceptions to the sexual orientation rules will be applied restrictively, as they are exceptions to the principle of non-discrimination on grounds of sexual orientation. Again, the close scrutiny given by the Tribunal to the decision making of the Bishop is noteworthy, and again treads the fine line between judging the beliefs, and judging their implementation.

5. Future religious employment disputes?

Although there has been much discussion about the extent to which religious communities can retain their religious autonomy with regard to staffing, so that they are able to require staff to remain loyal to the religious group, there has in fact been little case law on the issue. More contentious currently in Great Britain has been the freedom of religious staff in secular employment to request exemption from dress codes and also from work tasks on religious grounds. Thus far, the courts have treated the dress codes as indirect discrimination cases. Employers who impose requirements on staff, for example as regards dress codes which are potentially discriminatory, are able to justify such requirements where they have good, objective reasons to apply the requirement. Where they have not given good grounds for imposing the requirement, such requirements are not justified. Thus the requirement for a teacher to remove the *niqab* when teaching was

24 C.f. the tests of reasonableness used in unfair dismissal cases, discussed above.

justified as the employer had established with evidence that communication was enhanced when the face was visible. In contrast, an employer which claimed that a staff member wearing a headscarf would have an adverse effect on business was unsuccessful as no evidence of the impact on business was provided.[25]

It is interesting to note the similar outcomes in these cases with those which have been brought in Germany, despite differing legal bases. It seems that the approach based on anti-discrimination law reaches very similar results to that based on the German approach of a fundamental right of religious freedom. In the case of a freedom based approach to the wearing of a headscarf, the freedom can be limited only if the headscarf prevents the employee doing a good job. In the case of the indirect discrimination approach to the same issue, a ban will be discriminatory unless justified, for example because the headscarf prevents the employee doing a good job. It may well be that these different structures for protecting religion in the workplace result in very similar outcomes.

However, there appears to be a difference in approach between Germany and Great Britain with regard to the value given to neutrality of state employment. In the case of teachers in state schools and workers in hospitals and government offices, Great Britain generally accepts individual religious expression as long as it does not interfere with the performance in a role, whereas in Germany greater emphasis is given to state neutrality in the public sector. The indirectly discriminatory effect on the female Muslim community of requiring visible neutrality (female members of the community would be excluded from public sector workplaces) is perhaps given greater weight in Great Britain than in Germany, and religious dress in state employment is common. For example, army, police and judicial uniforms can be adapted to allow for Sikh men and Muslim women to wear head coverings. This may reflect a different weight being applied to the value of state neutrality, although in the schools cases in Germany it is also worth pointing out that the courts were concerned to protect the interests in children in being free from religious influence, particularly because they do not have a choice about being confronted with religion in school as they are obligate to be in class.

To an extent the legal protection available to religious workers in secular employment in state employment is therefore likely to vary as between the two countries, as they seem to give different weight to the value of visible state neutrality in the public workplace when determining proportionality. Given that both situations are governed by the same EU derived equality laws, it will be interest-

25 *Noah v Desrosiers t/a Wedge* (13 Jun 2008; ET/2201867/07).

ing to see which approach is given precedence should the issue come before the ECJ for resolution.

A second more contentious strand of cases is emerging, regarding the freedom of staff to opt out of certain work tasks on religious grounds. Two high profile cases have involved this clash, *Ladele* v. *Islington Borough Council*[26] and *McFarlane* v *Relate Avon Ltd.*[27] Ms Ladele claimed she was discriminated against for refusing, on religious grounds, to carry out civil partnerships as part of her job as a registrar. Mr McFarlane claimed that he was discriminated against for refusing, on religious grounds, to provide psycho-sexual therapy to same sex couples as part of his work as a relationship counsellor. In both cases, the religious claimants were unsuccessful. The court held that the indirect religious discrimination involved in requiring that the staff comply with equal opportunities policies was justified.

What made the refusal to allow staff to opt out of certain work tasks on religious grounds proportionate in the *McFarlane* and *Ladele* cases was the fact the opt out involved discrimination on grounds of sexual orientation. What is not examined in these cases, therefore, is whether the courts would have been sympathetic to attempts by religious workers to opt out of tasks for religious reasons that did not involve discrimination on other grounds. It may well be that the indirect discrimination rules would require that opt outs be allowed where to do so does not involve too much disruption to the employer. This is because any refusal to accommodate such a request will be potentially indirectly discriminatory and it will not be justified as proportionate to refuse, unless there are good reasons.

6. Conclusion

The challenges facing the courts in dealing with religion in an increasingly secular world remain profound. In this context, it is worth ending with two comments. First, the cases discussed above illustrate a broader debate in human rights thinking about competing rights, the details of which are beyond the scope of this paper, but which involves engaging in the conflict between the right to religious autonomy for religious individuals and communities on the one hand, and the equality and dignity rights of workers on the other. Resolving this conflict may be beyond us at the moment, but in the shorter term we need to find a way to create some equilibrium between these competing interests. In the employ-

26 UKEAT/0453/08, and [2009] EWCA Civ 1357.
27 [2010] EWCA Civ B1.

ment context, this equilibrium may be found by reliance on the concept of proportionality in resolving employment disputes, a concept that is usually the determining factor, legally, in deciding the scope of protection against discrimination: indirect discrimination is justified where proportionate, and GORs can be relied on where proportionate. It is also the factor in human rights discourse which governs how to resolve competing rights. In determining proportionality, a wide range of factors can be taken into account, such as the range of other jobs available to job applicants, how religious the organisation is, how close to the religious function the particular job is, and how »core« the employment is to the religious aims of the group. This makes cases very fact sensitive, but also enables nuanced decisions to be made, reflecting the complexity of individual situations.

In considering proportionality it is worth considering a second comment, which relates to the relative importance of the employment in religious life. Clearly employment is a key issue in this context. Work for most people is an economic necessity, and to deny work to individuals because of disputes about religion would seem unreasonable as a matter of principle. Equally, religious organisations will need, at times to engage workers, and they have a right to preserve their religious integrity while they do so. However, despite the importance of employment both to religious communities and religious individuals, it may sometimes be the case that religious freedom is best protected by avoiding the employment relationship, in particular by maintaining the »right to resign«. This is because although religious freedom remains a fundamental right, it does not include a right to a job. Thus, if religious scruple means that an individual cannot carry out some functions of the job, religious freedom is not removed by allowing the employer to dismiss. Equally, religious communities may wish to carry on other functions beyond those involving worship or religious practice, such as running book shops, or hospices, but again, restrictions on these activities in the name of equality does not interfere with the core of religious practice, such that autonomy is entirely compromised. This is not to say that we should have no protection against religious discrimination or of religious autonomy in the employment context, merely that in the final analysis, when compromise cannot be reached, the proportional response may not be to protect the religious interest, because employment is only one part of life, albeit an important one. Thus, although the challenges facing courts in reconciling conflicting rights are profound in the employment context, it should not be forgotten that the employment context is only one context in which the issues arise. The issues raised in the employment context are clearly important, and often create analogies with the issues raised in public life more generally, but care should be taken before drawing conclusions about the correct balance between competing rights in the broader context of public life, from the particular context of employment.

THE GERMAN PERSPECTIVE – Hinnerk Wißmann

1. Introduction

(a) Comparative Approach UK – Germany

A comparative approach to religious disputes in state courts in the UK and Germany should first highlight the differences: From a German perspective, the legal situation in the UK is characterized by the unique mixture of tradition and flexibility. Due to its content, the common law seems to be »beyond time« while on the other hand Parliament in principle enjoys full sovereignty. The resulting constitutional practice established over centuries also seems to incorporate the binding nature of European Law - which is of particular interest to the question we are concerned with - in its distinct way.

German law, in contrast, is characterized by its written constitution. Consequently, the German Constitution can protect a certain status against changes at least for a limited time. Nevertheless, changes in the social realities can be taken into account in the application of law, but only to some extent. For fundamental changes, there has to be a political decision to formally amend the constitution; on the other hand, the legislator and government are virtually not bound by any unwritten principles. As in the UK, the European integration presents a challenge to this internally consistent system. In this context, Article 23 of the German Constitution establishes a new and flexible arrangement for a system of multilevel governance that is based on mutual recognition and respect. However, as the debate about the Lisbon judgment of the *Bundesverfassungsgericht* shows, in this context the legal culture in Germany seems to be only at the early stages. Overall, German law is characterised by a complex interaction between the Constitution, European Law and the margin of appreciation of the legislator and the administration and, in cases of disputes by judgments, in particular of the German *Bundesverfassungsgericht (BVerfG)*.

(b) Cases of religious disputes

This general conclusion is particularly valid in cases of religious disputes. This is so because the relevant special provisions, the »Weimarer Kirchenartikel« (Article 140 of the constitution (GG)), have been in force since 1919.[1] In this respect, the constitution provides the following starting point:

1 BVerfGE 19, 206 (219); 226 (236).

(aa)

The individual freedom of religion in Article 4 of the constitution guarantees, according to the interpretation of the BVerfG, a right to a lifestyle which is extensively defined by religious rules. The State is only allowed to set limitations if these limitations can themselves be based on the constitution.[2] For example, this affects directly the core areas of public service and public schools.[3] But equally, private employers must face certain restrictions, since the State is bound by fundamental rights if it adjudicates in cases of conflict and has to protect the freedom of religion equally in this relationship.[4]

(bb)

How is the situation of freedom of religion *within* a religious group to be treated? Here, a conflict between the freedom of religion of e.g. a church which requires certain behaviour from their employees and the freedom of religion of the employee that does object to these requirements might arise.[5] In this context, first one has to bear in mind: The collective and co-operative freedom of religion is protected equally by the constitution. The German constitution (Art. 140 GG) expressly incorporates Article 137 (3) of the constitution of the Weimar Republic (WRV) which protects the self-determination of the religious communities. This includes the freedom to organise its structure: The legal structure should as far as possible be customised according to the needs of the religious communities. In the light of the historical situation, which cannot be explained in the context of this short paper, this means that: Even though a state church has not existed in Germany since 1919, according to Article 137 (5) of the WRV religious communities can (still) be organised as public bodies (»*Körperschaft des öffentlichen Rechts*«) which, however, are not considered to be part of the state institutions but enjoy the freedom of religion.[6] Christian as well as other religious communities often are organised in such a way. In addition there are countless (Christian and other) religious communities organised in a private, non-public way. The way in which these religious communities are organised has consequences in many different legal areas but especially with regard to judicial review.[7]

2 BVerfGE 93, 1 (21).
3 See below 2. a).
4 For example in the case »headscarf of a shop assistant«, see below 2. a).
5 BVerfG, Beschluss vom 30.7.2003 - 1 BvR 792/03 -, NJW 2003, 2815.
6 BVerfGE 102, 370 (386 ff.) – Zeugen Jehovas.
7 BVerfGE 83, 341 (355 ff.) – Baha'i.

(cc)

Another aspect must be added: It can be inferred from the particularly »pro-religious« case law of the BVerfG that the extensive right of protection also applies to collective religious freedom. In practice, this means that not only the church service but also many mixed activities with a commercial aspect have been considered to be an exercise of the freedom of religion – the related expansion of »*Diakonie*« and »*Caritas*« was at the same time an important element of the expansion of German public service into the so called »third sector«. As a result the Evangelical and Catholic Church are the largest employers after the State: The employment in a hospital, a welfare centre, or a drug-counselling service is ascribed to the church, independently of the legal status of the provider, if the Church itself considers this service as ascribed to it.[8] Thus, the right of self-determination of the religious communities pursuant Article 137(3) of the »*Weimarer Reichsverfassung*« applies to all these areas. Hence, in these cases a conflict between the individual freedom of religion of the employee and the institution's collective freedom of religion might arise.

2. What does this mean for the state courts in cases concerning religious disputes?

(a) Disputes between religious employees and non-religious employers

In German employment law, there are two main codifications that apply in cases of religious disputes. Concerning dismissal, it is the KSchG (Dissmissial Protection Act) that has to be observed. In cases of discrimination, the AGG (General Equality Treatment Act) applies. Whereas in Great Britain the headscarf of a shop assistant is a matter of indirect discrimination, as L. Vickers pointed out above, German courts decided on a more fundamental, rights driven basis. According to the highest labour court (the German *Bundesarbeitsgericht* - BAG), the employer in general has the right to advise his employees concerning their appearance. But he is obliged to respect the freedom of religion of his employees and therefore cannot keep a shop assistant from wearing a headscarf for religious reasons if it does not prevent the employee from doing a good job.[9]

8 BVerfGE 46, 73 (85 ff.); 53, 366 (392 f., 399); 57, 220 (243); 70, 138 (163).
9 BAGE 103, 111 (119 f.) – Kopftuch.

In the case of a teacher insisting on wearing the headscarf during her classes, things are different as this concerns public service law. The public servant is seen as part of the State and therefore both parts are subjected to stricter legal bounds. The *Bundesverfassungsgericht* granted political discretion to the federal state legislator because here it is necessary to find a compromise between the religious freedom of the teacher on the one hand and the negative religious freedom of pupils and parents on the other hand. The legislation thereafter gave priority to neutrality and prohibited clear signs of religious belief in the classroom in general. Again, the German jurisdiction took a material fundamental rights driven point of view.

Concerning the cases of religious employees facing discrimination because they refuse to act against their beliefs, the *Bundesarbeitsgericht* gave the individual freedom of conscience priority over the rights of the employer. Again, it is a question of practical coherence of competing fundamental rights that needs to be solved.[10] It seems that the German material perspective is more likely to strengthen the individual rights in these cases.

(b) Disputes within religious organisations

(aa)

First, two areas have to be distinguished: Traditionally, *in cases of priests or clerks about their status,* the BVerfG does not offer any access to state courts when religious communities are organised as a public body (»*Körperschaft des öffentlichen Rechts*«). Instead, such actions were considered inadmissible due to the right of self-determination of the religious communities. The decisive point thus seems to be not the religious motivation of the activity but instead the right of the churches to regulate their service, which leads to an exclusion from the realm of the (public) rule of law.[11] This case law has been long and unanimously criticised.[12]

Concerning the question whether clergy in general are protected by regulation on unjustified dismissal, L. Vickers showed that for the UK this is not the case. In Germany, the jurisdiction not only refuses to apply employment law but cler-

10 BAGE 47, 363; 62, 59.

11 BVerfGE 18, 385 (387 f.); 42, 312 (334 f.); 111, 1 (5). BVerwGE 95, 379 (381 ff.); 117, 145 (146 f.).

12 Korioth in Maunz/Dürig, GG, Art. 140 GG/137 WRV Rn. 50 ff. In contrast to the jurisdiction of BVerfG and BVerwG the highest civil court accepted the suit of a clergy, BHGZ 154, 306 (309 ff.).

gy cannot even take legal action. As a genuine matter of self-determination of religious organizations these cases cannot be brought to court. Whereas in Great Britain priests still find shelter in discrimination legislation, the German discrimination regulations (AGG) expressively do not apply to dismissals.

(bb)

On the other hand, there are cases on the right of self-determination in other employment relationships that are governed by employment law. In those *cases of individual employment law*, the courts do not seem to work with an exclusion from the rule of law. Instead, the issues here are the duties of loyalty known from classical employment law which in these cases are reinforced by the idea of a »*Dienstgemeinschaft*«. As a result, the right of the religious communities takes precedence over the freedom of religion of the individual employee, respectively over the general freedom to determine one's own way of life. Hence, the religious communities are frequently successful before courts if a case is brought and not settled beforehand. The controversial issue in those cases has for a long time been whether such wide duties of loyalty, which might even be related to the entire way of life, can be imposed in every employment relationship because of the community aspect (»*Dienstgemeinschaft*«), or whether one should distinguish between different areas of employment.[13]

By contrast to the cases of priests or other religious leaders, the German KSchG applies to employees of religious organisations just like the Employment Rights Act does in Great Britain. However, concerning dismissal because of religious reasons, the German courts do respect the autonomy of religious organisations by not questioning the religious teaching but only checking whether the religious organisation preserved their own principles and did not act disproportionately.[14]

It was pointed out for Great Britain that actual or prospective adherents of religious organisations may face discrimination for religious reasons. In Germany, the AGG applies in these cases.[15] Due to § 9 (1, 2) AGG, there are exclusions for so called »different treatment because of religion« as a parallel to the British Employment Equality (Religion and Belief) Regulations. Discriminating behaviour towards employees is lawful if there is a »justified occupational requirement« in respect of the concrete work or the religious beliefs of the employer.

13 BVerfGE 70, 138 (162 ff., 165 ff.); BAGE 34, 195; 47, 144.
14 BAGE 30, 247.
15 LAG Hamburg, Urteil vom 29.10.2008 - 3 Sa 15/08 -, ArbR 2009, 97.

This concerns only the requirement of adherence to a certain religion. Disregard for religious principles and lifestyle guidelines may also be met with disciplinary measures as here, again, the religious employer is allowed to demand a certain degree of loyalty and sincerity towards the religious lifestyle. The argument is that the religious employer needs to preserve his credibility. This also applies to dismissals, as the BAG pointed out in the case of a Charity-employee whose dismissal, which was based on the fact that she got divorced and then married again, was considered lawful by the court.[16]In general, I suggest that the assumptions given by the British discrimination regulation (religiously permeated workspace) provide a better protection for the employees whereas in Germany religious employers can exert influence on the private way of living of their employees on a larger scale.

However, it is important to insist on equal treatment in those cases. If far reaching duties are retained as a reserve competence for individual cases, this would violate the prohibition of arbitrariness which pursuant to Article 137 (3) of the German Constitution equally binds the churches as general law.

(cc)

With regard to the *collective labour law*, collective agreements with unions are avoided and other rules about workers' participation are modified due to the right of self-determination – churches apply the so called model of the »Third Way« which emphasises common decisions of the »*Dienstgemeinschaft*«, instead of an open conflict of interests between employee and employer. In this regard, cases brought, e.g. by the Unions, have not been successful so far.

3. The religious pluralisation as well as the Europeanisation require adjustments of the German system, which, however, should not undermine the substance of freedom of religion:

The State and the two »public churches« do not form an identical personal basis anymore. The freedom that is granted to religion is increasingly utilised by different religious groups. More and more, the collective freedom of religion is affecting citizens who themselves are not religiously bound, especially if the religion is visible in the public sphere and has not retreated into not encapsulated area.

16 BAGE 47, 144.

With regard to European law, which is until now debated mainly in terms of the anti-discrimination directive, two aspects need to be pointed out: Article 10 and 19 TFEU are strengthening the anti-discrimination task with regard to primary law, which in turn binds the churches as employers and imposes new burdens regarding justification. On the other hand, one has to bear in mind that the European Union has finally incorporated a reference to religious communities into primary law (Article 17 TFEU). The primary law serves in this regard as a new yardstick for secondary Union legislation which affects the status of religious communities. The mainly economically orientated secondary law, which combines its aim to implement the internal market with a reflex against any special rules which are »discrimination-friendly«, will have to adjust its position vis-à-vis the area of religiously oriented economic activity of the *Diakonie* und *Caritas*.

Drawing a final comparison I suggest that the British approach incorporates anti-discrimination and protection of workers in established rules on »fair proceedings' and sound reasons for the unequal treatment which are mainly focused on disclosure and comprehensibility. The common law in this regards moves away from a material system towards a system of procedural protection – which seems to be rooted in fundamentals.

German law, which has worked with a territorial understanding of self-determination, seems to have a much longer way ahead. With regard to this development it has to be called for the following:

1. The rights of the religious communities should be recognised only at a secondary stage instead of defining areas which are outside the (public) rule of law, which tends to surrender the involved citizens to intra-religious arbitrariness.

2. In cases where churches due to reasons of self-determination restrict the freedoms of their members or employees they have to justify where, why, and to what extent the religion requires special protection or support. It seems natural that in this regard, the issue has to be decided according to a sliding scale which takes account of the nature of the activity. This seems to be a reasonable contribution of the religions to an open constitutional state which is woven into the European system of multi-level governance and thus goes beyond building on (religious) exchange rather than separation.

V. BALANCING RELIGIOUS AUTONOMY AND OTHER HUMAN RIGHTS UNDER THE EUROPEAN CONVENTION – Ian Leigh

1. Introduction

The purpose of this chapter is to analyse ways in which the law can reconcile conflicts between collective religious freedom, individual religion freedom and other human rights, particularly in a European context.

Religious liberty is a collective as well as an individual right. Article 18 of the ICCPR refers to the right of freedom of thought, conscience and religion, including »either individually *or in community with others* and in public or private, to manifest his religion or belief in worship, observance, practice and teaching« (italics added); equivalent wording appears in Article 9.1 ECHR.

Famously the 1st Amendment to the US Constitution joins together in a single sentence separation of church and state and the free exercise of religion.[1] Even countries that do not make this link, for example European countries with state or established churches, nonetheless prize a certain degree or non-interference or religious autonomy as an important aspect of collective religious liberty. Reflecting this collective dimension to religious freedom religious organizations seek the right to determine their own structure, personnel, policy, objectives and so on.[2] Perhaps the fullest statement of this collective dimension to religious liberty comes in the UN Declaration on the Elimination of All Forms of Intolerance and of Discrimination Based on Religion or Belief 1981[3] which refers to, inter alia, the right to »train, appoint, elect, or designate by succession appropriate leaders« (Article 6(g)) and the right to »establish and maintain appropriate charitable and humanitarian institutions« (Article 6(b)).

Although in large part the right of religious autonomy comprises claims that the state should not interfere in the affairs of religious organisations in such matters it can also potentially conflict with the rights of individuals within those organisations. Thus, for example, an ordained minister whose teaching departs from the doctrine of his or her church can, on the one hand, claim to be exercising an individual right of freedom of religion or expression but this can be seen, on the other hand, as challenging the right of the organisation to constitute itself according to a set of distinctive beliefs. Corresponding points can be made about

1 'Congress shall make no law respecting an establishment of religion, or prohibiting the free exercise thereof'.

2 For a significant recent contribution to the literature see J. Rivers, *The Law of Organized Religions: Between Establishment and Secularism*, (Oxford, 2010).

3 Adopted by the UN General Assembly, 25 November 1981.

other ways in which individual and collective rights may conflict; the applicability of non-discrimination norms or standards for individual sexual behaviour falling within the ambit of the right to respect for private life are other instances. Similar issues may arise too in the context of legally recognised religious adjudication, whether applicable in clergy discipline cases or to other individuals by consent. Here questions may be raised about the conformity of the process with procedural human rights standards.

Claims that the collective interests of the religious body should take priority in these cases are often represented in contemporary public debate as »special pleading« or exceptionalism, with the organisation cast in the role of the human rights oppressor. However this is to over-simplify since the collective right of the organisation in these cases can also be seen as an aggregation of the rights of its individual members to compose themselves into a like-minded association.[4] From this perspective denial of the ability for religious organisations, for example, to exclude those who do not share their beliefs or values diminishes the freedom of the individual members who do subscribe to the beliefs or values in question. Of course this does not entail that the group's interests should always prevail but it does mean that human rights arguments must be counted on both sides of the legal equation and not just on behalf of the dissenting member.

In the sections that follow the question of the conflict between religious autonomy and other human rights is discussed with reference to the European Convention on Human Rights. After a brief discussion of the status of religious organisations the treatment of collective religious liberty under the Convention is analysed, together with the implications for the state, before attention turns to various ways in which conflict with individual rights may occur and the main approaches to dealing with them.

2. The Status of Religious Organisations

The justifications for *non-applicability* of human rights norms to religious organisations depend of several familiar arguments: separation of the state from religious bodies, lack of competence to intervene in religious disputes, and respect for individual and collective religious choices.[5]

4 For a recent study see: V. Bader, *Secularism or Democracy?: Associational Governance of Religious Diversity,* (Amsterdam University Press, 2007).

5 See also N. Doe and A. Jeremy, '*Justifications for Religious Autonomy*' in R. O'Dair and A. Lewis (eds.), Law and Religion, (Oxford, 2001); R. Minnerath '*The Right to Autonomy in Religious Affairs*' in T. Lindholm, W. Cole Durham and B. Tahzib-Lie (eds.), Facilitating Freedom of Religion or Belief: A Deskbook (Leiden, 2004).

It can be argued that pluralism requires the recognition of a non-state sphere where religious bodies and individuals are free to apply their own standards (or to do so within limits) in a way that departs from the prevailing societal ethos.[6] This is a guarantee of diversity within liberal society according to which individuals and groups are free to pursue their own conceptions of the good, including religious ones.

The non-applicability of human rights standards against religious bodies can also be justified on the basis that the state should remain separate from religious bodies. Intervention even according to state procedural standards can be said to be inconsistent with church-state separation or with the doctrine of state neutrality in religious matters. Some US decisions under the First Amendment certainly take a strong view of separation of this kind and as a consequence exempt from judicial scrutiny even procedural questions.[7]

As a matter of law, however, the boundaries of this non-state sphere depend on the juridical status of the religious bodies in question. State churches or those with the character of public corporations or church courts integrated into the legal system arguably have a responsibility to protect human rights in a way that their non-state counterparts do not as the price of their distinctive legal status.[8]

Even where a strict version of religion-state separation does not apply, however, judges tend to be wary of their lack of competence to rule on theological matters. Indeed in the case of religious arbitration agreements the parties' unwillingness to subject their disputes to non-religious judges is a prime motivation for using these alternatives to the conventional courts in the first place. It can be

6 R. Ahdar and I. Leigh, *Religious Freedom in the Liberal State*, (Oxford, 2004), 334 ff.

7 For example in *Serbian Eastern Orthodox Diocese v Milivojevich* 426 US 696, 713 (1976) Brennan J stated: »For civil courts to analyze whether the ecclesiastical actions of a church judicatory are in that sense »arbitrary« must inherently entail inquiry into the procedures that canon or ecclesiastical law supposedly requires the church judicatory to follow, or else into the substantive criteria by which they are supposedly to decide the ecclesiastical question. But this is exactly the inquiry that the First Amendment prohibits; recognition of such an exception would undermine the general rule that religious controversies are not the proper subject of civil court inquiry, and that a civil court must accept the ecclesiastical decisions of church tribunals as it finds them.«

8 In the UK the question arises as to whether they are 'public authorities' for the purposes of s. 6 of the Human Rights Act 1998. It is clear that the ecclesiastical courts of the Church of England have this status because of the source of their jurisdiction and their integration into the legal system as a whole (see for example *Re Crawley Road Cemetery, Luton* [2001] Fam 308 in the case of the Consistory Court) whereas a Parochial Church Council does not: *Aston Cantlow Parochial Church Council v Wallbank* [2003] UKHL 37, [2004] 1 A.C. 546.

argued then that state respect for individual religious liberty entails recognition of freedom to agree on private religious adjudication.[9]

The voluntary nature of religious organisation can also be seen as a bar. It is arguable that a clergyman who has consented to be bound by doctrinal and moral standards at ordination should not be allowed to override these by invoking human rights norms. Similarly, in religious courts the fact that jurisdiction is derived from consent it is claimed sets such religious adjudication apart from legal rules applicable at the fiat of the state. Common law courts have therefore used the consensual basis argument to decide that judicial review should not apply to decisions of some religious tribunals.[10]

At the Convention level after initially refusing standing to churches,[11] the European Commission of Human Rights accepted that it was artificial to distinguish between rights of the individual members and of the religious body itself.[12]It is now clearly established that a Church or an religious body may, as such, exercise on behalf of its adherents the rights guaranteed by Article 9 of the Convention.[13]

9 But note the decision of the ECtHR in *Refah Partisi v. Turkey*, (2003) 37 EHRR 1 that there was no violation of Article 9 in the prohibition for unconstitutional activities of Refah Partisi, a political party that supported the introduction of plural legal systems (according to which Muslims would be bound in private law matters by sharia). The Grand Chamber characterised Refah Partisi's policy as applying some of the precepts of sharia law to the majority of the population (Muslims) within the framework of a plurality of legal systems. This went beyond freedom to follow religion as a matter of individual conscience since it assigned private law obligations according to membership of a religious group (see especially paras. 127 and 128).

10 Thus in the UK the Administrative Court has declined to supervise the Provincial Court of the Church in Wales in a clergy discipline case since the clergyman has consented to the procedures in the Church's Constitution: *R v Provincial Court of the Church in Wales ex p. Williams* [1998] EWHC Admin 998 (23rd October 1998). The Administrative Court has likewise declined also to review the withdrawal by the Beth Din of a claimant's *kashrut* licence (ie the recognition that food served was kosher) because of the consensual nature of the Beth Din's jurisdiction: *R v London Beth Din (Court of the Chief Rabbi) e p Michael Bloom* [1997] EWHC Admin 1028 (18th November, 1997). And see B. Berkovits, 'Beth Din Arbitration and the Human Rights Act, section 6', (2005) 71 (3) *Arbitration*, 189.

11 *Church of X v. UK*, App. No. 3798/68, (1968) 13 Year Book European Convention on Human Rights 306. See C. Evans, *Freedom of Religion under the European Convention*, (Oxford, 2001) 12–14.

12 *X and the Church of Scientology v. Sweden* (1979) 16 DR 68.

13 See for example *Cha'are Shalom Ve Tsedek v. France* [Grand Chamber], no. 27417/95, § 72, ECHR 2000-VII. A company may also be able to claim Art. 9 rights: *Kustannus Oy Vapaa Ajattelija Ab v Finland* (1996) 2 ECHR CD69 (publisher established to promote freethinking literature).

Moreover it has been recognised that protection of collective religious liberty may require the giving of legal status or personality to religious organizations.[14] This enables them to hold property[15] (important for establishing premises[16] in which to meet and to fund-raise), to employ staff, to enter binding contracts, and to sue and be sued. The European Court of Human Rights has held that the discriminatory denial of legal personality to some churches, so that they are unable to litigate unless registered with the state, violates Articles 6 and 14 of the Convention.[17] Where a state chooses to institute a system for registration of religious organisations denial of or delay in registration can amount to interference with Article 9 in conjunction with Article 11 (the right of freedom of association) as the ECtHR explained in the leading decision of *Moscow Branch of the Salvation Army v Russia*:[18]

> »Since religious communities traditionally exist in the form of organised structures, Article 9 must be interpreted in the light of Article 11 of the Convention, which safeguards associative life against unjustified State interference. Seen in that perspective, the right of believers to freedom of religion, which includes the right to manifest one's religion in community with others, encompasses the expectation that believers will be allowed to associate freely, without arbitrary State intervention. Indeed, the autonomous existence of religious communities is indispensable for pluralism in a democratic society and is thus an issue at the very heart of the protection which Article 9 affords. The Court further reiterates that the right to form an association is an inherent part of the right set forth in Article 11. That citizens should be able to form a legal entity in order to act collectively in a field of mutual interest is one of the most important aspects of the right to freedom of association, without which that right would be deprived of any meaning. The way in which national legislation enshrines this freedom and its practical application by the authorities reveal the state of democracy in the country concerned. Certainly States have a right to satisfy themselves that an association's aim and activities are in conformity with the rules laid

14 See e.g. *Metropolitan Church of Bessarabia* v. *Moldova* (2002) 35 EHRR 1. For extended discussion of the human rights of religious organizations see Rivers, op. cit., ch. 2.

15 Churches can assert rights to property in their own name e.g. *Holy Monasteries v Greece* (1995) 20 EHRR 397.

16 It is clear that legal formalities concerning the establishment of a place of worship fall within the ambit of Article 9: *Manoussakis v. Greece* (1996) 23 EHRR 387; *ISKCON v UK*, Appl. No. 20490/92.

17 *Canea Catholic Church v.Greece* (1999) 27 EHRR 521.

18 (2007) 44 EHRR 46. A prohibition on religious manifestation if group is unregistered has been held to violate Art. 9: *Church of Bessarabia v. Moldova* (2002) 35 EHRR 1. See also *Masayev v. Moldova* [2009] Appl. No. 6303/05; *Supreme Holy Council of the Muslim Community v. Bulgaria* (2005) 41 EHRR 43; *Svyato-Mykhaylivska Parafiya v. Ukraine*, 14 May 2007; *Church of Scientology Moscow v. Russia* (2008) 46 EHRR 16. Lengthy delay in state registration may violate Art. 9: *Verein der Feunde der Christengemeinschaft and Others v. Austria* [2009] Appl. No. 76581/01 (violation of Article 14 ECHR (discrimination) taken in conjunction with Article 9 arising from 10 year waiting period for registration); *Kimlya and Others v. Russia* [2009] Appl. Nos. 76836/01 & 32782/03 (fifteen year qualifying period for registration violated Article 9): interpreted in the light of Article 11.

down in legislation, but they must do so in a manner compatible with their obligations under the Convention and subject to review by the Convention institutions«.

In this key passage the ECtHR endorses a vision of religious organisations free of state interference allowed to take their place in civil society as one of the building blocks of pluralism.

3. Clashes between autonomy and other human rights

(a) Internal Disputes

A helpful place to begin discussion of conflict between collective religious liberty and individual rights is with the position of religious organizations in disputes with their own members.

In the event of conflict between religious groups the state's role is to be a »neutral and impartial organiser of the exercise of various religions, faiths and beliefs« and its »role is conducive to public order, religious harmony and tolerance in a democratic society.«[19] So far as *intra*-religious disputes are concerned it is clear that the state must avoid taking sides since freedom of religion »excludes any discretion on the part of the State to determine whether religious beliefs or the means used to express such beliefs are legitimate.«[20] In a series of decisions from Eastern Europe the Court has found that Article 9 is violated when state authorities interfere in religious disputes and schisms over leadership. As the European Court of Human Rights put in a 2009 ruling against Bulgaria:

> »The State's duty of neutrality and impartiality, as defined in the Court's case-law, is incompatible with any power on the State's part to assess the legitimacy of religious beliefs. Furthermore, in democratic societies the State does not need to take measures to ensure that religious communities remain or are brought under a unified leadership. . …. State measures favouring a particular leader of a divided religious community or seeking to compel the community, or part of it, to place itself under a single leadership against its will would constitute an infringement of the freedom of religion«[21]

The capacity for individual congregations to use the Convention in disputes against church episcopal or denominational authorities (or for individual church

19 *Refah Partisi v. Turkey*, (2003) 37 EHRR.1, 33. For an example of liability for failure to deal with religious persecution see *Gldani Congregation of Jehovah's Witnesses v Georgia* (2008) 46 EHRR 623.

20 *Manoussakis v. Greece*, Appl. No. 18748/91, 23 EHRR 387, 400-01 (1996).

21 *Holy Synod of the Bulgarian Orthodox Church (Metropolitan Inokentiy and Ors v Bulgaria* [2009] Appl. Nos. 412/03 & 35677/04 (22 January 2009). See also *Serif v Greece* (1999) 31 EHRR 561; *Hasan and Chaush v Bulgaria* (2000) 34 EHRR 55; and *Metropolitan Church of Bessarabia v Moldova*, judgment of 13 December 2001.

members to invoke the Convention against the congregation or clergy) in doctrinal, liturgical or disciplinary disputes is virtually non-existent. This is for two connected reasons. Firstly, there are structural reasons concerning standing to bring a complaint and, correspondingly, state liability. The European Convention of Human Rights makes a clear distinction between state institutions (which can be liable for human rights violations) and non-state actors: only individuals and non-state bodies can petition the European Court of Human Rights under Article 34 of the Convention. Religious organisations can therefore petition as non-governmental organisations but cannot be respondents directly. That distinction can be seen in an admissibility decision of the European Commission in which it held to be manifestly ill-founded a complaint that a prohibition concerning the form of liturgy to be used in the Church of Sweden violated Article 9.[22]

The implication of this distinction is that an individual is only able to bring an action at the Convention level arising from alleged violation of his or her rights by a religious organisation if the question can somehow be »triangulated« so that it is argued as a failure of the respondent state to protect the petitioner's rights. The process of doing so is no means straightforward in conceptual terms, however, since it depends on the extent of a person's Convention rights in the first place. Put simply: if Article 9 does not apply to between an individual and his or her church then there is nothing for the state to be responsible *for*.

It might be thought that domestic courts are free to grant additional constitutional protection against non-governmental bodies where Strasbourg would not do so but even this raises potential difficulties. Religious organisations have Convention rights of their own and to tip the balance too far in favour of the individual at the domestic level could leave the state open to challenge by the organisation at the Strasbourg level.

The second limitation arises because the Convention organs have clearly recognised that religious group autonomy requires limits to the freedom of individuals. This point is exemplified in *X v. Denmark* in which the Commission stated:

> »A church is an organised religious community based on identical or at least substantially similar views. Through the rights granted to its members under Art. 9, the church itself is protected in its right to manifest its religion, to organise and carry out worship, teaching practice and observance, and it is free to act out and enforce uniformity in these matters. . . [The church's servants'] individual freedom of thought, conscience or religion is exercised at the moment they accept or refuse employment as clergymen, and their right to leave the church guarantees their freedom of religion in case they oppose its teachings. In other

22 *Hautaniemi* v. *Sweden* (1996) 22 EHRR CD155, arising from the prohibition on use of a form of liturgy in the Finnish Evangelical-Lutheran Church (the parish was Finnish-speaking).

words, the church is not obliged to provide religious freedom to its servants and members, as is the State as such for everyone within its jurisdiction.«[23]

The freedom that an individual has to leave a religious organization in the event of a dispute is fatal to bringing a religious liberty claim against it under the Convention. This gives practical effect to the principle of voluntariness as an important basis for religious liberty.

While this exit/ surrender principle might appear clear arguably it undervalues what may be the high costs for those involved of exercising it. For example a woman who feels increasingly called to ordained ministry within a religious denomination that does not recognise the ordination of women will be faced with the stark choice between following her vocation and continuing in the church, unless the denomination itself moves its doctrinal stance (in which case traditionalists may be put to the same choice, perhaps even more invidious in their case).

Moreover at a purely technical level the application of the principles under the Convention leaves room for debate. Does the principle apply only to claims to the exercise of Article 9 rights or may other human rights be deemed to have been surrendered in the same way? A partial answer can be given by examining how claims involving the right to a fair trial by an independent and impartial tribunal (Article 6) and the right to respect for private and family life (Article 8) have fared in cases involving religious organisations.

(b) Procedural Standards, Human Rights and Religious Adjudication

For many religious organisations self-governance is an important attribute of religious autonomy. Systems of canon law remain in many European as the formal reminder of what historically was a much broader jurisdiction, extending not only to clergy but also to the laity.[24] In the UK ecclesiastical courts are now are only concerned with internal church affairs but in some other countries vestiges of this broader jurisdiction remain. The questions raised by these internal legal regimes concern the extent to which in the name of religious autonomy they should be free to apply their own distinctive standards and procedures or whether general legal or human rights norms should apply and concerning the supervisory role of the regular legal system.Moreover with the rise in popularity of religious arbi-

23 (1976) 5 DR 157, 158.

24 For the law of the Church of England see: M. Hill, *Ecclesiastical Law* (3rd ed., Oxford, 2007); N. Doe, *The Legal Framework of the Church of England* (Oxford, 1996).

tration among Jewish and Muslim communities in Europe these questions are likely to arise in new forms and to an increasing extent in future.[25]

The main procedural requirement of the European Convention of relevance is Article 6(1):

> »In the determination of his civil rights and obligations or of any criminal charge against him, everyone is entitled to a fair and public hearing within a reasonable time by an independent and impartial tribunal established by law. Judgement shall be pronounced publicly but the press and public may be excluded from all or part of the trial in the interest of morals, public order or national security in a democratic society, where the interests of juveniles or the protection of the private life of the parties so require, or the extent strictly necessary in the opinion of the court in special circumstances where publicity would prejudice the interests of justice«

Before an applicant can succeed under this provision several hurdles have to be successfully negotiated: it must be shown that a »civil right or obligation« or a »criminal charge« is in issue, that one of the relevant procedural standards has been violated, and that the violation is by a body for which the state is responsible. The first and third of these are particularly problematic in the context of religious disputes. Even where it is found that Article 6 does apply there is scope for the European Court of Human Rights to adapt its requirements, taking account of the religious institutional setting in which dispute resolution occurs. Moreover, the question of waiver of rights or consent by a party to a procedure that might otherwise be taken to violate Article 6 is all pervasive.

The decision in *Tyler v UK*[26] in which a Church of England clergyman unsuccessfully invoked Article 6 in respect of disciplinary proceedings taken against him in church courts for an allegation of »conduct unbecoming« illustrates application of these principles. The Commission proceeded on the assumption that the decision could be taken to affect the clergyman's »civil rights«[27] but nevertheless failed to find that the composition of the courts (appointed by church authorities) breached the independence requirement under Article 6. The Commission argued that it was appropriate forwhat were essentially disciplinary matters to be dealt

25 For discussion of Shari'a law see: R. Ahdar and N. Aroney (eds.), *Shari'a in the West* (Oxford University Press 2010); J. Nielsen and L. Christoffersen, *Shari'a As Discourse*, (Ashgate, 2010). In the UK see especially: R. Williams, 'Civil and Religious Law in England: A Religious Perspective' (2008) 10(3) *Ecc LJ* 262 <http://www.archbishopofcanterbury.org/1575>; Lord Philips, 'Equality Before the Law' <http://www.matribunal.com/downloads/LCJ_speech.pdf>.; S. Bano, 'In Pursuit of Religious and Legal Diversity: A Response to the Archbishop of Canterbury and the »Sharia Debate« in Britain' (2008) 10(3) *Ecc LJ* 283; A. Tucker, 'The Archbishop's Unsatisfactory Legal Pluralism' [2008] *Public Law 463.*

26 Appl. No. 212183/83, 5 April 1994.

27 The disciplinary proceedings were, however, insufficiently penal in character to constitute a 'criminal charge'.

with by a tribunal containing representation from the body concerned and that there were other guarantees of independence that were relevant (such as security of tenure and the judicial oath).

The Strasbourg Court has also invoked the danger of interfering with religious autonomy as a reason for finding that Art. 6 (1) did not apply to proceedings in which priests of the Czechoslovak Hussite Church challenged termination by the church authorities of their clerical service.[28]

Strictly speaking there is no scope for qualifying the state's responsibilities under Article 6 as the limitations on the right are specific and do not to the »necessary in the interest of a democratic society« (proportionality) test that applies under Articles 8- 11. Nevertheless, these decisions show the Court acknowledging the religious autonomy interests inherent in religious adjudication by what can be termed definitional balancing,[29] finding that Article 6 does not apply in certain contexts.

One might have expected perhaps that the treatment by the Strasbourg court would give less latitude to adjudication by religious bodies where this affects lay members or where the ecclesiastical decision affects a person's legal rights in general and in effect substitutes for a temporal one. In these instances it can be argued that the religious autonomy interest is less pressing. In two significant decisions from Italy, the European Court of Human Rights has found that Article 6 can apply where the decision of a religious body is recognised by other state institutions as affecting the applicant's rights.

Where orders of ecclesiastical courts affect a person's rights in law within the ambit of Article 6 the state has a duty to ensure that Article 6 is observed by the church courts. In *Pellegrini v Italy*[30] the applicant successfully argued that the article had been breached by nullity proceedings taken against her by her husband. The decree of nullity had been made by a Vatican ecclesiastical court and en-

28 *Duda and Dudova v Czech Republic*, Appl. No. 40224/98, 30 January 2001, affirming the reasoning of the Czech Constitutional Court, decision of 26 March 1997.

29 The distinction between 'definitional balancing' and 'ad hoc' balancing of rights originates in discussion of US First Amendment jurisprudence. See M. B. Nimmer, 'The Right to Speak From *Times* to *Time*: First Amendment Theory Applied to Libel and Misapplied to Privacy', (1968) 56 *Cal. L. Rev,* 935, arguing in favour of definitional balancing especially on grounds of certainty. For systematic discussion of proportionality with regard to religious freedom, R Ahdar and I. Leigh, *Religious Freedom in the Liberal State* (Oxford 2004), ch. 6 and as regards clashes between religious expression and limitation of homophobic speech: I. Leigh, 'Homophobic Speech, Equality Denial and Religious Expression' in I. Hare and J.Weinstein (eds.), *Extreme Speech and Democracy*, (Oxford University Press, 2009), ch. 19.

30 Appl. No. 30882/96, ECtHR, 7.July 2001.

dorsed by the Italian civil courts. Quite apart from the ecclesiastical nature of the initial proceedings, the Vatican, of course, is not a party to the Convention. The Italian courts endorsed under the terms of the Concordat with the Holy See the decision of an ecclesiastical court in declaring the applicant's marriage a nullity.[31] The applicant had commenced judicial separation proceedings in the civil courts but was unaware of the separate nullity proceedings instituted by her husband until she responded to a summons to an order to be questioned in the ecclesiastical court. She was given no advance notice of the nature of the proceedings, had no legal representation and was not informed that a declaration of nullity would have serious consequences for the maintenance payments to which she would otherwise have been entitled. Her appeal to a higher ecclesiastical court failed as did her appeals in the civil courts.

The European Court of Human Rights found that the Italian courts had failed in their duty to adequately verify that Article 6 had been complied with before executing the nullity decree issued by the ecclesiastical courts. A review of this kind was necessary where the original decree emanated from a country which had not ratified the Convention and where a matter of importance for the parties was at stake inexecuting that decree. The proceedings had breached the equality of arms principle under Article 6(1) because the conditions under which the initial hearing had taken place put her at a substantial disadvantage since she had not been able to see and contest the evidence relied on by her husband and she had no access to a lawyer.

A variation on this approach was applied in *Lombardi Vallauri v. Italy*[32] in which the European Court of Human Rights found a violation of Articles 10 and 6 of the ECHR arising from the refusal to re-employ a lecturer in legal philosophy at a Catholic university in Milan. The applicant had worked on temporary contracts at the university from 1976 to 1998 but in 1998/99 the Faculty of Law decided not to examine his application for an advertised vacancy since he did not have the approval of the of the Congregation for Catholic Education (one of required conditions of the post). The Congregation for Catholic Education, an institution of the Holy See, had written to the President of the University stating that some of the applicant's views were »in clear opposition to Catholic doctrine« and that »in the interests of truth and of the well-being of students and the University« the applicant should no longer teach there.

31 As second cousins the couple were within the prohibited degrees of kindred and the officiating priest had failed to obtain the necessary dispensation before their canon law ceremony of marriage.

32 Appl. No. 39128/05.

Vallauri's attempts to challenge the university's decision in the Italian courts failed. The Lombardy Regional Administrative Court rejected his argument that the decision breached his constitutional rights to equality, freedom of instruction and freedom of religion. The Court foundthat adequate reasons had been given for the Faculty Board's refusal to consider the applicant's candidacy, and that the revised Concordat between the Holy See and the Italian Republic did not lay down any requirement to state the religious grounds for refusing approval. The court further held that neither the Faculty Board nor the court itself had jurisdiction to examine the legitimacy of the Holy See's decision, which had emanated from a foreign State. Moreover, teaching staff were free to choose whether or not to adhere to the principles of the Catholic faith. The applicant's appeal to the Consiglio di Stato likewise failed. The Consiglio di Stato applied existing doctrine according to which the fact that teaching appointments at the Catholic University were subject to the approval of the Holy See was compatible with the constitutional guarantees of freedom of instruction and freedom of religion.[33] The Consiglio di Stato stated that »no authority in the Republic may rule on the findings of the ecclesiastical authority«.

The European Court of Human Rights found that having regard to the habitual renewal of the applicant's temporary teaching contracts for in excess of 20 years, the refusal to consider his application on this occasion had therefore amounted to interference with his right to freedom of expression. Although the interference had been prescribed by Italian law and could be said to have had the legitimate aim of protecting the »rights of others« (namely, the University's interest in basing its teaching on Catholic doctrine), it had not been »necessary in a democratic society« and so breached Article 10.The basis for so holding was that, although it was not for the domestic authorities to examine the substance of the Congregation's doctrinal stance, the administrative courts, in the interests of »the principle of adversarial debate«, should have addressed the lack of reasons for the Faculty Board decision. For similar reasons by a majority of 6 to 1 the Court also found a breach of Article 6 because the lack of reasons impaired the applicant's effective access to a court.[34]

The Court's use of Article 10 to imply a procedural guarantee based on a supposed principle of adversarial debate is striking and curious, especially when the same conclusion could more naturally be reached under Article 6. While recognition of religious autonomy could justify the university's refusal to employ someone who in its view did not conform to its religious ethos, this could not ex-

33 Judgment of 18 June 2005.

34 The Court considered that there was no need to examine separately the applicant's complaints under Articles 9, 13 and 14.

tend to a point blank refusal to explain the basis for that conclusion. The Vallauri decision therefore is better understood as endorsing a procedural limitation or constraint on claims of religious autonomy.

As these decisions show even where the European Court of Human Rights is satisfied that it is dealing with a violation by a state body- for example because of legal status of the religious courts - this is not in itself determinative. There still remains some scope for the requirements of Article 6 to be tempered to take account of religious autonomy, especially in clergy discipline and doctrinal dispute cases. On the other hand in the examples of the effective adoption of the clerical decisions by state entities and claims brought against religious bodies that enjoy a measure of autonomy (eg religious universities) Article 6 has been applied.

In contrast to these decisions on fair procedure a quite different approach can be seen operating in recent cases concerned with conflict between Article 9 and Article 8, to which we now turn.

(c) Private Life Cases

Two recent cases from Germany involving the dismissal of employees of religious organisations for adultery raise the question of conflict between religious autonomy on the one hand and the right to private life of the employees concerned. What is striking about these judgments from the European Court of Human Rights is their use of a different approach to the conflict of rights- one of ad hoc balancing or proportionality- as the standard for reviewing the treatment of the issues at the domestic level.[35]

The *Obst* case involved the dismissal of an employee of the Mormon church for adultery.[36] He unsuccessfully challenged his dismissal before the Federal Labour Court, which found that the dismissal had been necessary in order to maintain the credibility of the church, particularly with regard to the representative capacity in which Mr Obst was employed as an international officer (he was Europe Director in its public relations department). The domestic court had taken account of the claimant's background in having grown up in the church. He was

35 An earlier decision in which the Commission declared inadmissible an Anglican clergyman's claim that the General Synod approval of the ordination of women perhaps anticipates this approach by entertaining the claim in principle but using Art. 9.2 to dismiss it (although the reasoning is far from clear): *Williamson v UK*, Appl. No. 27008/95; for criticism of the decision see Rivers, op. cit., 58.

36 *Obst v Germany*, Appl. No. 425/03 (23 September 2010).

or should have been aware of the importance to his employer of conformity to its teaching on marital fidelity particularly in the high profile role that he occupied. The ECtHR found that in considering these factors the Federal Labour Court was entitled to give priority to the church's interests after having engaged in a thorough and careful balancing of the respective rights of the parties.

By contrast in the *Schüth* case[37] (involving the dismissal for adultery of an organist employed by the Catholic Church) the ECtHR found that the assessment by the domestic courts had not satisfied the requirements of Article 8. The Federal Labour Court had failed to consider the effects on Mr Schüth's de facto family or his limited prospects for finding alternative work.[38] It had also too readily accepted the church's assertion that the organist's functions were so closely connected with the church's proclamatory message that dismissal was necessary. Moreover, in the ECtHR's view the contract of employment could not be interpreted as a clear commitment to a life of sexual abstinence in the event of divorce or marital separation.

The difference between the outcomes in these decisions is instructive and in effect gives guidance on how in the Strasbourg Court's view such cases should be approached in future: by carefully weighing the impact on both the religious organisation and the employee. This should be approached through the lens of Article 8.2 , which permits restrictions on the right to respect for private life in the interests of the rights and freedoms of others (in this instance, the right of freedom of thought, conscience and belief of the religious organisation) where it is prescribed by law and necessary in a democratic society. The Court found that the domestic court in *Obst* had properly carried out this proportionality exercise whereas in *Schüth* it had failed to do so.

In view of fact that the approach approved by the European Court of Human Rights was one that the one that the German courts had used (albeit inadequately in *Schüth*) it is easy to overlook the broader significance of these decisions. In practice *Obst* and *Schüth* are very clear examples of the horizontal application of rights against non-state employers. To German eyes, accustomed to *Drittwirkung*, this may not appear as exceptional as does from a common law perspective.

The question of whether or how Convention rights apply to private actors has been much debated in the UK especially since the introduction of the Human

37 *Schüth v Germany,* Appl. No. 1620/03 (23 September 2010).

38 He subsequently found part-time work for a Protestant parish but employment prospects for a non-protestant within Protestant churches were limited.

Rights Act 1998.[39] Indeed in the case of an employee in secular employment whose employer's demands conflicted with his religious practice, the Court of Appeal has (with some misgivings) followed the Strasbourg approach that Article 9 rights had been »surrendered« by the employee in entering the employment, with the result that that there was no need to »balance« this right against the employer's.[40]

The European Court of Human Rights itself has previously taken the view that an employee faced with a conflict between the demands of a religiously informed conscience and duties under his contact of employment cannot invoke Article 9, rather freedom of religion is guaranteed by the right to resign from the employment in question.[41] This approach has been followed both in relation to state employees[42] (where the Convention more directly binds the employer) and in relation to (failure to protect) private employees.[43] As we have seen similar principles have been applied in doctrinal disputes between individual clergy and their church employers in the few instances that these have arisen under the Convention system. This approach is quite different, of course, to the balancing of the employee's and employer's rights endorsed in *Obst* and *Schüth*.

Since in its recent decisions the Court does not explicitly address the apparent inconsistency with its earlier jurisprudence it is not clear to what extent the difference in approach is a conscious one. There are several possible explanations, however.

The least satisfactory possibilities are that Article 8 is deemed to have horizontal application whereas Article 9 is not or that religious employers are for some reason to be treated differently to other non-state employers. The former possibility would suggest an unfortunate hierarchy of rights that is inconsistent with the Convention text. Critics often suggest that since (from one viewpoint anyway) the adoption of a religion is voluntary that this justifies the restriction on the right to manifest one's religion. Leaving aside whether this is an accurate depiction of religious affiliation, if this is true of religion it is certainly true of the formation of a sexual relationship which, whether extra-marital or not, is a voluntary act also. This would give no reason then to treat Article 8 on a higher plane in cases like *Obst* and *Schüth*. Nor is there any reason to subject religious

39 I. Leigh and R. Masterman, *Making Rights Real: the Human Rights Act in its First Decade* (Oxford, 2008), ch. 9.

40 *Copsey v WWB Devon Clays Ltd* [2005] EWCA Civ 932.

41 *Stedman v United Kingdom* (1997) 23 EHHR CD168.

42 *Ahmad* v. *United Kingdom* (1981) 4 EHRR 126; *Kontinnen* v. *Finland*, Appl. No. 24949/94, 3 December 1996. See also *Kalaç* v. *Turkey* (1999) 27 EHRR 552 in the special context of voluntary military service.

43 *Stedman v United Kingdom* (1997) 23 EHHR CD168.

employers to the horizontal application of rights where other non-state employers would not be so regarded- if anything quite the reverse since this is one category of employers that clearly do have Convention rights of their own.[44]

Discounting these explanations there remains the possibility that in effect these cases signal a new approach which, if it is applied consistently, will have implications in other contexts too. There are indeed good reasons why it is preferable to treat employment disputes with a religious element as involving clashing rights that need to be appropriately balanced, rather than treating some of them as a zone in which human rights do not apply in the first place.[45] In principle this approach is more nuanced and context sensitive than the Court's earlier jurisprudence. Proportional balancing acknowledges the relevance of the various rights and even where one is displaced by another, this is because of factors that tip the scales in that direction rather than on the artificial basis that the right do outweighed was not relevant in the first place. This approach admits that changes in the context can tip the scales in the other direction, as indeed happened comparing the ECtHR's decision in *Schüth* with that in *Obst.*

In many ways these decisions can be seen as preliminary skirmishes in battles that have yet to reach the European Court of Human Rights concerning the reach of equality law to religious organizations. Where the dust will settle as regards the growing recognition of collective freedom of religion in the coming battles over discrimination on grounds of sexual orientation cannot be predicted, although same-sex relationships clearly fall within the right to respect for private life under Article 8. The Equality Framework Directive granted a narrow exception for religious bodies, hedged around with multiple qualifications[46] which has been implemented in a variety of ways by EU states that could potentially be open to challenge on Convention grounds either by religious bodies or by homosexuals or lesbians excluded from employment with them.[47] If, as is likely, this

44 Cf. *Aston Cantlow and Wilmcote with Billesley Parochial Church Council v Wallbank* [2003] UKHL 37; [2004] 1 AC 546 in which the House of Lords were influenced by the fact that a Parochial Church Council enjoyed Convention rights to find that it was not therefore a core public authority bound by Convention rights for the purpose of Human Rights Act 1998.

45 Arguably the failure of the ECtHR to develop such an approach earlier to protect manifestation of religious belief in secular employment led to a serious lacuna, filled only by the arrival of the principle of non-discrimination on grounds of religion in EU law.

46 Employment Directive 2000/78, Art. 4(2), discussed in Ahdar and Leigh, op. cit, 319 et seqq.

47 The UK Regulations dealing with employment discrimination on grounds of sexual orientation give a limited exception for 'employment for purposes of an organised religion' that allows an employer to apply a requirement related to sexual orientation to comply with the doctrines of the religion, or to avoid conflicting with the strongly held religious convictions of a significant number of the religion's followers: The Employment

issue finally reaches the European Court of Human Rights it is now clear that it should be approached through the same balancing approach applied in the recent German decisions.

4. Conclusion

After decades of relative inactivity the jurisprudence of Article 9 of the European Convention of Human Rights is now undergoing rapid development. As the European Court of Human Rights increasingly recognizes the collective dimension to religious liberty, the potential for conflict between it and individual human rights increases.

In early decisions in this field the ECtHR tended to resolve disputes between religious adherents and their churches by finding that individual religious liberty had been surrendered or amounted only to the right of »exit«. The Court's more recent rulings, however, mark an important new development in treating religious autonomy as a consideration subject to balancing against other rights. This is preferable, it is submitted, to the Court's earlier approach holding that religious autonomy crowds out the possible application of other human rights- for instance rights to fair procedure- so that they do not apply in the first place. In principle proportionality is more nuanced and context sensitive approach than the definitional balancing approach that characterized the court's earlier jurisprudence.

Resolving these conflicts is a delicate but important task. The contribution that religious bodies make to the continued diversity and vitality of civil society is at stake in these clashing rights cases. If religious organizations are to continue to flourish in Europe it is crucial that the process of balancing pays careful attention to their character, history and doctrine while also protecting individual human rights.

Equality (Sexual Orientation) Regulations 2003, 2003 SI/1661, Reg. 7(3). The High Court rejected a challenge to this provision in *R (on the application of Amicus et al) v. Secretary of State for Trade and Industry* [2004] EWHC 860 (Admin). Richards J. stated (at para. 186) that the provision appropriately balanced the rights of homosexuals against those of followers of organized religions.

SCOPE AND LIMITATIONS OF FREEDOM OF RELIGIOUS ASSOCIATIONS UNDER THE EUROPEAN CONVENTION ON HUMAN RIGHTS – Katharina Pabel

1. Introduction

This article is supposed to give an overview and an analysis of the case-law of the European Court of Human Rights (ECtHR) concerning the protection of religious communities and churches by fundamental rights enshrined in the European Convention of Human Rights (ECHR). For this purpose two preliminary remarks should be made:

First, the ECHR does not contain any provision regulating the relationship between the State and religious communities or churches as such. Statements concerning the relationship between States and religious communities from the perspective of the ECHR can only be derived from the fundamental rights it enshrines – especially the freedom of religion under Article 9 ECHR. Therefore, only individual (but important and crucial) aspects of the relationship between the State and religious communities are determined by the ECHR.

Second, the ECtHR rules on individual cases. It is only able to decide on those legal questions which are brought to it by way of individual applications. The sum of the specific decisions and judgments is the basis from which more general statements on legal issues can be derived.

Considering both remarks, the requirements for the regulation of the relationship between the State and religious communities by the European Convention on Human Rights develop little by little, partly they unfold accidentally, and they are fragmentary.

2. Religious Communities and Religious Freedom

In the Member States to the ECHR, religious communities in general and – more specifically – churches enjoy quite different legal statuses. Legal orders in the Member States typically provide for religious communities to enjoy legal personality and all connected benefits. Furthermore, religious communities are sometimes allowed to organise as associations of private law. Beyond that, religious communities may under particular conditions obtain specific legal status as religious associations. This status, which often requires an act of recognition by the authorities, is typically connected to a range of additional rights or privileges.

The fundamental rights guaranteed by the ECHR are firstly designed to protect individuals against State actions. Moreover, legal persons can rely on the fundamental rights. This is shown by Article 34 ECHR, according to which not only individuals but also non-governmental organisations are enabled to submit applications to the Court. Consequently, the ECtHR has approved that religious communities or churches as legal persons can rely on the fundamental rights, especially on the freedom of religion.[1]

According to German constitutional law, religious communities can be granted legal personality under public law if they fulfil certain conditions.[2] This specific status might lead to the discussion of whether a legal person under public law in general and, more specifically, churches enjoy fundamental rights (or whether they are bound by them). From the perspective of the ECtHR, the assignment of a legal person to private or to public law is not decisive for the reference to fundamental rights. What is relevant is that the concerning entity does not exercise authority but is an association separate from the State. Accordingly, the ECtHR recently confirmed that the Catholic Church despite of its status as a legal person under public law in Germany does not exercise authority and, therefore, it can rely on human rights.[3]

3. The Freedom of Religious Associations

By now, it can be regarded as established case-law of the ECtHR that religious freedom is not only a matter of individual conscience, but also implies collective aspects. The Court implies the collective perspective of religious freedom in the individual right of religious freedom. It refers to the wording of Article 9 ECHR, according to which the guarantee implies, inter alia, the freedom to manifest one religion »alone and in private or in community with others …«.[4] Another argument for the integration of collective aspects in the scope of Article 9 ECHR is the reference to religious communities traditionally existing in the form of organ-

1 ECtHR, *Canea Catholic Church v. Greece*, judgment of 16 December 1997, no. 25528/94, § 31; ECtHR, *Cha'are Shalom Ve Tsedek v. France*, judgment of 27 June 2000, no. 27417/95, § 72. See *Walter*, Religions- und Gewissensfreiheit, in: Grote/Marauhn (ed.), Konkordanzkommentar. EMRK/GG, 2006, chapter 17 para. 90 et seq.

2 See, basically, Bundesverfassungsgericht, decisions of the Bundesverfassungsgericht, vol. 102, p. 370; for an overview see *v. Campenhausen/de Wall*, Staatskirchenrecht, 4th ed. 2006, § 17.

3 ECtHR, *Schüth v. Germany*, judgment of 23 September 2010, no. 1620/03, § 54 with reference to former decisions.

4 From the rich case law see, e.g., ECtHR, *Church of Scientology Moscow v. Russia*, judgment of 5 April 2007, no. 18174/02, § 72; ECtHR, *Svyato-Mykhaylivska Parafiya v. Ukraine*, judgment of 14 June 2007, no. 77703/01, § 112.

ised structures.[5] Therefore, the Court held that Article 9 ECHR must be interpreted in the light of Article 11 ECHR, which safeguards associative life against unjustified State interference. These guarantees of the Convention establish the right to obtain legal recognition as a religious community and effective enjoyment of the right to freedom of religion and association in any organisational form.[6]

The case-law of the European Court of Human Rights has not yet clarified the relationship between Article 9 and Article 11 of the Convention regarding the collective dimension of the freedom of religion.[7] Sometimes the Court does not decide in the individual case whether it examines a violation of the freedom of religion pursuant to Article 9 ECHR or a violation of the freedom of association pursuant to Article 11 ECHR. Moreover, the ECHR seems to rely on Article 11 of the Convention if the individual application concerns matters of registration or recognition of religious communities.[8] At first sight, the differentiation between the two fundamental rights is not very important because the justification for interferences with either guarantee is quite similar.[9] Regarding Article 11 ECHR, the Court has held that States have a right to satisfy themselves that an association's aim and activities are in conformity with the rules laid down in legislation.[10] For the future it will be crucial whether and in what manner the ECtHR will consider the specific features of religious communities when dealing with Article 11 ECHR. In the light of Article 9 ECHR, it might be unacceptable to provide for democratic structures of an association when determining the legal conditions for the recognition or the registration of religious communities.[11]

5 Cf. ECtHR, *Jehova's Witnesses of Moscow v. Russia*, judgment of 10 June 2010, no. 302/02, § 99; ECtHR, *Kimlya and Others v. Russia*, judgment of 1 October 2009, no. 76836/01, § 81.

6 ECtHR, *Kimlya and Others v. Russia*, judgment of 1 October 2009, no. 76836/01, § 88; ECtHR, *Jehova's Witnesses of Moscow v. Russia*, judgment of 10 June 2010, no. 302/02, §§ 101 et seq.

7 See, e.g., ECtHR, *Svyato-Mykhaylivska Parafiya v. Ukraine*, judgment of 14 June 2007, no. 77703/01, §§ 121, 123 (»an interference with the applicant association's right to freedom of religion under Article 9 of the Convention, taken alone or read in the light of Article 11«). See *Stelzer*, Korporative Aspekte der Religionsfreiheit in der Rechtsprechung des EGMR, in: Kohlhofer (ed.), Religionsgemeinschaftenrecht und EMRK, 2009, p. 18.

8 See, e.g., ECtHR, *Kimlya and Others v. Russia*, judgment of 1 October 2009, no. 76836/01, § 81.

9 Exception: the specific possibilities to restrict the freedom of association for members of the armed forces, of the police or of the administration of the State according to Article 11 para. 2 in fine, and the possible restrictions according to Article 16 ECHR.

10 ECtHR, *Sidiropoulos and others v. Greece*, judgment of 10 July 1998, no. 57/1997/841/1047, § 40.

11 See *Stelzer* (ref. 7), p. 18.

Based on the established case-law, two elements of the religious freedom in a collective dimension can be identified: First, the freedom of religious association, and second, the autonomy of religious communities. The specific contents of the freedom of religion seen together with the freedom of association can be identified as the *freedom of religious communities*. In the following, the two aspects will be analysed in the light of the case-law of the ECtHR.

(a) The Freedom of Religious Association

The Court stressed in a couple of cases that the right of believers to freedom of religion encompasses the expectation that believers will be allowed to associate freely, without arbitrary State intervention.[12] In this context, the State's duty of neutrality and impartiality is seen to be incompatible with any power on the State's part to assess the legitimacy of religious beliefs.[13]

Consequently, the refusal by the domestic authorities to grant the status of legal entity to an association of believers amounts to an interference with the right to freedom of religion under Article 9 ECHR[14] and to freedom of association under Article 11 ECHR.[15] What is decisive for the assumption of an interference is that, by reason of the refusal, the religious group concerned is restricted in its ability to exercise the full range of religious activities and activities normally exercised by registered non-governmental legal entities.[16] Therefore, there also is an interference with the right to freedom of religion if a religious group obtains a specific status without being legally recognised. The Court considers the right to own or to rent property, to maintain bank accounts, to hire employees, and to ensure judicial protection of the community, its members and its assets to be essen-

12 ECtHR, *Metropolitan Church of Bessarabia v. Moldova*, judgment of 13 December 2001, no. 45701/99, §§ 118, 123; ECtHR, *Hasan and Chaush v. Bulgaria*, judgment of 26 October 2000 (GC), no. 30985/96, § 62; ECtHR, *Svyato-Mykhaylivska Parafiya v. Ukraine*, judgment of 14 June 2007, no. 77703/01, § 113.

13 ECtHR, *Metropolitan Church of Bessarabia v. Moldova*, judgment of 13 December 2001, no. 45701/99, §§ 118, 123; ECtHR, *Hasan and Chaush v. Bulgaria*, judgment of 26 October 2000 (GC), no. 30985/96, § 62; ECtHR, *Svyato-Mykhaylivska Parafiya v. Ukraine*, judgment of 14 June 2007, no. 77703/01, § 113.

14 ECtHR, *Metropolitan Church of Bessarabia v. Moldova*, judgment of 13 December 2001, no. 45701/99, § 105; ECtHR, *Kimlya and Others v. Russia*, judgment of 1 October 2009, no. 76836/01, § 84; *Jehova's Witnesses of Moscow v. Russia*, judgment of 10 June 2010, no. 302/02, § 101.

15 ECtHR, *Sidiropoulos and others v. Greece*, judgment of 10 July 1998, no. 57/1997/841/1047, §§ 31 et seq.; ECtHR, *Gorzelik and others v. Poland*, judgment of 17 February 2004 (GC), no. 44158/98, §§ 52 et seq.

16 ECtHR, *Svyato-Mykhaylivska Parafiya v. Ukraine*, judgment of 14 June 2007, no. 77703/01, § 123.

tial for exercising the right to manifest one's religion in community.[17] If, according to national law, a religious group without legal personality is not able to exercise those rights or some of those rights, the refusal to recognise a religious community or to register it amounts to an interference with Article 9 ECHR. The authorities' refusal to recognise or to register a group directly affects both, the group itself as well as its presidents, founders or individual members.[18]

For example, the Court observed an interference with the right to freedom of religion under Article 9 of the Convention interpreted in the light of Article 11 if the religious community was granted the status as a legal person but not the status as a registered religious organisation; the latter status was a precondition to exercise the right to establish places of worship, the right to hold religious services in places accessible to public, the right to produce, obtain and distribute religious literature, the right to create educational institutions, and the right to maintain contacts for international exchanges and conferences which were recognised as fundamental aspects of religious practice by the Court.[19]

In the case of *Zeugen Jehovas vs. Austria*, the ECtHR considered that under Austrian law religious societies enjoy privileged treatment in many areas. In consideration of the number and the quality of these privileges the Court assessed the advantage obtained by religious societies as being substantial. In respect to Article 9 ECHR, the Court found that the special treatment undoubtedly facilitates a religious society's pursuance of its religious aims.[20]

Under these conditions the States' obligation to remain neutral in exercising its power relating to the recognition of religious communities means that the State has to set up a legal framework for conferring legal personality on religious groups to which a specific status is linked. Furthermore, all religious groups wishing to obtain this status must have a fair opportunity to apply for the status.

17 ECtHR, *Religionsgemeinschaft der Zeugen Jehovas and Others v. Austria*, judgment of 31 July 2008, no. 40825/98, § 66; ECtHR, *Metropolitan Church of Bessarabia v. Moldova*, judgment of 13 December 2001, no. 45701/99, § 118; ECtHR, *The Canea Catholic Church v. Greece*, judgment of 16 December 1997, no. 143/1996/762/963, §§ 30, 40 et seq.; ECtHR, *Kimlya and Others v. Russia*, judgment of 1 October 2009, no. 76836/01, § 85; ECtHR, *Jehova's Witnesses of Moscow v. Russia*, judgment of 10 June 2010, no. 302/02, § 102.

18 ECtHR, *Religionsgemeinschaft der Zeugen Jehovas and Others v. Austria*, judgment of 31 July 2008, no. 40825/98, §§ 79 et seq.; ECtHR, *Kimlya and Others v. Russia*, judgment of 1 October 2009, no. 76836/01, § 84; ECtHR, *Metropolitan Church of Bessarabia v. Moldova*, judgment of 13 December 2001, no. 45701/99, § 105.

19 ECtHR, *Jehova's Witnesses of Moscow v. Russia*, judgment of 10 June 2010, no. 302/02, § 102.

20 ECtHR, *Religionsgemeinschaft der Zeugen Jehovas and Others v. Austria*, judgment of 31 July 2008, no. 40825/98, § 92.

And, finally, the criteria established by the legal framework must be applied in a non-discriminatory manner.[21]

The Court considered that, given the importance of the right to freedom of religion, there was an obligation on State authorities to keep the time during which an applicant waited for conferment of legal personality reasonably short. The imposition of a waiting period before a religious community that has already been granted legal personality can obtain a more privileged status as a public-law body can be justified under specific conditions. According to the Court, such a waiting period could be necessary in the case of newly established and unknown groups.[22] On the other hand, in cases of religious groups with a long-standing existence – as the Jehovah's Witnesses in the present case – the authorities should be able to verify whether a group fulfils the criteria of the relevant legislation within a short period.[23]

The refusal to recognise a religious community or to grant it a specific status must be proportional in the sense of Article 9 para. 2 and Article 11 para.2 ECHR. If the refusal leads to a refusal of central and important aspects of the freedom of religion and, therefore, amounts to a serious interference with fundamental rights, the ECtHR examines the proportionality of the measure in a very detailed manner. It requires that the national authorities not only allege that the religious group represents a danger to the rights of others or to public interests, but also that it supplies evidence for the allegations.[24]

(b) The Autonomy of Religious Communities

The ECtHR perceives the autonomous existence of religious communities as indispensable for pluralism in a democratic society. It locates that issue at the very heart of the protection which Article 9 ECHR affords.[25] According to that case-law, the right to freedom of religion encompasses the expectation that a commu-

21 ECtHR, *Religionsgemeinschaft der Zeugen Jehovas and Others v. Austria*, judgment of 31 July 2008, no. 40825/98, § 92.

22 ECtHR, *Religionsgemeinschaft der Zeugen Jehovas and Others v. Austria*, judgment of 31 July 2008, no. 40825/98, § 98.

23 ECtHR, *Religionsgemeinschaft der Zeugen Jehovas and Others v. Austria*, judgment of 31 July 2008, no. 40825/98, § 98.

24 ECtHR, *Jehova's Witnesses of Moscow v. Russia*, judgment of 10 June 2010, no. 302/02, §§ 109 et seq.

25 ECtHR, *Metropolitan Church of Bessarabia v. Moldova*, judgment of 13 December 2001, no. 45701/99, §§ 118, 123; ECtHR, *Hasan and Chaush v. Bulgaria*, judgment of 26 October 2000 (GC), no. 30985/96, § 62; ECtHR, *Jehovahs's Witnesses of Moscow v. Russia*, judgement of 10 June 2010, no. 302/02, § 99.

nity will be allowed to function free from arbitrary State intervention in its organisation.[26]

Whereas in the legal order of some Member States to the Convention there are long traditions in interpreting what »church autonomy« encompasses,[27] there is no such tradition in the case-law of the European Court in Strasbourg. Moreover, only some aspects of the content of the guarantee of the »autonomous existence of religious communities« can be extracted from the judgments.

One first aspect concerns the determination of membership of the religious communities. Religious associations are free to determine at their own discretion the manner in which new members are admitted and existing members are excluded.[28] Consequently, the principle of autonomy bans the State from obliging religious communities to accept new members or to exclude others.[29]

Another aspect of the autonomous existence is related to the internal structure of a religious community. In this context autonomous existence of religious communities means self-organisation. The Court considered that the internal structure of a religious organisation must be seen as a means by which such organisations are able to express their beliefs and maintain their religious traditions. Also in this respect (as in respect of the membership), the Court points out that the right to freedom of religion excludes any discretion on the part of the State to determine whether the means used to express religious beliefs are legitimate.[30]

Some cases ruled on by the ECtHR pertain to State measures deciding on the internal leadership of a religious community. The Court does not consider that, in democratic societies, the State needs to take measures to ensure that religious communities remain or are brought under unified leadership.[31] Because the personality of the religious leader is of importance to the members of the commu-

26 ECtHR, *Holy Synod of the Bulgarian Orthodox Church (Metropolitan Inokentiy) and Others v. Bulgaria*, judgment of 22 January 2009, no. 412/03 and 35677/04, § 103.

27 See for Germany, e.g.,*v. Campenhausen/de Wall* (as above 2), § 14; *Korioth*, Art. 137 WRV, in: Maunz/Dürig et al. (ed.), Grundgesetz Kommentar, para. 17 et seq. (»Selbstbestimmungsrecht«).

28 ECtHR, *Svyato-Mykhaylivska Parafiya v. Ukraine*, judgment of 14 June 2007, no. 77703/01, § 150.

29 ECtHR, *Miroļubovs and Others v. Latvia*, judgment of 15 September 2009, no. 798/95, § 80.

30 ECtHR, *Svyato-Mykhaylivska Parafiya v. Ukraine*, judgment of 14 June 2007, no. 77703/01, § 150; ECtHR, *Hasan and Chaush v. Bulgaria*, judgment of 26 October 2000 (GC), no. 30985/96, § 78; ECtHR, *Mannoussakis v. Greece*, judgment of 26 September 1996, no. 18748/91, § 47.

31 ECtHR, *Agga v. Greece*, judgment of 17 October 2002, no. 50776/99 and 52912/99, § 59.

nity, it forms a part of the organisational life of the community that should not be affected by the State.[32] Therefore, it amounts to an interference with the freedom of religion if a State takes action which has the effect of terminating the autonomous existence of one of two opposing groups in a religious community by resolving a leadership dispute in a divided religious community by assisting one of the opposing groups to gain full control, to the exclusion of the rival group.[33] If tension is created in situations where a religious community becomes divided, the Court considers that this is one of the inevitable consequences of pluralism. The role of the authorities in this case is not to remove the cause of tension by eliminating pluralism but to ensure that the competing groups tolerate each other.[34]

It has to be taken into account that many of the cases concerning State intervention concerning the person of a religious leader come from only a few member states to the Convention. In the case of Bulgaria, the ECtHR has shown impressively that State intervention on the internal organisation of the Orthodox Church had a long tradition. Therefore, statements by the Court on church autonomy have always to be seen in the light of the State concerned. Any generalisation has to be done quite carefully.

Also in this context, the Court referred to the State's duty under Article 9 ECHR to remain neutral and impartial. Neither is it the Court's task, nor the task of any authority outside the religious community and its institutions, to assess the validity under canon law of the opposing claims to legitimacy made by rival leaderships.[35] The need to restore legality and to secure public order could only justify neutral measures ensuring legal certainty and foreseeable procedures for the settling of disputes in the community.[36]

32 ECtHR, *Holy Synod of the Bulgarian Orthodox Church (Metropolitan Inokentiy) and Others v. Bulgaria*, judgment of 22 January 2009, no. 412/03 and 35677/04, § 103.

33 ECtHR, *Holy Synod of the Bulgarian Orthodox Church (Metropolitan Inokentiy) and Others v. Bulgaria*, judgment of 22 January 2009, no. 412/03 and 35677/04, § 103, §§ 112, 120.

34 ECtHR, *Agga v. Greece*, judgment of 17 October 2002, no. 50776/99 and 52912/99, § 60, referring to ECHtR, *Plattform Ärzte für das Leben v. Austria*, judgment of 21 June 1988, Series A no. 139, § 32.

35 ECtHR, *Holy Synod of the Bulgarian Orthodox Church (Metropolitan Inokentiy) and Others v. Bulgaria*, judgment of 22 January 2009, no. 412/03 and 35677/04, § 137.

36 ECtHR, *Holy Synod of the Bulgarian Orthodox Church (Metropolitan Inokentiy) and Others v. Bulgaria*, judgment of 22 January 2009, no. 412/03 and 35677/04, § 139 mit deutlichem Bezug zu dem konkreten Fall.

However, Article 9 ECHR does not require the States to give legal effect to religious weddings and religious courts' decisions.[37] If weddings celebrated by ministers of a religion are assimilated to civil ones and the ministers have competence to adjudicate on certain family and inheritance disputes between the adherents to that religion the State may take special measures to protect from deceit those whose legal relationships can be affected by the acts of religious ministers.[38] The guarantee of the autonomous existence of religious communities does not include recognition of internal decisions by the national authorities. If, according to the legal order of a Member State to the Convention, actions of a religious leader are recognised in the legal order of that State, it seems to be legitimate that the State imposes specific requirements on the internal structure of the religious community, especially the clear identifiability of the religious leader. Such requirements add to legal certainty.

4. The Limitation of the Freedom of Religious Associations

In a review of the judgment that the ECtHR held on the different aspects of the freedom of religious association, one has to note that the limitations of this guarantee given by Article 9 para. 2 and Article 11 para. 2 ECHR had not yet been specified.[39] The Court circumscribes in a very general way that States may take measures to ensure the peaceful coexistence of different religions in a democratic society. Moreover, the ECtHR often quotes the principle of neutrality and impartiality in religious affairs.[40] This principle does not seem to be a separate content of the guarantee of »autonomous existence of religious communities«, but merely a formula to limit the influence of the authorities in the area of religion. Therefore, the reference to that formula can be seen as a specific limitation to interferences with the right to freedom of religious associations.

37 ECtHR, *Agga v. Greece*, judgment of 17 October 2002, no. 50776/99 and 52912/99, § 57; ECtHR, *Savez Crkava »Riječ Života« and Others v. Croatia*, judgment of 9 December 2010, no. 7798/08, § 56.

38 ECtHR, *Agga v. Greece*, judgment of 17 October 2002, no. 50776/99 and 52912/99, § 57.

39 See *Walter* (ref. 1), para. 132.

40 *Walter* (ref. 1), para. 132.

5. Particular Cases

(a) The Regulation of employment in Churches

Recently, the Court had to decide a number of cases against Germany concerning different aspects of employments in churches. In Germany, the Protestant and the Catholic Church as well as other religious communities, for example the Salvation Army, employ a great number of persons who work in institutions run by the churches. These employments underlie specific regulations set up by the religious communities concerning the comportment of the employees during the working time but also in their daily life. The churches impose specific contractual obligations on persons working for them which include duties of loyalty requiring him (or her) to lead his (or her) life in conformity with the doctrine of the church. In the case of a breach of those rules the churches as employers can take a range of measures, including, in the case of a severe and continuing violation, the dismissal of the employee.

Domestic courts, that is to say the labour courts in up to three instances, examine the lawfulness of a dismissal based on the internal rules of the churches and the specific obligations in the labour contracts. The procedures before the labour courts in those cases comply with the requirements of Article 6 ECHR. In particular, they are decided by a tribunal in conformity with Article 6 ECHR in a fair proceeding. In the examination of the lawfulness of a dismissal, the courts consider the decision of the German Constitutional Court of 1985 which forms a guideline for the labour courts dealing with dismissals of church employees. In that decision, the Constitutional Court recognised the right to self-determination of the churches in respect to the possibility of imposing specific duties of loyalty on a person working for the church.[41] At the same time, it pointed out the particular importance of the employees' protection against unfair dismissal by the law and carefully struck a balance between the two rights concerned. This landmark decision of the Constitutional Court is not only the basis for the jurisdiction of the labour courts in Germany concerning labour contracts with churches but also had an important influence on labour law itself and the drafting of labour contracts.

By now, this well-established system has been examined by the Strasbourg Court. In three cases employees who were dismissed because of having violated duties of loyalty deriving from their working contracts applied at the ECtHR.

41 Bundesverfassungsgericht, decision of 4 June 1985, decisions of the Constitutional Court, vol. 70, p. 138 (p. 168 et seq.).

In the first case of *Obst*,[42] the applicant belonged to the religious community of the Mormons and got married according to his conviction in 1980. Until 1993 he worked as a regional director for public relations of the Mormon Church when he confided to a pastor that he had a relationship to a woman out of wedlock. On strong advice of the pastor he informed his superior about the relationship. A few days later he has been dismissed and, later on, he was excluded from church.

The applicant in the second case, *Mr Schüth*,[43] was employed as a church musician at a Catholic parish since the middle of the 1980s. In 1994 he separated from his wife and lived together with another woman without being formally divorced. When it became public that the new woman was expecting a child, the applicant was dismissed. The dismissal dated from July 1997 and entered into force in April 1998. It was based on a breach of the »Basic Order for Service concerning Church Employments« where the Catholic Church defined basic principles for the engagement, the content and the termination of employment contracts for persons working for the church.[44]

In the third case the applicant, *Mrs Siebenhaar*,[45] worked in a playschool run by the Protestant Church. In 1998 the Protestant Church was informed that the applicant was member of a religious community called »Universal Church« and that she held initiation courses for this community. Therefore, she was dismissed with immediate effect.

The three employees first applied to the German labour courts,[46] and subsequently appealed to the Federal Constitutional Court. By reference to its established case law, the Constitutional Court rejected the applications. The ECtHR found an interference with the right to respect for private and family life according to Article 8 of the Convention in the cases of *Obst* and *Schüth* because of the dismissals' being connected with the way the applicants lived their private and sexual life. In the case of *Siebenhaar* there had been an interference with the right to freedom of religion. Finally, it found a violation in the case of *Schüth*, but not in the cases of *Obst* and *Siebenhaar*. The ECtHR examined whether the German Labour Courts found a fair balance between the applicant's right to re-

42 ECtHR, *Obst v. Germany*, judgment of 23 September 2010, no. 425/03.

43 ECtHR, *Schüth v. Germany*, judgment of 23 September 2010, no. 1620/03.

44 Grundordnung des kirchlichen Dienstes im Rahmen kirchlicher Arbeitsverhältnisse, <http://www.dbk.de/fileadmin/redaktion/diverse_downloads/VDD/db051_11_auflage.pdf > (proved: 2 may 2011). In this Basic Order a graded system of specific duties of loyalty and possible reactions to a violation of such duties is provided.

45 ECtHR, *Siebenhaar v. Germany*, judgment of 3 February 2011, no. 18136/02.

46 First instance: Labour Court, second instance: Regional Labour Court; third instance: Federal Labour Court.

spect for private life and to religious freedom on the one side, respectively, and the rights of the church in question (in its function as an employer) on the other side and whether the courts provided for an adequate protection against dismissal. The Court emphasized that the autonomy of the churches is an integral part of the religious freedom guaranteed by Article 9 read together with Article 11 ECHR. It found that in general, Germany has fulfilled its positive obligations vis-à-vis applicants in labour law cases by way of establishing labour courts and a supervisory control by the Federal Constitutional Court. But the Court reviewed the balancing of the rights concerned taken by the labour courts in detail. It weighted the different aspects of the three cases and, by this, it decided itself whether the dismissal led to an inadequate inference with the applicants' rights.

All three cases mentioned resulted from judicial proceedings concerning civil rights which had been decided by national courts in favour of one litigant, here in favour of the churches as employers. In the applications brought to the ECtHR, both of the litigants, the employee as well as the employers, rely on human rights and freedoms. The Court has to strike a fair balance between the rights concerned. In these settings, where the case brought to the Strasbourg Court is based on a judicial proceeding concerning civil rights, it should be borne in mind that in the case of a decision by the national court in favour of the applicant, the other litigant had the opportunity to bring an action before the Court. If the German labour courts decided in favour of the employee, the churches could lodge an application relying on Article 9 ECHR. The ECtHR should avoid acting as another labour court instance. In order to do so, it would have to leave a wider margin of appreciation to the authorities of the Member States.[47] This is not at all the case in the recent judgments.

In abstracto, the ECtHR, referring not only but also to Article 9 and Article 11 ECHR, describes the scrutiny in examining possible violations as follows: It is not for the Court to decide instead of the national authorities and to substitute its own view for that of the relevant national authorities. Rather, it has to review the decisions they made exercising its discretion. The ECtHR has to satisfy itself whether the national authorities exercised their discretion reasonably, carefully and in good faith. Furthermore, it must look at the interference complained of in the light of the case as a whole and determine whether the reasons adduced by

47 The German Constitutional Court (Bundesverfassungsgericht) is in the same situation if it has to decide on an individual application against a court decision (Urteilsverfassungsbeschwerde). It limits its scrutiny to the examination of a possible violation of constitutional law (»spezifisches Verfassungsrecht«) by stressing that it would not act as another instance (»Superrevisionsinstanz«), see, with reference to the case-law, *Hillgruber/Goos*, Verfassungsprozessrecht, 3rd ed. 2011, para. 181.

the national authorities are relevant and sufficient.[48] This is how the Court characterised the very high level of scrutiny as it has been shown in the judgments concerning church employment, as mentioned above. Whether the requirement not to replace the national authorities has been respected is open to question. In sum, in these cases the ECHR acts in the same manner as a national labour court. It must be questioned whether it is the function of an international court to decide in this detailed manner a case which four national courts, including the constitutional court, had decided with due reasoning.

In respect of the fundamental rights of the churches, one has to note that in the labour law cases the Court took into account the »autonomy of the churches«. In consideration of its previous case law, the ECtHR underlines the importance of the protection not only of the individual right to freedom of religion but also of religious communities as a specific kind of association. Furthermore, it stressed the autonomy of religious communities in organised structures.[49] What is missing is a deeper analysis concerning what encompasses »autonomy«. The case-law of the ECtHR develops some aspects of »autonomy« in specific cases, but does not develop a concept of »autonomy«.[50] In the context of the labour law cases it would have been necessary to decide whether and to what extent church autonomy means that churches may impose special duties of loyalty on their employees and whether they may sanction a violation of such duties by dismissal.

(b) »Procedural Standards, Human Rights and Religious Adjudication«

Under the abovementioned heading, *Ian Leigh* discussed a number of cases decided by the European Court of Human Rights (and the former European Commission of Human Rights).[51] He raised the question of whether and to what extent internal legal regimes of churches (or other religious communities) should be free – in the name of religious autonomy – to apply their own standards and procedures or whether general legal or human rights norms should apply. In terms of the ECHR, this question mainly touches the applicability and the scope of the right of access to court and the procedural guarantees enshrined in Article 6 ECHR.

In the following some remarks on this question should be given:

48 See, e.g., ECtHR, *Church of Scientology Moscow v. Russia*, judgment of 5 April 2007, no. 18147/02, § 87.
49 ECtHR, *Obst v. Germany*, judgment of 23 September 2010, no. 425/03, § 44.
50 See *Stelzer* (ref. 7), p. 24 et seq.
51 See above, p. 125 et seqq.

The structure of Article 6 ECHR requires a two-step examination. First, it has to be established whether Article 6 ECHR is applicable in a specific case. Second, it has to be examined whether the right of access to court or one of the procedural guarantees has been violated. In most of the interesting cases, it is the right of access to court that is in question. In so far it must be kept in mind that this guarantee not only requires the mere »access« to court but also asks for the competent court to be able to decide on all legal topics which arise in a case.[52] Taking a look at the relevant judgments of the Court it can be noticed that the Court acknowledges church autonomy and restricts the right of access to court in favour of the applicant. But it seems to be unclear on which stage of the examination the restriction is located: it may be a question of applicability of Article 6 ECHR, or it may be a question of the scope of Article 6.

Despite of the fact that interferences with Article 6 ECHR are not subject to a proportionality test as it is provided in Articles 8 to 11, the Court accepts that there are immanent limitations of the right of access to court. Church autonomy as guaranteed by Article 9 ECHR could be seen as such a limitation to procedural rights under specific conditions. But again – similar to the cases concerning the dismissals of church employees – one has to ask for a more detailed analysis of the scope of church autonomy in the light of Article 9 of the Convention. So far, the Court seems to weigh just one part of the two-part relationship, that is to say the applicant.

52 *Grabenwarter*, Europäische Menschenrechtskonvention, 4. ed. 2009, chapter 24 para. 28 et seq.

VI. AUTONOMY AND ESTABLISHED CHURCHES: THOUGHTS ON ENGLISH ESTABLISHMENT(S) IN THE TWENTY-FIRST CENTURY – Peter W. Edge

1. Introduction

The establishment of the Church of England has had a significant impact on the global structuring of church/state relations, most notably through the legacy of British colonialism.In North America, the British colonies were influenced by the experience of establishment in England in seeking their own, diverse, forms of the relationship.[1] Early efforts towards political union needed to balance politic unity with religious diversity, including Puritan, Calvinist, Catholic and Quaker colonies.[2] The second Constitutional Congress (1775-1789) acted in a way consonant with a relationship between religion and state much closer than strict separation. It created chaplains for the army and the legislature; accommodated the needs of religious pacifists; issued a series of proclamations calling for public humiliation, fasting and prayer for the care of a kind Providence, and an overtly Trinitarian Thanksgiving Day proclamation; sought to suborn British allies and soldiers by offering them freedom of religion; included religious liberty clauses in treaties with the Netherlands, Sweden and Prussia, and endorsed a privately funded translation of the Bible, as well as encouraging the States to take steps to procure Bibles, and even voted to import 20,000 bibles for distribution in the states, although this never took place.[3]

The Confederation was a flawed relationship, and in 1787 a Constitutional Convention was convened in order to prepare the United States Constitution, which came into effect in 1789. Witte identifies four »heuristic models – typical clusters of argument and adherence, distinct and distinguishable contributions to eighteenth century American debates about religious rights and liberties« in the work of the Founders.[4] It is important to understand the constitutional text against this rich background – silence in the original Constitution, and brevity in the Bill of Rights which quickly followed, did not reflect an indifference to religious issues, but rather a shared understanding that religious issues were to be

1 Contrast Fundamentals of West Jersey (West Jersey), 1681, art.X, with Connecticut Code of Laws, 1650 (Connecticut), both in D.S. Lutz (ed.), *Colonial origins of the American Constitution: A documentary history*, Liberty Fund: Indianapolis, 1998.

2 New England Confederation, 1643 in D.S. Lutz (ed.), *Colonial origins of the American Constitution: A documentary history*, Liberty Fund: Indianapolis, 1998.

3 J. Witte, *Religion and the American Constitutional Experiment*, Boulder: Westview Press, 2005 at 25.

4 Witte, *ACE*, 23.

resolved by the states and the people, not the federal government.[5] The most significant clause of the original constitution in relation to religion prohibits religious tests in regard to any federal office.[6] As Madison argued, »A religious sect may degenerate into a political faction in a part of the Confederacy; but the variety of sects dispersed over the entire face of it must secure the national councils against any danger from that source«.[7] A particularly influential strand in the adoption of this clause was that of equality between these diverse religions – the prohibition on religious tests put all on a level with regard to the federal government, and allowed all citizens to be eligible for federal office.[8] Additionally, the prohibition on a federal religious test was a significant support for the authority of the states over religious matters.[9]

The Bill of Rights similarly, on its face, included a restriction on the power of federal government. The First Amendment provides:

> »Congress shall make no law respecting an establishment of religion, or prohibiting the free exercise thereof; or abridging the freedom of speech, or of the press; or the right of the people peaceably to assemble, and to petition the government for a redress of grievances«[10]

The First Amendment was, for a considerable period, read as relevant to the federal authorities only.[11] During this period, the principal responsibility for regulating the relationship between law and religion lay with the States. By the 1930s, however, the Supreme Court accepted that the 14th Amendment required all state and local governments to adhere to the fundamental principles of liberty and justice which lay at the base of the civil and political institutions of the country, and which could be found stated authoritatively in the Bill of Rights, even those which on their terms bound only the national government.[12] In *Cantwell v Connecticut*,[13] the Supreme Court found that the 14th Amendment »has rendered the legislatures of the states as incompetent as Congress to enact such laws«. Free exercise rights of individuals were thus applicable against the States under the 14th Amendment. Perhaps more controversially, in *Everson v Board of Edu-*

5 Witte, *ACE*, 76-9.
6 US Constitution, Article I, section 7(2).
7 James Madison, Federalist Paper no. 10: The utility of the Union as a safeguard against domestic faction and insurrection, 1787.
8 Witte, *ACE*, 49.
9 D.L. Dreisbach, 'The Constitution's forgotten Religion Clause: Reflections on the Article VI religious test ban', (1996) 38 *Journal of Church and State* 261 at 286.
10 US Constitution, 1st Amendment.
11 Consider Barron v Mayor and City Council of Baltimore, 32 US (7.Pet.) 243 (1833), US SCt.
12 Palko v Connecticut, 302 US 319 (1937), US SCt; see also Hamilton v Regents of the University of California, 293 US 245 (1934), US SCt.
13 Cantwell v Connecticut, 310 US 296 (1940), US SCt.

cation,[14] the court led by Black J ruled that the 14th Amendment also imposed the limits of the establishment clause upon the states. It is not quite the case that the 1st Amendment binds the States since the passage of the 14thAmendment. The Supreme Court has never accepted that the 14th Amendment incorporated the Bill of Rights. Rather, the 14th Amendment imposes obligations and sets limits for the states based on the fundamental values of the United States – values laid out in the Bill of Rights. From the 1960s onwards, however, the Supreme Court has looked ever more closely to the Bill of Rights in developing the content of these guarantees, so that is fair to talk of thenationalization of the First Amendment guarantees.

Within the context of this collection, there are perhaps interesting lessons to be learnt for the Europeanisation project from this nationalisation of disestablishment in the US. For this paper, however, it is primarily of interest for the contrast it provides to the experience of establishment in England. Here, the story of church/state relations from the Reformation to theearly twentieth century can largely be framed in terms of increased tolerance of religious communities, and their members, falling outside of the established church; occurring alongside a retention of the paramount position of the Church of England in public life, and involvement of the state in that Church. In the twentieth and early twenty-first centuries, however, this increase in toleration has been combined with an increased separation of the Church of England from the United Kingdom state. It would be easy to see this as simply positive in terms of religious liberty and autonomy. The transformation of Church/State relations has occurred, however, in the absence of a UK framework guaranteeing the autonomy of religious organisations, and prohibiting state involvement in religious matters. In this paper I will argue that in the early twenty-first century there is evidence of an attenuation of some elements of the special relationship between the Church of England and the UK state, but that this is being matched by an intensification in the relationship between Islamic religious organisations and the UK state which raises the possibility of asymmetrical disestablishment where the state is increasingly insulated from religious organisations, but religious organisations are subject to state involvement in religious issues.

14 Everson v Board of Education, 330 US 1 (1947), US SCt.

2. What is meant by establishment?

The term establishment has been used in a variety of ways in the context of Church/State relations.[15] In the English context, it has been required to bear meanings as disparate as the role of the Church of England in the creation of shared values, the demographics of worshippers, and the legal status of church law.[16] One useful way of looking at Establishment is as a special relationship, consisting of both benefits and burdens, between the Church of England and the English – later British and then United Kingdom – state.[17] I have argued elsewhere, however, that establishment may be best understood as a non-exclusive relationship between a state and a religious organisation, so that:

> »A religious organisation is established where there are laws which apply to that particular religious organisation, *qua* that religious organisation, which do not apply to the majority of other religious organisations«.[18]

Within the UK, there is no doubt that the religious organisation - or perhaps better - constellation of religious organisations within a single ecclesiastical hierarchy, which is *most* established is the Church of England. Other religious organisations are governed by special laws, for instance »the legal framework within which the Methodist Church is governed«[19] is drawn from the Methodist Church Act 1976, an Act of the UK Parliament. The entanglement of the Church of England and the state, and the sheer volume of laws applying to it, is considerably greater than that of others. For that reason, it may be useful to distinguish between Establishment for that religious organisation, and establishment more broadly.

15 For instance, see P. Hammond, *Religion and Personal Autonomy: The Third Disestablishment in America*, (University of South Carolina Press, 1992).

16 See Lord Selborne, *A Defence of the Church of England Against Disestablishment*, (MacMillan, 1987) at 10. Consider Norman, »The Unravelling of Church and State«, *The Times*, October 17, 1992, which refers to »a relationship between law and opinion«. In a legal context, see the review of English meanings by Gibbs J. in *Attorney General for the State of Victoria ex rel. Black v Commonwealth of Australia* (1980) 146 CLR 559.

17 For a fuller review see P. Cumper and P.W. Edge, »First amongst equals: The English State and the Anglican Church in the 21st Century?«, (2008) 83 *University of Detroit Mercy Law Review* 601-623.

18 See further P.W. Edge, »Reorienting the Establishment Debate: From the Illusory Norm to Equality of Respect«, [1998] *Anglo-American Law Review* 265-284.

19 *The Constitutional Practice and Discipline of the Methodist Church*, 2005, vol I, p.iii.

3. The developing situation

(a) Church of England involvement with the State

The Christian church in England predates England itself:

> »When England gained a unifying monarchy and became a single state in the ninth and tenth centuries, the archbishopric of Canterbury and the church had already been functioning as a unifying factor for two centuries«[20]

Initially part of a broader European church accepting, albeit not always uncritically, some papal authority, the Reformation of the sixteenth century initially aimed at a separation of a national, Catholic, church under the King from »Roman« Catholicism under the Pope. Although subsequently coming to incorporate Protestant elements into its theology and practice, the Anglican Church retained elements of Catholicism, and today is a broad national church, so that particular adherents may stress either the Protestant or the Catholic elements in its composition.[21] The establishment of a non-Roman Catholic identity for this national church was intimately tied to the needs of the English State, and a number of key legal elements retain this linkage, although other forms of religious belief, and religious organizations, are now accepted as legitimate.[22] The Church of England no longer retains an effective monopoly over public life and positions in the State.[23] Nonetheless, the position of the Church of England in the life of the State remains exceptional.

The Sovereign is the Supreme Governor of the Church of England,[24] although not *ipso facto* a minister of that Church.[25] The control of the Sovereign over the Church of England was declared[26] by the Act of Supremacy 1558, which united and annexed all ecclesiastical powers of visitation, reformation and correction of the Church of England with the Crown.[27] The Sovereign also possesses very

20 A. Hastings, *Church and State: The English experience*, (Exeter: University of Exeter Press, 1991) at 10.

21 See T. Thomas (ed.), *The British: Their religious beliefs and practices, 1800-1986*, (London: Routledge, 1988) especially T. Thomas, »Introduction«.

22 See K. Hylam-Smith, *The churches in England from Elizabeth I to Elizabeth II: Volume II, 1833-1998*, (London: SCM Press, 1988) 211-33; E. R. Norman, *Church and society in England 1770-1970*, (Oxford: Clarendon Press, 1976) at 416-75; G. Davie, *Religion in Britain since 1945: Believing without belonging*, (Oxford: Blackwell, 1994) at 139-161.

23 For a discussion of the key moves away from this monopolistic position, see St.J.A.Robilliard, *Religion and the Law*, (Manchester: Manchester University Press, 1984) at 199-203.

24 See Act of Supremacy 1558 s.9.

25 Articles of Religion 37.

26 *Caudrey's Case* (1591) 5 Co.Rep.1a at 8a.

27 Act of Supremacy 1558 s.8.

wide powers of appointment to offices within the Church of England.[28] Although the Sovereign is responsible for a range of functions within the life of the Church of England, there is no provision for delegation of these functions in the event that the Sovereign should be of a different denomination or religion. Rather, there are absolute limits on the religion of the Sovereign.

In 1688 the Protestant Parliament offered the Crown to the Protestant William and Mary, Prince and Princess of Orange. As part of the Bill of Rights 1688, which confirmed this constitutional change, Parliament excluded those in communion with the Roman Catholic Church, or professing its religion, or marrying such a person would be unable to inherit or hold the Crown.[29] The Bill of Rights also contains, by implication, a positive requirement that the person becoming Sovereign should be a Protestant at that time.[30] These provisions were supplemented by a requirement that the Sovereign take an oath, normally at Coronation, renouncing certain aspects of Roman Catholic doctrine,[31] replaced in 1688 by an obligation to protect the Protestant religion,[32] and in 1910 by a shorter form containing a positive declaration that the Sovereign was »a faithful Protestant«.[33] In 1700, the succession to the Crown was laid down by statute, and limited to Protestants.[34] The same Act reaffirmed the relevant provisions of the Bill of Rights,[35] and provided that »whosoever shall hereafter come to the possession of this Crown shall join in communion with the Church of England as by law established«.[36]

The position of the Church of England in relation to the Sovereign, then, remains uniquely powerful. Important though the position of the Head of State is, however, both in practical and rhetorical terms, in the UK the Head of Government is the Prime Minister. In contrast with other members of the executive, there is an important limitation, based on religious affiliation, on this post. The Roman Catholic Relief Act 1829 was primarily intended to remove restrictions upon the role of Roman Catholics in public life. A number of sections, however, were intended to ensure that particular functions were not discharged by Roman Catholic officials. Under the Act, »It shall not be lawful for any person professing the Roman Catholic religion directly or indirectly to advise His Majesty ...

28 See Halsbury's Laws of England, vol. 14 para. 358.
29 Bill of Rights 1688 s.1 (the spelling has been modernised).
30 ibid.
31 ibid.
32 Coronation Oath Act 1688.
33 Accession Declaration act 1910, Schedule.
34 Act of Settlement 1700 s.1.
35 ibid, s.2.
36 ibid, s.3.

touching or concerning the appointment to or disposal of any office or preferment in the ... Church of England ... or in the Church of Scotland; and if such person shall offend in the premises he shall, being thereof convicted by the due course of law, be deemed guilty of a high misdemeanour, and disabled for ever from holding any office, civil or military, under the Crown.«[37] This provision was repeated, in relation to Jews, in the Jews Relief Act 1858.[38] A problem arises when these limits make it a high misdemeanour for an individual to fulfil some of the duties of their office, even though it is lawful for them to hold the office. Statutory provision has been made for such functions to be transferred from a Roman Catholic, although not a Jewish, Lord Chancellor to another Minister of the Crown.[39] No provision has been made, however, concerning the functions of Prime Minister. Along with their other legal and political powers, the Prime Minister is responsible for advising the Sovereign on a range of key appointments within the Church of England, including appointment of Bishops. Although it should be remembered that the Prime Minister acts on the advice of others, notably the Crown Nominations Commission which consists almost entirely of Church of England officials and representatives. The Sovereign is bound to accept this advice. The effect of this is that although there is no bar on a Roman Catholic or Jew occupying the post of Prime Minister, and discharging most functions, properly carrying out some of the duties is not only unlawful, but would expose the Prime Minister to criminal sanctions, including being barred from any office under the Crown - which would include ministerial and Prime Ministerial office. In practice, a Roman Catholic or Jewish Prime Minister would exercise a slightly different conception of the post from their predecessors. The post of Prime Minister is mainly a creature of convention, and so can be changed informally.[40] It would not be impractical for the duties of the Prime Minister that would expose them to prosecution under this Act to be exercised by another Minister of the Crown, or for swift legislation to formalise such an arrange-

37 Roman Catholic Relief Act 1829 s.18; as amended by the Statute Law Revision (no.2) Act 1888; Statute Law Revision (Northern Ireland) Act 1976. See *R v Kennedy* (1902) 86 L.T. 753.

38 Jews Relief Act 1858 s.4; Statute Law Revision (Northern Ireland) Act 1980 s.1, Schedule, Pt. XIV.

39 Lord Chancellor (Tenure of Office and Discharge of Ecclesiastical Functions) Act 1974 s.1,2; the situation is complicated by the Jews Relief Act 1858 s.3, which expressly barred Jews from the office of Lord Chancellor, but was repealed by the Promissory Oaths Act 1871, which was itself repealed. Currently »it is unclear whether a person professing the Jewish religion would be appointed Lord Chancellor without clarifying legislation« (Halsburys Laws of England, vol.8, para. 477 fn.7), although Sir Rufus Issacs occupied the post during the existence of the 1871 Act.

40 See McEldowney, op.cit., at 78-81, 265.

ment.[41] This is unsatisfactory however, as the Prime Minister would in effect be occupying an office with slightly fewer powers than if they held the office as a member of any other religious community. This may explain why Tony Blair, Prime Minister from 1997 to 2007 begun formal conversion to the Roman Catholic Church at the very end of his term, rather than while active as Prime Minister.[42]It might be possible to justify this differential treatment if only Prime Ministers in communion with the Church of England could exercise authority over ecclesiastical appointments, as there seem strong arguments for only members of a particular religious community deciding on senior appointments within that community. It is clear, however, that a non-Roman Catholic, non-Jewish, Prime Minister can exercise these powers without being a member of the Church of England. The distinction between a Roman Catholic Prime Minister, and, for instance, a Muslim Prime Minister, seems one without difference.

As well as the connection between the Church of England and the State in relation to the Head of State and Head of Government, the Church enjoys a unique position in the national legislature. The bicameral Houses of Parliament are dominated by the directly elected House of Commons, which having lost its last remaining religious limit on membership,[43] is composed of individuals of a range of religious backgrounds. The second chamber of Parliament, the House of Lords, however, retains an element of privilege for the Church of England. In 2000, of the 665 members of the House of Lords, 92 were hereditary peers who had inherited their position in the legislature;[44] 520 were life peers, who were elevated to the peerage in recognition of distinction in public life, often service within the political system;[45] 27 were Law Lords, the most senior British judges appointed to the Lords primarily to perform its judicial tasks, but with a role in legislation; and 26 Lords Spiritual.[46] The Lords Spiritual are all members of the

41 Consider the developments when the possibility of Tony Blair, the serving Prime Minister, converting to Roman Catholicism was publicly aired - (1998) *The Guardian* 12 February.

42 For a maximal version of this view, see S Bates, »After 30 years as a closet Catholic, Blair finally puts faith before politics«, (2007) *The Guardian* 22 June.

43 House of Commons (Clergy Disqualification) Act 1801, repealed by House of Commons (Removal of Clergy Disqualification) Act 2001.

44 This is a useful simplification. In 1999, 665 of the 1321 members of the House of Lords were hereditary peers. As the first stage of the reform of the House, the House of Lords Act 1999 reduced this number to 92, elected by the existing hereditary peers.

45 For instance, former Prime Ministers James Callaghan (Lord Callaghan of Cardiff) and Margaret Thatcher (Baroness Thatcher). The statement in the text is an obvious simplification of the forces which lead to the appointment of a life peer to the House of Lords.

46 See *Modernising Parliament: Reforming the House of Lords*, (1998) Cm. 4183 para. 3.2-3.5.

Anglican hierarchy.[47] Originally, all Bishops of the Church of England sat in the Lords, but the increase in the number of bishoprics was not met by an increase in the number of seats.[48] Today, both Archbishops, the Bishops of London, Westminster and Durham, and the twenty-one most senior of the remaining Bishops, sit in the House of Lords.[49] They retain their position so long as they hold their bishopric, effectively retiring from both roles before the age of seventy.[50]

It is possible for other religious organisations to gain a voice in the national legislature, through the appointment of a life peer with strong links to the organisation.[51] An obvious example is the appointment of the Chief Rabbi as a life peer. There are, however, significant differences between even this peer and a Lord Spiritual. A life peer effectively retains their position for life, while a Lord Spiritual who ceases to hold their position in the Church of England hierarchy loses their place in the Lords. The appointment of a Lord Spiritual is effectively automatic, and as of right to the most senior Bishops, while appointments such as that of the Chief Rabbi are ad hoc and at the discretion of the political figures recommending the creation of life peers. Weller sees these appointments as having:

> »been solely on the basis of a recognition of the individual concerned, rather than as part of an explicit attempt to reflect the wider range of religious traditions and communities now present in our increasingly pluralizing society«.[52]

It follows that the selection of which religious figure to appoint as a representative of a religious organisation or community can be contentious. In discussing the Chief Rabbinate, Newman notes:

> »the extent to which the »host society« has welcomed the intervention of successive chief rabbis in politics - even to the extent of awarding one of them a seat in the House of Lords - might well in itself have weakened the status of the chief rabbinate within the Jewish

47 The Human Rights Act may have impacted on the appointment of these officials – see J. Rivers, »From toleration to pluralism: Religious liberty and religious establishment under the United Kingdom's Human Rights Act« in R.J. Ahdar, *Law and religion*, (Aldershot: Ashgate, 2000) at 144.

48 See Halsbury's Laws of England, vol.14, para. 528.

49 See Bishoprics Act 1878. This excludes the Bishop of Sodor and Man, who has a seat in the legislature of the Isle of Man; and the Bishop of Gibraltar in Europe. See P. Goodrich, »A Bishop in the house of Lords« [1997] *Law and Justice* 63.

50 Ecclesiastical Offices (Age Limit) Measure 1975; Bishops (Retirement) Measure 1986.

51 »Other ecclesiastical groupings may be represented through the nomination of Life Peers. The Roman Catholic Archbishop of Westminster is not included, and only recently the Chief Rabbi, head of the Jewish faith, has been made a Life Peer« - J.F. McEldowney, *Public Law*, (London : Sweet and Maxwell, 1994) at 55. Additionally, members of the House may themselves follow a particular faith – see for instance A. Versi, »House of Lords loses a Muslim«, (1999) *Muslim News* 26 November.

52 P. Weller, *Submission to the Royal Commission on the Reform of the House of Lords*, (Unpublished, 29 April 1999) at para. 6.5.

community itself. And the extent to which the State has turned to the chief rabbinate and regarded it as the official spokesman of the community has further alienated those groups within the community who are unhappy about many of its aspects.«[53]

The composition of the House of Lords was radically changed in 1999, with the removal of the majority of the hereditary peers from the House, causing it to be numerically dominated by life peers. This measure was seen by its supporters as Stage I of a more far reaching reform, however, which could include consideration of the position of the Lords Spiritual. The Royal Commission, reporting in 2000, recommended a reduction in Church of England representation, addition of other Christian representatives, and using other appointed places to represent other religious communities. The White Paper which followed endorsed a reduced, but remaining, Church of England presences, and using appointed places to represent other religious group, including other Christian groups. As Parliament, and the executive, moved implementation of the White Paper forward they became increasingly cautious on religious representation, and difficulty with reform generally led to dropping of the legislative plans in 2004. It is striking, in relation to the position of the Lords Spiritual, that an equality narrative initially pushing towards extension of places in the legislature to other religious groups, when faced with the practical difficulties of doing so, began to transform into an argument for abolition of the special treatment of the Church of England. A second White Paper, in 2007, put forward a number of possibilities for the future shape of the House of Lords, all with a reduced Church of England representation. As of 2010 the new Prime Minister of a coalition government - itself something of a novelty for the United Kingdom – has announced proposals for an entirely, or mainly, elected House of Lords. The coalition consists of two parties, the Conservatives and the smaller Liberal Democrats. Liberal Democrat policy has explicitly excluded the Lords Spiritual from a reformed second chamber, even one which was not wholly elected. The Conservative position is less clear. The end result may be fewer Lords Spiritual in a partly elected chamber, but it may be their removal, or relegation to non-voting members.

This review of the formal involvement of the Church of England in the key organs of the United Kingdom suggests that the Church of England enjoys considerable privileges in relation to control of state power. This risk is being misleading. The role of the Sovereign should not be overstated; the difficulties of a Prime Minister faced with the limits on Roman Catholic and Jewish advisors to the Crown are surmountable; and as we have seen the small minority of the

53 See A. Newman, »The office of Chief Rabbi: A very English institution«, in N. Aston, *Religious change in Europe, 1650-1914*, (Oxford : Clarendon Press, 1997); R. Gledhill, »Chief Rabbi post for progressives«, (1999) *Times* 17 February.

House of Lords who sit as representatives of the Church of England are by no means certain to continue to hold their place.

(b) State involvement in Church of England doctrine

During the twentieth century, state involvement in the doctrine of the Church of England through law has declined markedly.

Although Parliament has the authority to legislate over the internal affairs of any religious community, in practice legislation tends to be limited to the Church of England. After the Reformation, the bulk of ecclesiastical legislation was passed by Parliament. The doctrinal inheritance of the Church of England therefore includes state laws, both legislation and decisions of state courts. As a result, the national courts still have a role in resolving doctrine, for instance the question of whether a structure referred to as an altar rather than a table was permissible.[54] By the early twentieth century the extent of the legislative programme made this inconvenient for Parliament, which in any case was no longer composed exclusively of members of the Church of England. In 1919 an Act of Parliament created the National Assembly of the Church of England,[55] later renamed the General Synod.[56] Although Parliament retains the authority to legislate over the Church of England the General Synod is now the principal legislature for the Church of England.[57] The General Synod has the authority to legislate by Measure on matters concerning the Church of England, which include fundamental issues concerning the constitution, doctrine, conventions, customs and practices of the Church.[58] A Measure may even amend or repeal an Act of Parliament, and for most purposes has the same effect as an Act of Parliament.[59]

Any Measure intended to have the effect of an Act of Parliament must be referred to the Legislative Committee of the General Synod. The Legislative

54 Re St Stephen's (1987) 2 All ER 578.

55 Church of England Assembly (Powers) Act 1919.

56 Synodical Government Measure 1969. See also Church of England (Worship and Doctrine) Measure 1974.

57 See *ex parte Haynes-Smith* [1928] 1 K.B. 411. The General Synod has a range of legislative powers, of which only the Measure is discussed in the text. For other forms of legislation, see L. Leeder, *Ecclesiastical Law Handbook*, (London: Sweet and Maxwell, 1997) para. 2.29, 2.23-4.

58 *R v The Ecclesiastical Committee of the Houses of Parliament, ex parte the Church Society* (1993) Times November 4.

59 See Church of England Assembly (Powers) Act 1919 s.3,4; *ex parte Haynes-Smith*, op.cit.; *ex parte Williamson* (1994) Times 9 March (CA). It will be recalled that, for the purposes of the Human Rights Act, these measures are to be treated as primary legislation.

Committee must then submit this Measure, along with any comments, to the Ecclesiastical Committee of Parliament. This Committee is composed of members of both Houses of Parliament, and consults formally and informally with the Synodical Committee. The Ecclesiastical Committee then reports on the proposed Measure to Parliament. The proposed Measure, along with the reports of the Legislative Committee of the General Synod, and the Ecclesiastical Committee of Parliament, is then laid before both Houses of Parliament. If both Houses of Parliament pass a resolution directing that the Measure should be approved, it will pass to the Sovereign for Royal Assent. Parliament has no authority to amend a proposed Measure as such.

While the State has become much less directly involved in the creation of Church of England law, including ecclesiastical law concerning doctrine, it has also become less involved in the protection of that doctrine. Formerly, doctrines of the Church of England had special protection under the law of blasphemy. The core of the offence was publication of blasphemous material – blasphemy came to require a combination of substance and manner of expression, but the substance had to be in conflict with the doctrines of the Church of England. Any protection to other religious communities, including other Christianities, was only in relation to shared doctrines. So an attack on Judaism through the Old Testament was potentially blasphemeous, as »the Old Testament is so connected with the New that it is impossible that such a publication as this could be uttered without reflecting upon Christianity itself«.[60] An attack on religious doctrine not shared by the Church of England was not prohibited by the law of blasphemy.[61] As with religious representation in the House of Lords, equality concerns played an important part in consideration of reform of this law, with extension to other religious communities being rejected as impractical, and replaced with a decision to abolish the protection of Church of England doctrine.Blasphemy has now been abolished.[62] All religions now receive some protection through crimes of religious hatred, but this does not protect doctrine.[63]

(c) State involvement in Islamic doctrine

Outside of the Church of England, the general position of the UK state in relation to religious doctrine is fairly categorically stated. A very recent statement by Eady J may serve to illustrate the general position:

60 Williams (1797) How St TR 654.
61 See for instance *ex parte Choudhury* (1982) 3 WLR 986.
62 Criminal Justice and Immigration Act 2008 s.79.
63 Crime and Disorder Act 1998 as amended.

»the courts will not attempt to rule upon doctrinal issues or intervene in the regulation or governance of religious groups. [this is] partly a matter of a self-denying ordinance, applied as a matter of public policy, and partly a question of simply recognising the natural and inevitable limitations upon the judicial function«.[64]

There are well-established instances when this is not possible, for instance where the doctrinal issue is tied to property rights, the terms of a trust or the like; or where the doctrinal issues have been stated in an Act of Parliament. As mentioned earlier, some non-Anglican religious organisations have made use of Acts of Parliament to provide a foundation for their legal organisation. As an example of this, The Methodist Church Act 1976 provides that »the constitution of the Methodist Church and the doctrinal standards shall be as declared and defined in the Deed of Union«,[65] and that »Conference shall be the final authority within the Methodist Church with regard to all questions concerning the interpretation of its doctrines«.[66] A more disturbing development, however, concerns state involvement in Islamic doctrine.[67]

Following the 7/7 bombings of London, the Prime Minister Tony Blair expressed a commitment to British Muslims to »work with you to make the moderate and *true* voice of Islam heard as it should be«,[68] and later described other Muslims as »fanatics, attached to a completely wrong and reactionary view of Islam«.[69] This may be seen with some justification as a misspeak – the Prime Minister was not genuinely asserting an ability to determine true Islam, but rather reacting to the fear of Islamophobia immediately after the bombings. Later state actions, however, cannot be explained quite so easily. A significant thread of UK counter-terrorism strategy has been the use of soft power to support Islamic groups compatible with that strategy, even to the extent of seeking to influence doctrinal arguments within Islam to promote a form of Islam compatible with State goals. In the aftermath of 7/7, Islamic working groups taking part in the government review Preventing Terrorism Together recommended a new national advisory body of mosques and imams; creation of continuous professional development programmes for imams and mosque officials; and »particular empha-

64 In Singh Ji Maharaj v Eastern Media Group (2010) EWHC 1294.
65 Methodist Church Act 1976 s.3(1).
66 Ibid, at s.3(2).
67 For a fuller discussion of the issues in this section, see PW Edge, »Hard law and soft power: Counter-terrorism, the power of sacred places, and the establishment of an Anglican Islam«, (2010) *Rutgers Journal of Law and Religion* 12(2), 382.
68 Statement to Parliament on the London Bombings, 11 July 2005, at <www.number10.gov.uk/page 7903> (accessed 31 March 2009).
69 A Blair, »A renaissance in Foreign Policy«, Los Angeles World Affairs Council August 1 2006, at <http://www.lawac.org/speech-archive/pdf/2006/Blair_609.pdf> (accessed 12.10.2012).

sis on developing skills around interfaith dialogue, youth work, counselling, management, communication, citizenship and English«.[70]

There then followed the launch, in 2006, of the Mosques and Imams National Advisory Board (MINAB) as »an independent community led initative«.[71] Despite this emphasis on its independence, however, it has been identified as an integral part of the UK counter-terrorism strategy CONTEST, and been extensively criticised for receiving a substantial amount of state funding.[72] On the second point, continuous professional development has been supported by initiatives such as the Preventing Violent Extremism Community Leadership Fund, which provides ongoing support for capacity building and training of imams, including providing a course to equip newly qualified imams »to engage with British culture and humanitarian values, and *to find parallel values within the Qur'an*«.[73] A similar doctrinal approach can be found under Foreign and Commonwealth Office projects under CONTEST to »challenge extremist ideology and support mainstream voices«.[74] Recipients of this funding do not necessarily see it as problematic. Maajid Niwaz of Quilliam, for instance, explained that his organisation's »long term ambition is to be fully independent of government. I would also emphasis here though, at this stage, that I don't think there is anything beside the perception problems, which of course pose real strategic concerns, I don't think that intellectually there is anything wrong with governments providing grants to secure their country«.[75]

4. Asymetrical disestablishment?

This brief, and very selective, review of Establishment, and establishments, in England raises an interesting line of speculation. The constitutional order of the United States, although its interpretation has changed greatly since its creation, both limits and protects religious organisations in their relationship with the state. Elements of the relationship of the Church of England to the state would clearly be unacceptable under the US constitutional order. It is difficult to imag-

70 »Preventing Extremism Together« Working Groups August-October 2005, at 69.

71 See minab.org.uk (accessed 30 March 2009).

72 See I Bunglawala, »Minab: Community initiative, or quango?«, (2009), <http://www.guardian.co.uk/commentisfree/belief/2009/may/15/minab-mosques-imams-islam> (accessed 28 July 2009).

73 Hansard HC 12 Jan 2009, col. 236W (Sadiq Khan, Parliamentary Under-Secretary (Community Cohesion and Fire and Rescue Service)).

74 <http://www.fco.gov.uk/en/fco-in-action/counter-terrorism/counter-terrorism/preventing-extremism/> (accessed 19 June 2009).

75 Maajid Nawaz, interviews on PM, Radio 4, 23 June 2009, my transcript.

ine a Congress containing members directly appointed by a religious organisation for instance. A great strength of this formalisation of the relationship between religious organisations and the state, however, is that it sets an element of religious corporate and communal autonomy – of non-interference with religious organisations – into the state constitutional order. In England, however, our development of Church/State law has been much more piecemeal. As I have briefly noted above, Islamic organisations do not receive the same constitutional privileges as the Church of England. This has not meant, however, that their autonomy has been protected. Instead, the English absence of a constitutional guarantee of religious autonomy may leave open the path to asymmetrical disestablishment, whereby religious organisations lose, or do not gain, power within the state order; while the state retains, or even increases, its power over these organisations.

A particularly interesting manifestation of this would be if the UK were to become more intimately involved in doctrinal disputes within religious organisations and communities in order to mould them more closely into conformity with state values. In this brief paper I have discussed the particular issue of Islam, human rights, citizenship, and interfaith dialogue. It will be interesting to see if other state values are used to justify state support for particular doctrinal positions in a range of religious organisations – for instance non-discrimination on the grounds of gender or sexual orientation in relation to the appointment of religious leaders. These are issues currently debated by members of the Church of England itself. It would be fascinating, but perhaps in the light of the last decade no longer startling, if the state supported those members whose doctrinal views match state values on these issues.

C. Questions of Status and Organisation

VII. *THE PARTICIPATION OF RELIGIOUS COMMUNITIES IN PUBLIC LIFE – THE BRITISH EXPERIENCE – Peter Cumper*

1. Introduction

At first sight one might assume that, in Britain, religious communities would play an important role in public life.[1] After all, Britain is home to an Established Church (the Church of England), a monarch who takes a coronation oath to defend the Protestant reformed tradition, and a Parliamentary Chamber (the House of Lords) that guarantees ex officio membership to the nation's 26 most senior Anglican Bishops.[2] Yet, on closer inspection, such assumptions may be erroneous because of the apparent demise of organised religion,[3] and the considerable influence of secularism on public life.[4]

Today Britain is arguably the most religiously diverse nation in Europe, with Britons classified as being affiliated to at least 170 different faiths and systems of belief.[5] Yet, at the same time, the increasing influence of secularism has contributed to what has been termed the »death of Christian Britain«.[6] Indeed, as a senior British judge has succinctly put it: »One of the paradoxes of our lives is that we live in a society, which is at one and the same time becoming both increas-

1 This chapter will cover Great Britain (ie England, Scotland and Wales, but not Northern Ireland which is part of the United Kingdom, rather than Great Britain). Due to constraints of space its primary focus will be on England, the largest of the three regions that compose Great Britain. That said, many of the points made in relation to England apply equally to the other British regions.

2 See Norman Doe, *The Legal Framework of the Church of England A Critical Study in a Comparative Context* (Clarendon, Oxford, 1996).

3 See Cole Moreton, *Is God Still an Englishman?: How We Lost Our Faith (But Found New Soul)* (Little Brown, 2010) and Grace Davie, *Religion in Britain Since 1945: Believing without Belonging (Making Contemporary Britain)* (Wiley Blackwell, 1994).

4 The increasing influence of secularism appears to explain why even former Prime Ministers are in apparent disagreement as to whether Britain can still be thought of as a 'Christian country. Gordon Brown's bold affirmation that Britain is still a Christian country appears not to be shared by Tony Blair. See, respectively, »Gordon Brown insists Britain is still Christian country«, *The Daily Telegraph*, 7 August 2009 and »Tony Blair: Mention God and you're a 'nutter'«, *The Daily Telegraph*, 25 November 2007.

5 See the 2001 census for England and Wales: <http://www.statistics.gov.uk/census2001/profiles/commentaries/ethnicity.asp>.

6 C. Brown, *The Death of Christian Britain* (Routledge, 2000, London).

ingly secular but also increasingly diverse in religious affiliation«.[7] As a consequence, Britain's judges, legislators and policy makers face a particularly difficult challenge – they have to make and apply laws for a nation with an Established Church and a longstanding Judaeo-Christian heritage that is, increasingly, both multi-faith and secular in ethos. Nowhere are these challenges more apparent in British public life than in the area of education, which will be the main focus of this chapter.

Education tends to provide a particularly useful vehicle through which the participation of religious communities in public life can be measured. After all, whilst there is general agreement that education is a basic human right, secularists and people of faith often fundamentally disagree on questions such as the nature and purpose of education, especially where matters of religion and education are concerned.[8] Accordingly, in examining the role of faith and participation of religious communities in public life through the prism of education, this chapter will: (i) consider the role and status of maintained (state funded) and independent (privately financed) religious schools; (ii) examine the way in which British schools offer pupils lessons on religious education; and (iii) explore the extent to which religious communities are able to manifest their faith in publicly funded schools.

2. The role and status of religious schools

It is a characteristic of religious communities the world over that they wish to transmit their faith and values to future generations. International human rights law takes cognisance of this principle, for it guarantees, in both public and private spheres, the right of parents to ensure that their children are educated »in conformity with their own religious and philosophical convictions«.[9] In this regard British parents have a range of options when it comes to religion and the selection of a school. First, they may choose to send their child to a maintained

7 Munby LJ in *Singh v Entry Clearance Officer New Delhi* [2004] EWCA Civ 1075, para.62.

8 In the liberal tradition, there is general agreement that education (in the sphere of religion, as elsewhere) should empower pupils to realise their full potential and empower them to lead autonomous lives. See, eg., H.J. Blackham (ed) *Education For Personal Autonomy* (Bedford Square Press, London, 1978). However, many religious organisations view education in much more restrictive terms. See, eg., Y. Zaki, »The teaching of Islam in schools: A Muslim view« (1982) *British Journal of Religious Education* 5(1), pp.33-38.

9 See, for example, Art. 2 Protocol 1 of the ECHR (1950) and Art. 18(4) of the International Covenant on Civil and Political Rights (1966).

non-denominational school (of which there are approximately 13,000),[10] where religion is taught in formal religious education (RE) lessons. Secondly, they can opt for a maintained faith school (of which there are approximately 7,000), where RE lessons are based on the prevailing religious ethos of a particular school.[11] And thirdly parents, for whom faith is a particularly important matter, may look outside the public educational sector and send their children to one of the nation's privately funded independent faith schools, of which there are currently 957, educating just over 21,000 pupils.[12]

The involvement of religious communities in the public sphere of education is long-standing, for Britain's first religious schools were established at the beginning of the 19th century by the Anglican Church.[13] Yet in spite of the apparent decline of organised religion with the passage of time, matters pertaining to faith and education continue to be inextricably bound in British public life. As will be explored in more detail, below, the state today funds a high number of religious schools, many of which are massively over-subscribed, even though organised religion is apparently in decline.[14] In seeming defiance of the inexorable rise of secularism, it will be suggested that there are at least three reasons for the enduring appeal of religious schools in Britain.

First, a significant number of parents choose schools with a religious ethos for their children, as a response to the increasing secularisation of British public

10 <http://www.education.gov.uk/schools/leadership/typesofschools/b0066996/faith-schools/>.

11 See <http://www.education.gov.uk/aboutdfe/foi/disclosuresaboutschools/a0065446/> maintained-faith-schools. There are different types of faith school. These include: Voluntary Controlled Faith schools; Voluntary Aided Faith schools; Foundation Faith schools; and, Religious Academies. All such faith schools are often oversubscribed, so places tend to be in short supply.

12 It has been claimed that a significant number of religious parents are so alienated by the increasing secular influence of the maintained sector, they choose instead to send their children to privately funded faith schools: L. Philip Barnes »An alternative reading of modern religious education in England and Wales« (2009) *British Journal of Sociology of Education*, 30(5) pp.607-619. See, also, G. Walford, »The Christian Schools Campaign - a successful educational pressure group?« (1995) *British Educational Research Journal* 21(4), pp.451-464.

13 By 1870, when the elementary education in England became compulsory, 70 per cent of the school population attended Church of England schools. Thus, state permitted religious schools to exist alongside non-religious state schools, paving the way for the current dual system of faith and non-faith maintained schools. See M. Cruickshank, *Church and State in English Education* (London, 1964), p.190.

14 See Cole Moreton, *Is God Still an Englishman?: How We Lost Our Faith (But Found New Soul)* (Little Brown, 2010). For recent statistics on changes in belief in Britain see <http://www.brin.ac.uk/figures/#ChangingBelief>.

life.[15] Secondly, there is a widely held perception that maintained faith schools offer children a superior education to that provided by non-faith establishments.[16] And thirdly, successive British governments have, in recent decades, sought to endear themselves to faith groups by supporting the growth of state funded religious schools.[17]

It should of course be pointed out that, in view of the popularity of religious schools, many parents struggle to secure places for their children in maintained faith schools.[18] Given that faith schools usually give preference to their co-religionists, this has led to allegations that many parents only attend church or have their children baptised so as to increase their chances of winning entry for their offspring in oversubscribed public schools.[19] Indeed, the statistical breakdown of the number of such schools reveals that a parent's chances of obtaining a place for their child are significantly improved if they happen to be a member of the Catholic or Anglican traditions.

According to the Department for Education, of England's 7000 maintained faith schools, the vast majority of these are classified as being either Church of England (68 per cent) or Roman Catholic (30 per cent) schools.[20] The remaining two per cent are associated with a range of different groups that include: other Christian denominations (61); Judaism (38); Methodism (26); Islam (11); Sikh-

15 See, for example, Shaikh Abdul Mabud, »A Muslim Response to the Education Reform Act 1988«, (1991-92) *British Journal of Religious Education*, vol. 14, p.89.

16 For a recent example, see »High marks for C of E primary schools in tests«, *The Church Times*, 17 December 2010.

17 See Department for Children, Schools and Families, *Faith in the System: the role of schools with a religious character in English education and society* (London, 2007) p 3, where the previous Labour government recognised »the benefits to society« of state funded religious schools. This policy has now been re-affirmed by the current Conservative and Liberal Democrat coalition government: See *The Coalition: Our programme for government* (HM Government, 2011) para.26 <http://www.direct.gov.uk/prod_consum_dg/groups/dg_digitalassets/@dg/@en/documents/digitalasset/dg_187876.pdf>.

18 See, for example, »School admissions misery prompts appeal rise«, *The Daily Telegraph*, 4 March 2009. Note also that a faith school may not refuse to offer a non-faith student a place, if there is not a faith candidate to fill it: the School Standards and Framework Act 2006, s 86(2).

19 Baptism and active church membership are factors that maintained faith schools will take into account in offering places to prospective pupils. Critics of the current system claim that there is a correlation between parents wishing to secure places for their children, and a dramatic recent increase in child baptisms. For example, according to the Pastoral Research Centre Trust, the number of baptisms of children (below 13) into the Catholic church has risen by almost a quarter since 1958. See <http://www.brin.ac.uk/news/?tag=pastoral-research-centre>.

20 <http://www.education.gov.uk/schools/leadership/typesofschools/b0066996/faith-schools/>.

ism (4); the Greek Orthodox faith (1); Hinduism (1); Quakerism (1); the Seventh Day Adventist faith (1); and the United Reform Church (1).[21]

The fact that the vast majority of maintained faith schools are from the Christian tradition has, perhaps unsurprisingly, often led to allegations of discrimination against minority faith groups (especially Muslims).[22] A prominent British sociologist has, for example, warned that there is presently »an anti-Muslim wind blowing across the European continent« and that this is accompanied by the perception that Muslims are making »culturally unreasonable« demands, especially in the field of education.[23] Certainly a significant number of Muslim parents, unable to send their children to a maintained faith school, and unwilling to utilise the state educational sector, are only left with the option of sending their child to one of the nation's 118 privately funded Muslim schools.[24] Such independent faith schools may apply to join the maintained (ie., state funded) sector, and success is contingent on the Department for Education accepting that they meet the criteria for maintained status.[25] The advantages of faith schools being in receipt of state funding are clear. Aside from the obvious financial benefits,[26] state funded religious schools may, as a general rule: adopt admissions policies that (in the event of pupil over-subscription) afford a higher priority to their co-religionists;[27] show preference to teachers from their own faith tradition in matters of recruitment;[28] and organise both religious education lessons and statutory acts of collective worship in accordance with the school's particular faith.[29] That said, there are also a number of similarities between maintained

21 *Ibid.* For a breakdown of religious schools in England see also <http://www.brin.ac.uk/figures/#ChangingBelief>.

22 See J. M. Halstead, *The Case for Muslim Voluntary-aided Schools: some philosophical reflections*(Cambridge, Islamic Academy, 1986).

23 See T. Modood, »Muslims and the Politics of Difference« (2003) *The Political Quarterly*, p.100.

24 Of England's 957 independently funded faith schools, the vast majority (786) are based on a Christian ethos, with a lower number of Muslim (118), Jewish (49), Hindu (2), Buddhist (1) and Sikh (1) privately funded religious schools currently in operation.

25 An independent faith school must satisfy certain criteria including, for example, an appropriate site and any necessary capital funding, to be recognised as a maintained faith school. On this generally see the Education and Inspections Act 2006.

26 For example, in the case of voluntary aided faith schools, the Local Authority provides all running costs and 90 per cent of the building coasts. See, also, the School Standards and Framework Act 1998, Sch 3, para 3.

27 It is important to note that there are differences in the admissions policies employed by the various faiths. For example, Church of England schools has tended to be much more willing to admit children of other faiths or none than their Catholic counterparts. See *The Way Ahead* ('The Dearing Report'), (London, 2001) para.4.44 <http://www.natsoc.org.uk/schools/the_way_ahead/wa-whole.pdf>.

28 The School Standards and Framework Act 1998, s 60(5).

29 The School Standards and Framework Act 1998, Sch.19, para.4.

faith schools and other (non-faith) maintained schools, in that they are all subject to the National Curriculum and the School Admissions Code of Practice, so an independent faith school which chooses to move from the private to the public sector, sacrifices a degree of its autonomy.[30]

In recent years eleven independent Muslim schools have, to date, been approved for public funding, and many of the fears that were expressed in the past about the creation of state funded Muslim schools have proved to be unfounded.[31] But the principle of equality demands that Muslims (and other minority faith groups) are granted an additional number of state funded schools, commensurate with the size of their communities – a scenario that is, as yet, clearly some way off! Whilst the facilitation of such reform inevitably takes time, progress in this area has been undeniably slow. In effect, it means that Christians continue to enjoy much greater choice when it comes to being able to send their children to state funded religious schools than their non-Christian neighbours. As a consequence, it is hard to avoid the suspicion that many in the Britain's corridors of power remain wary about according maintained status to Muslim and other minority faith schools.

Long standing claims of religious bias and Islamophobia in Britain aside,[32] it is perhaps unsurprising that decisions to grant maintained status to Muslim and other minority faith schools are often controversial. After all, the history of religious schools in England reveals that they have long been dogged by controversy. For example, in the 19th century, Protestant non-conformists and Catholics objected to Church of England schools that offered (mainly to the poor) an education based on the tenets of the established church,[33] and many of their objections are today mirrored in the opposition of secular groups to the state funding religious schools.[34]

The argument as to whether the government should continue to fund faith schools continues to arouse heated debate in Britain.[35] It tends to pitch secular-

30 On the National Curriculum see <http://curriculum.qcda.gov.uk/>. On the School Admissions Code see <http://www.education.gov.uk/schools/adminandfinance/schooladmissions/a00195/currecu-codes-and-regulations>.

31 See generally P. Cumper, »Muslims Schools and the Education Reform Act« (1990) 16(3) *New Community*, pp. 379-391.

32 For example see John Richardson, *(Mis)representing Islam: the racism and rhetoric of British broadsheet newspapers* (Amsterdam, 2004), and the Runnymede Trust, *Islamophobia: A Challenge To Us All* (London, 1997).

33 See M. Cruickshank, *Church and State in English Education* (London, 1964), p 2.

34 For example, see the British Humanist Association, »Faith Schools«, <http://www.humanism.org.uk/campaigns/religion-and-schools/faith-schools>.

35 See Robert Jackson, »Should the State Fund Faith Based Schools? A Review of the Arguments« (2003) *British Journal of Religious Education*, 25(2) pp.89-102; Jo Cairns, Roy

ists,[36] who maintain that the government should not fund *any* religious schools, against people of faith, who insist that faith schools contribute positively to the wider society.[37] However, in a sense, such debate is misleading. Even if, at some point in the future, a British government were to abolish maintained faith schools and merge them into the state sector, religion would not be totally removed from the educational public sphere.[38] On the contrary, *public* money – the issue that tends to generate the most consternation amongst secularists – would *still* be spent on lessons about religion in Britain's maintained schools. It is thus to this issue – of religion being taught in the classrooms of maintained schools (ie., RE) – that I now turn.

3. Religious Education

Britain is one of the 25 member States of the Council of Europe where lessons on religion in school are compulsory.[39] Whilst RE is a compulsory subject in all maintained British schools,[40] an important caveat is that parents have an unqualified right to withdraw their children from such lessons.[41] The *way* in which it is taught depends ultimately on the nature of a particular school. In contrast to

Gardner, Denis Lawton (eds), *Faith Schools. Consensus or Conflict?* (Routledge, 2005); and S. J. McKinney, »Catholic schools in Scotland and divisiveness« (2008) *Journal of Beliefs & Values*, 29(2), pp.173-184.

36 The British Humanist Association argues that »Ultimately, all faith schools should be absorbed back into the secular schools sector, becoming inclusive community schools.« See BHA <http://www.humanism.org.uk/campaigns/religion-and-schools/faith-schools>.

37 See Christina Odone, *In Bad Faith. The New Betrayal of Faith Schools* (Centre for Policy Studies, 2008), pp.19-27. Also, according to Professor David Jesson, faith secondary schools contribute more by way of social and community cohesion than equivalent non-faith schools. See <http://www.natsoc.org.uk/jessonreportnov09.pdf>.

38 Such a hypothetical scenario seems unlikely, for, as noted above, state funded religious schools tend to be popular with parents, so it would be a brave (or some might even say fool-hardly) government that were to risk incurring the political wrath of parents and religious groups by abolishing the nation's state funded religious schools.

39 The European Court has noted that RE is a compulsory subject in 25 member States of the Council of Europe, and that there are significant differences between states where the obligation to attend classes in RE is absolute, and others that permit exemptions under certain conditions: *Hasan and Eylem Zengin v Turkey* (2008) 46 *EHRR* 44, para.31.

40 There has, however, been some longstanding opposition to RE being a compulsory subject in Britain's schools. For example, see John White, »Should religious education be a compulsory school subject?« (2004) *British Journal of Religious Education*, 26(2), pp.151-164.

41 In England and Wales parents have the right under s.71 of the School Standards and Framework Act 1998 to withdraw their children from RE lessons in all maintained schools, including faith ones. An equivalent right exists for parents in Scotland under the Education (Scotland) Act 1980, s.9.

maintained faith schools, where classes on RE reflect the tradition of the sponsoring faith, lessons on religion in non-denominational schools must be based on alocally »agreed syllabus«. The content of this syllabus is determined by a Standing Advisory Council on Religious Education (SACRE), which is composed of Local Education Authority, teachers' and faith group representatives.[42]Each local syllabus must »reflect the fact that the religious traditions in Great Britain are in the main Christian« and must take »account of the teaching and practices of the other principal religions represented in Great Britain«.[43]

The rationale for the law governing RE is based, at least partly, on the premise that to understand British history properly (eg., the British Civil War in the 17th century, and the long standing conflict in Northern Ireland), young people need to have at least a basic knowledge of Christianity. Moreover, today the OSCE has recognised the value of religious education as a way of combating religious extremism in contemporary Europe, and in this regard has called on states to make provision for well trained RE teachers.[44] However in Britain there remains a shortage of staff properly qualified to teach RE,[45] and, as a result, religious education has often been regarded as »the »Cinderella« subject of the curriculum, under-financed and lacking in high-quality resources«.[46] But should the state even involve itself in the area of RE, and would it be better for Britain to, say, adopt the French model, where formal lessons on religion are not offered in the classrooms of publicly funded schools? In answering this question, there are often differences of emphasis and approach between secularists, Christians, and minority faith representatives. With this in mind, in order to analyse the various criticisms that can be made of the current British model for the provision of religious education in the classroom, I will focus on each of these three groups: (i) secularists; (ii) Christians; and (iii) minority faith groups.

42 The British Government was criticised recently by the UN Special Rapporteur on the basis that the local bodies responsible for devising RE policies (SACREs), which routinely include members of Christian and non-Christian traditions do not, as of right, include humanists. See *Report of the Special Rapporteur on freedom of religion or belief, Asma Jahangir, to the United Kingdom of Great Britain and Northern Ireland*, A/HRC/7/10/Add.3, 7 February 2008, p.20, para.70.

43 See Education Reform Act 1988, s.8(3) and the School Standards and Framework Act 1998, s.69. On the rules governing RE generally see *Religious education in English schools: non-statutory guidance* 2010, DCSF, 2010.

44 »Knowledge about religions and beliefs has the valuable potential of reducing conflicts that are based on lack of understanding for others' beliefs and of encouraging respect for their rights«: *Toledo Guiding Principles on Teaching about Religion and Beliefs in Public Schools* (OSCE, 2007), p.76.

45 See B. Gates, *Religious Education: Supply of teacher for the 1990s* (Religious Education Council, Birmingham, 1990).

46 V. Baumfield, »The place of religious education in the school curriculum« (2004) *British Journal of Religious Education* 26, p.2.

(a) The Secular Approach

At first glance one might suppose that Britain's secularists would be keen to remove all religion, including formal Religious Education lessons from public schools, and thereby emulate the French model.[47] Yet, on closer inspection, this is not actually the case. The fact that religious educations programmes are synonymous with a wide range of social, educational, and political benefits,[48] would appear to explain why some atheists/secularists are willing in principle for publicly funded schools to teach religion.[49] However, that said, the willingness of secular groups in principle to endorse neutral and objective Religious Education programmes about a wide range of religions and equivalent secular beliefs, is not always borne out in practise. As a consequence, a frequent criticism of secularists is that school lessons on religion may *indoctrinate* rather than *educate* young people about religion and belief.[50] A particular concern of some British atheists is the power of faith schools to determine the content of their RE classes,[51] which they claim gives religious schools an opportunity to indoctrinate their pupils.[52] It is perhaps hardly surprising that such charges are robustly denied by apologists for religious schools,[53] who maintain that a faith based education is fully compatible with contemporary societal norms,[54] and claim that »secular« forms of indoctrination are just as dangerous as those of a »religious« kind.[55] Moreover, the defenders of the current system for the provision of RE seem to have the law on their side. For example, if a secular group were ever (hypothetically) to bring a legal challenge to the right of maintained faith schools to formulate their own

47 See M. Estivalèzes, »Teaching about religion in the French education system« (2003) *Prospects*, 33(2), pp.179-190.

48 »Knowledge about religions and beliefs has the valuable potential of reducing conflicts that are based on lack of understanding for others' beliefs and of encouraging respect for their rights«: *Toledo Guiding Principles on Teaching about Religion and Beliefs in Public Schools* (OSCE, 2007), p.76.

49 For example, Richard Dawkins has said that a »good case can indeed be made for the educational benefits of teaching comparative religion«. See R. Dawkins, *The God Delusion* (Black Swan, 2007) p.340.

50 For example, on the negative consequences of RE programmes see Christopher Hitchens, *God is Not Great: How Religion Poisons Everything* (Atlantic, 2008) pp.2-4.

51 The right of faith schools (both maintained and privately funded) to determine the content of their RE classes is a legacy of the fact that RE in Britain, although compulsory, is not part of the state's National Curriculum.

52 See »Teach RE in schools – but do it properly says atheist Dawkins«, *The Times*, 18 August 2010.

53 See Christina Odone, *In Bad Faith. The New Betrayal of Faith Schools* (Centre for Policy Studies, 2008).

54 See T. Copley, *Indoctrination, Education and God* (SPCKL, London, 2005).

55 See T. Copley, »Non-Indoctrinatory Religious Education in Secular Cultures« (2008) *Religious Education,* 103(1) pp.22-31.

RE programmes, this would seem likely to fail, because British law gives parents an automatic right to withdraw their children from RE classes,[56] while human-rights law also grants denominational schools considerable freedom in the areas of curriculum design and delivery.[57]

(b) Christian criticisms of RE

There is, of course, no common Christian approach to RE. It is almost inevitable that some British Christians would prefer to *confine* education about religion to the home (like secularists), whereas others would *extend* RE school run programmes to cover more faiths (as will be discussed in more detail, below). However, for the purposes of this chapter, I will focus on a criticism that is frequently made by conservative Christian groups – that RE programmes in publicly funded schools fail to devote enough time to the study of the Christian faith.[58] It was in the late 1960s and early 1970s that British schools moved from a uniquely confessional »Christian« form of religious *instruction*, to a non-confessional or multi-faith religious *educatio*n approach,[59] and although an attempt was made by conservative Christians in 1988 to reverse the tide of multi-faith RE programmes,[60] young Britons still typically receive a broader education about religious and equivalent philosophical beliefs than many of their European counterparts.[61] For many liberals this is a cause for celebration, and a demonstration of the nation's inclusively and commitment to religious diversity in the classroom.[62] But for others, and in particular the nation's conservative Christian communities,

56 See s.71 of the School Standards and Framework Act 1998. The right of parental withdrawal is definitive test adopted by the European Court in this area: *Folgerø and others v Norway* (2008) 46 *EHRR* 47. That said, as evidence shows, parents are, in practise, often reluctant to exercise the right of withdrawal lest children are stigmatized as being different from their classmates.

57 On this generally see *W. Dalgado Paez v Colombia*, 12 Jul 1990, Human Rights Committee, Communication Number 195/1985, UN Doc A/45/40 vol.2 (1990), p.43, para.5.7.

58 See Penny Thompson, *Whatever Happened to Religious Education* (Luterworth Press, 2004).

59 A major influence in this change was the work of Ninian Smart. See N. Smart, *Secular education and the logic of religion* (1968, Faber and Faber).

60 The vehicle for this aattempt was the Education Reform Act 1988. On this generally see R. Watt, and C. Hamilton, »A discriminating education: religious education in school« (1996) *Child and Family Law Quarterly*, 8(1), pp.28 40.

61 See, generally, E. Kuyk et al., (eds.) *Religious Education in Europe. Situation and current trends in schools,* (Iko and ICCS, Oslo, 2007), and J. Lähnemann and P. Schreiner (eds.) *Interreligious and Values Education in Europe* (Comenius, Münster, 2008).

62 See, for example, K. O'Grady, »Professor Ninian Smart, phenomenology and religious education« (2005) *British Journal of Religious Education* 27(3) pp.227-237, and J.M. Hull, *Mishmash*, (Christian Education Movement, Birmingham, 1991).

the British experiment in RE has been a costly failure, which has led to children being taught a confusing mis-mash of beliefs, and schools trivialising every religion's claims of truth.[63]

(c) Minority Faith Perspectives

Young people attending Muslim and other minority faith maintained schools have the opportunity to receive RE based on the tenets of their particular tradition. But this is an opportunity denied to the vast majority of children from minority faith homes, because, as noted above, the vast majority of state funded religious schools are affiliated to the Anglican and Catholic churches. This means minority faith pupils must receive RE lessons in state funded non-denominational schools, where the classes are based on a syllabus which must »reflect the fact that the religious traditions in Great Britain are in the main Christian«, although those teaching RE in such schools are also required, by law, to take »account of the teaching and practices of the other principal religions represented in Great Britain«.[64]

Parents that are worried about the potential Christian influence of RE lessons can, as noted above, withdraw their children from RE lessons. But such parental »opt outs« are a very blunt and unsatisfactory way of maintaining religious freedom, for peer pressure may preclude minority parents from choosing to remove their children from RE classes,[65] an argument endorsed by the late British Muslim scholar Zaki Badawi, who pointed out that withdrawing a child in such circumstances is akin to saying the a »child is not a member of the group«.[66]

There would appear to be support from within Britain's numerous minority faith communities for publicly funded school RE programmes to take more account of their beliefs, but the challenges of doing this are considerable. For a start, there is the problem of agreeing which *religions* (other than Christianity) should be included on any »multi-faith« syllabus. Coverage of the world's most

63 See, for example, Copley, T. (2005), *Indoctrination, education and God: The struggle for the mind* (SPCK , London); L. P. Barnes, »The disputed legacy of Ninian Smart and phenomenological religious education: A critical response to Kevin O'Grady« (2007) *British Journal of Religious Education*29(2) pp.157-168; and L. P. Barnes, »Developing a new post-liberal paradigm for British religious education« (2007) *Journal of Beliefs and Values*, 28(1), pp.17-32.

64 Education Reform Act 1988, Section 8(3). On the rules governing RE generally see *Religious education in English schools: non-statutory guidance* 2010, DCSF, 2010.

65 See A. Mawhinney, »The opt out clause: imperfect protection for the right to freedom of religion in schools«, (2006) *Education Law Journal* 7(2), pp.102-115.

66 As cited in R. Tames, *Approaches to Islam* (John Murray, London, 1982) p.154.

long established religions (eg., Buddhism, Islam, Judaism, Sikhism) would seem necessary – yet British schools might be wary of amending RE programmes to ensure that their pupils had the chance to learn about *new* (and sometimes controversial) religious groups, such as Jehovah's Witnesses, Mormons, Rastafarians, Moonies, Scientologists, etc. However, if such an approach were to be taken, and a distinction drawn between long established faiths and more newly established religious movements, Britain could find itself accused of acting contrary to its human rights obligations, because the Human Rights Committee of the International Covenant on Civil and Political Rights (1966), has stated that it »views with concern any tendency to discriminate against any religion or belief for any reason, including the fact that they are newly established«.[67]

(d) RE, Faith and Religious Communities

In view of the points made above, it might seem that the strongest reason for retaining the current system of RE in British schools is quite simply the problem of finding a different model to replace it. Yet it is suggested that such an interpretation would be not entirely accurate. British law may appear to show preference to one religious community (Christians) at the expense of others, but this is to ignore the fact that since the syllabus for RE is locally designed, the RE that is taught will take account of local factors – so, for example, the RE taught in an overwhelmingly Muslim school will be significantly different from that taught say in an overwhelmingly Christian school. In each school, children will learn about their own and other faiths, but the emphasis will just be different.

Perhaps the strongest criticism of the law governing RE lies beyond the remit of this chapter – that British law confines the right of withdrawal from religious education lessons to parents alone – and fails thus to take account (subject to age and maturity) of the rights of the child. This issue has incurred the wrath of the UK Parliament's Joint Committee on Human Rights in recent years,[68] and brings me to the wider issue of human rights, and the extent to which members of religious communities have been able to manifest their faith in the classroom of publicly funded schools.

67 General Comment No. 22: »The right to freedom of thought, conscience and religion« (Art. 18), 30 July 1993, para.2.

68 See the Joint Committee on Human Rights, 28th Report, Education and Inspections Bill, HL 116 (13 October 2006) para.2.2.

4. Religious communities, human rights and publicly funded schools

In recent years Britain's religious groups have sought to invoke human rights law in a range of areas in order to manifest their faith in public. Such cases include: an unsuccessful attempt by Muslim parents to argue that the state should guarantee (on religious grounds) single-sex schooling for their daughter;[69] the rejection of a Muslim maths teacher's request to have time off work to attend Friday prayers;[70] the dismissal of a claim that a local Council should fund the transport of nine Jewish pupils, whose parents wanted them to be educated in Jewish schools in Manchester rather than in their home city of Leeds;[71] a refusal to sanction the use of corporal punishment at a privately funded Christian school;[72] a finding that an atheist employed as a teacher in a Catholic maintained school had been unfairly discriminated against following their unsuccessful application for a more senior post in the school;[73] and a number of successful claims, where religious organisations have been held to be vicariously liable for the physical and sexual abuse of pupils by staff at faith schools.[74] However, an area that has generated much litigation in recent years, and which neatly illustrates many of the challenges facing law and policy makers when dealing with the participation of religious organisations in public life in Britain and beyond,[75] is that of religious dress.

69 *K, R (On the application of) v London Borough of Newham* [2002] EWHC 405 (Admin) (19 February 2002).

70 *Mayuuf v Governing Body of Bishop Challoner Catholic Collegiate School* [2005] Employment Tribunal Case no. 3202398/04 (21 December 2005). Given the requirements of the school's teaching timetable, it was held that the school's policy was proportionate and thus did not constitute indirect discrimination contrary to the Employment Equality (Religion or Belief) Regulations 2003. See also, *Ahmad v UK* (1982) 4 EHRR 126, where a Muslim teacher claimed, unsuccessfully, that Article 9 of the ECHR entitled him to an extra long lunch break to attend Friday prayers in a local Mosque.

71 *R (on the application of) v Leeds City Council* [2005] EWHC 2495 (Admin) (11 November 2005).

72 *R (Williamson) v Secretary of State for Education and Employment* [2005] UKHL 15; [2005] 2 A.C. 246. The House of Lords rejected the claim that corporal punishment should be permitted, on the basis of the Biblical injunction, »He who spares the rod hates his son, but he who loves him is diligent to discipline him« (Matthew 22, vv 20-22.) Their Lordships held unanimously that whilst this was a manifestation of belief, it could be legitimately interfered with in order to protect the physical and mental well being of children.

73 *Glasgow City Council v McNAB* [2007] UKEAT 0037 06 1701 (17 January 2007).

74 *Various Claimants v The Catholic Child Welfare Society and Others* [2010] EWCA Civ 1106 (26 October 2010).

75 See L. Auslander, »Bavarian crucifixes and French headscarves: Religious Signs and the Postmodern European State« (2000) *Cultural Dynamics*, 12(3), pp. 283-309; and L.M. Liederman, »Religious Diversity in Schools: the Muslim headscarf Controversy and Beyond« (2000) *Social Compass*, 47(3), pp. 367-381.

An important starting point here is the Human Rights Act 1998 (HRA), which incorporated the European Convention on Human Rights (ECHR) into British law. As a result of this legislation, school children (and teachers) have the right to wear religious dress (as recognised under Article 9(1)), whereas restrictions on the display of such dress may be lawful, as long as they satisfy the criteria under Article 9(2) of the ECHR – ie., a restriction on the manifestation of a religion or belief must be prescribed by law, with a legitimate aim, and proportionate.[76]

It is a truism that religious believers tend to manifest their faith in a variety of different ways. Thus, for example, in *R (Playfoot) v Governing Body of Millais School*,[77] a Christian pupil complained that her school's no jewellery policy prevented her from wearing a »purity ring«, which she claimed was an expression of her commitment to premarital chastity. The Court, however, in rejecting her claim, took the view that there had not been any interference with the applicant's Article 9(1) right to manifest belief because the wearing of the ring had not been »intimately linked« to her belief in chastity before marriage – and even if Article 9(1) had been engaged, Playfoot's voluntarily acceptance of the school's uniform policy meant that the ring's ban had been justified. In essence the Court thus held that the ring was merely a piece of jewellery, rather than a religious artefact, and the school's prohibition of it had been justified.[78]

Similarly, in *R (X) v Y School, the Court* took the view that there had not been any interference with the claimant's right to manifest religious belief, following her complaint that her school had refused to let her wear the niqab (a veil that covered her entire face and head, except for her eyes) while attending school).[79]In accepting that the claimant's request had been based on a genuine religious faith, Silber J reasoned that there had *not* been any interference with her rights under Article 9(1) because the claimant had been offered a place at an equivalent school, with an excellent academic reputation, where she would have been allowed to wear the niqab. Indeed, even if Article 9(1) had been activated,

76 Article 9 of the ECHR provides as follows:
1. »Everyone has the right to freedom of thought, conscience and religion; this right includes freedom to change his religion or belief and freedom, either alone or in community with others and in public or private, to manifest his religion or belief, in worship, teaching, practice and observance.«
2. »Freedom to manifest one's religion or beliefs shall be subject only to such limitations as are prescribed by law and are necessary in a democratic society in the interests of public safety, for the protection of public order, health or morals, or the protection of the rights and freedoms of others.«

77 *R. (Playfoot) v Governing Body of Millais School* [2007] EWHC 1698 (Admin).

78 See generally R. Sandberg, »Recent controversial claims to religious liberty« [2008] *Law Quarterly Review* 213.

79 *R (X) v Y School* [2007] EWHC Admin 298, [2007] ELR 278.

Silber J held that the applicant's claim would still have failed on the basis of a number of grounds, including the fact that a common school uniform (excluding the niqab) was an important element in the headteacher's vision for the school, as well as the need to ensure that all pupils of faiths felt comfortable in the school environment. Thus, it was accepted that the ban on the niqab could (at least in part) be justified on the basis of a need to foster a sense of equality and cohesion for pupils within the school.

The most high profile case on religious dress to date in Britain is *R (Begum) v Governors of Denbigh High School*. A majority of the House of Lords held that there had been no interference with the Article 9(2) rights of a 15 year old schoolgirl (Shabina Begum) who had been refused permission to wear a *jilbab* (a long Islamic cloak) on the grounds that it contravened school uniform policy.[80]

Whilst accepting that the claimant's beliefs were genuine and sincerely held, the House of Lords (by a majority) dismissed Begum's complaint on the basis that she had not been greatly inconvenienced because she could have attended another local school which permitted students to wear the *jilbab*. Their Lordships also agreed that but that the school's policy, which accommodated to a large extent the beliefs of »mainstream« Muslim pupils by allowing the headscarf and *shalwar kameeze*, was justified, and that it was entitled to have a uniform policy which, in its view, best protected social harmony within the school and the rights of other pupils.[81]

A different approach was however adopted by the British Courts in *R (on the application of) v Aberdare Girls' High School & Another*,[82] where a Welsh Sikh girl (Watkins-Singh) had been refused permission by her school to wear a plain steel bangle (the Kara). The Court of Appeal, rather than examining the case under Article 9 of the ECHR, held that a school's ban on the Kara was contrary to section 71 of the Race Relations Act 2002, which required it to have »due regard« to the need to end unlawful racial discrimination. This case is unusual because one of the peculiarities of British law is that Sikhs (in contrast to say Christians and Muslims) are regarded as being members of both a religion and a race[83] – and had it not been for this fact and the opportunity for the litigant to rely on Race Relations legislation, it is perhaps questionable whether Watkins-

80 *R (Begum) v Governors of Denbigh High School* [2006] UKHL 15; [2005] 5 WLR 3372, per Lords Bingham, Hoffmann and Scott.

81 *Ibid,* Lord Bingham at [26]-[34]; Lord Hoffmann [58]-[68]; Lord Scott [86]-[88]; and Baroness Hale [94]-[98].

82 *R (on the application of) v Aberdare Girls' High School & Another* [2008] EWHC 1865 (Admin).

83 *Manda v Dowell Lee* [1983] 2 AC 548.

Singh would have been any more successful in invoking Article 9 of the ECHR than Begum and Playfoot.[84]

In analysing these cases, a number of observations can be made about the way in which Britain's Courts have recognised the right of religious communities to manifest their faith in public.

First, Britain's religious communities have, as a general rule, long been free to manifest their faith through their choice of dress within the nation's schools.[85] The British approach is accordingly very different from that of say France, where the law controversially bans the display of »conspicuous« religious symbols from the classrooms of all French public schools.[86] Thus in Britain there is no equivalent of »laïcité« – the principle that religion is fundamentally incompatible with the institutions of the secular French Republic, and that the public manifestation of one's beliefs should be confined to the private rather than public sphere.[87]

Second, whilst religious groups have considerable freedom to display the symbols and wear the clothes of their choice in Britain's schools, this freedom is not unlimited. On the contrary, Britain's Courts have generally interpreted Article 9 of the ECHR narrowly in relation to dress codes – especially in cases such as *R (X) v Y School* and *Playfoot,* where the claims of the litigants were not even regarded as falling within Article 9(1).

Thirdly, in relation to Article 9(2) of the ECHR, the Courts have doubtlessly been influenced by wider public policy considerations in balancing the religious dress claims of individuals against the more general interests of society. One could argue that, in striking this balance, the nation's judges should afford greater protection to the religious sensibilities of those, such as Begum and Playfoot, who appear to imbue certain garments (ie., the jilbab) and artefacts (ie., the chastity ring) with a degree of reverence that is not shared by most of their co-religionists. That said, it must also be acknowledged that situations where a per-

84 That said, it should be noted that in Playfoot the school which had lawfully prohibited the applicant from wearing a 'purity ring' had also permitted two Sikh girls to wear the kara bracelet, since it was considered as being an essential requirement of the Sikh religion.

85 See, for example, *Mandla v Dowell-Lee* [1983] 2 AC 548 UKHL 7 (24 March 1982), where (as noted, above) the House of Lords held that because Sikhs are a racial group for the purposes of the Race Relations Act 1976, a school's ban on Sikh pupils wearing the turbans had to be overturned.

86 Law No. 2004-228, of 15th March 2004.

87 For example, see S. Poulter (1997), »Muslim Headscarves in School: Contrasting legal approaches in England and France«, (1997) *Oxford Journal of Legal Studies* 17 at 43. See also J. Freeman, »Secularism as a barrier to integration – the French dilemma« (2004) *International Migration*, 42 (3), pp. 5-27.

son of faith is, in the words of Waldron, »torn between a requirement imposed by the state and another imposed by his church or community«[88] are relatively rare when it comes to religious clothing and related symbols being displayed in public

5. Conclusion

As demonstrated above, religious communities in Britain have considerable freedom to exercise their faith in public life. This is the position now, but what of the future? In this regard a number of questions need to be answered.

First, should religious communities be permitted to have a privileged position in public life? As noted above, faith communities in Britain are the beneficiaries of certain privileges, as evidenced by the fact that today 18 per cent of all secondary schools and 37 per cent of all primary schools are religious schools, funded by the state.[89]Since Britain is an increasingly secular nation, where less than 10 per cent of the population regularly attend a religious service,[90] is it inappropriate for the state to continue to fund such educational institutions? Most religious communities would answer this question in the affirmative but, as their numbers decrease, the moral authority of this argument tends to fall accordingly.

Second, if the law should accommodate religion in public life, as maintained by groups such as faith organisations,[91] this begs the question, what is so special about religion?[92] For many religious communities, their beliefs are special be-

88 J. Waldron, »One law all? The logic of cultural accommodation« (2002) 59 *Washington and Lee LR* 3 at 24.

89 See note 11, above.

90 See Cole Moreton, *Is God Still an Englishman?: How We Lost Our Faith (But Found New Soul)* (Little Brown, 2010), and Grace Davie, *Religion in Britain Since 1945: Believing without Belonging* (Wiley Blackwell, 1994).

91 Such an approach is also advocated by advocates of multi-culturalism: see B. Parekh, *Rethinking Multiculturalism: Cultural Diversity and Political Theory* (London: Macmillan, 2000). But for a different approach, on non-accommodation, see B. Barry, *Culture and Equality* (Cambridge, Mass: Harvard University Press, 2002).

92 See (albeit from a US perspective) S. G. Gey, »Why Is Religion Special?: Reconsidering the Accommodation of Religion Under the Religion Clauses of the First Amendment«, (1990) 52 *University of Pittsburgh Law Review* 182. For a defence of the accommodation of religion see M. McConnell, »Accommodation of Religion: An Update and a Response to the Critics,« (1992) 60 *George Washington Law Review* 685. For a different approach see C. Lupu, »Reconstructing the Establishment Clause: The Case Against Discretionary Accommodation of Religion« (1991) 140 *University of Pennsylvania Law Review* 555.

cause they are integral to their very identity, both collectively and individually.[93] But for Western liberalism, law and policy must be based, not on subjective faith, but rather on objective reason alone.[94] On that basis, religious organisations might advance the argument that religion is special because – in the sphere of education – faith schools and RE programmes make a particularly valuable contribution to society in terms of promoting moral values. But such matters are always difficult to quantify, and recent well published allegations of clerical child abuse in Britain and other parts of Europe rather detract from the view that there is an automatic correlation between faith and public morality.

Third, given that the common law demands that all faiths »are entitled to equal respect,«[95] one may ask, why should the law uniquely grant privileges to *religious* communities in an increasingly secular age, rather than to other socially worthy *secular* groups (eg., environmentalists, pacifists, human rights activists etc)?[96] After all, the European Court has held that Article 9 of the ECHR protects not just religious »believers«[97] but also »atheists, agnostics, sceptics, and the unconcerned,«[98] so given that the religious tenets of the nation's minority religious communities are incorporated in RE lessons, should not equivalent provision be made for the »philosophical« convictions of parents from *non-religious* traditions? Indeed, with such considerations in mind the British Humanist Association has asked, »Why aren't there any humanist schools?« in arguing that the existence of maintained *religious* schools justifies the creation of specialist state funded *secular* schools.[99]

93 See, for example, T. Modood and P. Werbner (eds) *The Politics of Multiculturalsim in the New Europe: Racism, Identity and Community* (London, 1997); and T. Ramadan, *To Be A European Muslim* (The Islamic Foundation, Leicester, 1999).

94 See Robert Audi, »The Separation of Church and State and the Obligation of Citizenship« (1989) 18 *Philosophy and Public Affairs* 259. However, even Kent Greenawalt, who is much more open to the influence of religious reasons in the public sphere than Audi, accepts that »the legislator should eschew reliance on religious premises insofar as he can«: Kent Greenawalt, *Religious Convictions and Political Choice*, (Oxford University Press, 1988) p.237.

95 *Munby Jin Sulaiman v Juffali* [2002] 1 FLR 479. See also Laws LJ in *McFarlane v Relate Avon Limited* [2010] EWCA Civ B1; [2010] I.C.R. 507 (EAT) at [17].

96 See, generally, M. Freeman, »The Problem of Secularism in Human Rights Theory«, *HRQ* 26 (2004) at 395.

97 *Kokkinakis v Greece* (1994) 17 EHRR 397 at 418.

98 *Ibid,* at 418. The European Court's approach is consistent with international human rights law generally. For example, the Krishnaswami Study suggested that the term 'religion or belief' should »include, in addition to various theistic creeds, such other beliefs as agnosticism, free thought, atheism and rationalism«: E/CN.4/Sub.2/200/Rev.1, p.1.

98 *X v UK*, App. No.18187/91, 10 February 1993.

99 <http://www.humanism.org.uk/education/education-policy/humanist-schools-why-not>.

Finally, if the law is to afford greater protection to minority faith communities and secular groups in public life, where does this leave the privileged position of Christians generally and Anglicans in particular? In the field of education, as elsewhere, there is a general feeling amongst Church leaders that the Christian faith in Britain is not merely often marginalised,[100] but is also under attack from secularism,[101] and liberal decision makers who are actively hostile to Christianity.[102] One of the greatest challenges that will face Britain's legislators and decision makers in the coming years will be the task of reassuring Christian groups that increasing state recognition of the rights of minority faith and secular communities will not constitute an indirect attack on Christianity. A particularly daunting challenge – and one that may – to use a Biblical phrase – require the proverbial »wisdom of Solomon«.

100 See, for example, 'Rowan Williams raps government for treating religion as a »problem«', *The Guardian*, 12 December 2009.

101 See, for example, 'Pope Benedict XVI goes to war with »atheist extremism«', *The Guardian*, 16 September 2010.

102 For example, the former Archbishop of Canterbury, Lord Carey of Clifton, recently accused the judiciary of having a »disparaging attitude to the Christian faith and its values« and of having a »clear animus« towards Christian beliefs: *McFarlane v Relate Avon Limited* [2010] EWCA Civ B1 at [17]; [2010] I.C.R. 507 (EAT).

PARTICIPATION OF RELIGIOUS COMMUNITIES IN PUBLIC LIFE – GREAT BRITAIN AND GERMANY – Antje von Ungern-Sternberg

1. Introduction

Religion is, in many respects, part of public life in Great Britain[1] and in Germany. The presence of religion can be illustrated by religious days of rest and religious holidays, by religious symbols in public buildings, or by religious ceremonies accompanying important political events. This contribution focuses on yet another, very sensitive issue of religious presence in public life, namely the dissemination and propagation of religion or information on religion, particularly in schools and universities. In Great Britain and Germany, religious education and theology is not only considered to be the – private – affair of the religious communities concerned, it also takes a place in state schools and state universities. In the following, I would like to look at the question underlying the whole book – how do established state-church relations respond to religious pluralisation – with regard to schools and universities. After distinguishing the British and the German model of the presence of religion in public life (I.), I would like to address the legal issues of equal access to religious privileges (II.) and of state neutrality (III.).

2. Religion in public life: two models

For the sake of simplification, one can distinguish a British and a German model of how religion or religious communities participate in public life. The *British* model is a dual system: On the one hand, churches and other religious communities set up institutions of their own such as (independent or state maintained) faith schools[2] and theological colleges in which they provide for religious education and theological studies according to their respective creed.[3] In England, for example, the state maintained faith schools (not including independent faith schools) account for 30% of all maintained elementary and for 15% of all main-

1 This article consciously leaves out the particular problems of state-religion relations in Northern Ireland.

2 For the history of the 'dual system' of secular and religious schools, see *Priscilla Chadwick*, The Anglican Perspective on Church Schools, Oxford Review of Education 27 (2001), 475 seqq.

3 *David McClean*, Staat und Kirche im Vereinigten Königreich, in Gerhard Robbers, Staat und Kirche in der Europäischen Union. 2nd ed., Baden-Baden 2005, 603 (616 seqq.); see also *Peter Cumper* in this book (p. 175 seqq.).

tained secondary schools.[4] On the other hand, state run institutions provide for religious needs themselves by organising religious education (a daily act of collective worship and religious education lessons) in state schools[5] and theology in public universities. By contrast to the situation in Germany, these religious activities by the State do not generally presuppose the consent and the cooperation of the religious communities[6], even if the State and some religious communities do cooperate, for instance by working out a school syllabus[7]. The *German* system primarily relies on state institutions, i.e. state schools and state universities. Only about 7.5 % of the pupils attend private schools[8] and only 0.9 % of university students attend private universities (including faith institutions and non-denominational private institutions).[9] Within state schools and state universities, religious instruction and theology are organised in cooperation with the Churches and other religious communities.

In this context, it is crucial to distinguish »religious instruction« and »theology« on the one hand from »religious education«/»ethical lessons« and »religious studies« on the other hand. The latter deal with religion from an outsider's perspective: Religion – a particular creed or several of its manifestations – is studied as an object of interest, like any other subject in school or university. The former, i.e. »religious instruction« and »theology«, however, look at a particular creed from an insider's perspective: Religious instruction shall raise the pupils in a particular faith; theology is understood to be academic discipline bound to a certain creed (»bekenntnisgebunden«). According to German constitutional law, the State by itself can only be in charge of religious education and religious studies, whereas it not by itself competent to engage in religious instruction or theology without a religious counterpart responsible for the insider's perspective. In

4 The figures date from 2007, *Philip Petchey*, Legal issues for faith schools in England and Wales, Ecc.L.J. 10 (2008), 174 (176).

5 S. 70 and 71 School Standards and Framework Act 1998 (c 31).

6 Cf. for the lack of church influence over theologians in state universities *Geoffrey Turner*, Großbritannien, in Adrian Lorentan, Theologische Fakultäten an europäischen Universitäten, Münster 2004, 123 (125).

7 *McClean* (n 3), 616. On public and private schooling in Germany, see *Lutz R. Reuter*, School Choice and Civil Values in Germany, in: Patrick J. Wolf, Educating citizens, Washington D.C. 2004, 213 seqq.

8 7.3 % in 2007/2008, 7.8 % in 2008/2009. <https://www.destatis.de/DE/ZahlenFakten/GesellschaftStaat/BildungForschungKultur/Schulen/Tabellen/SchuelerPrivatenSchulen.html>.

9 4.5 % of the students in tertiary education (including universities and universities of applied sciences) attend private institutions; figures 2009/2010 <http://www.destatis.de/jetspeed/portal/cms/Sites/destatis/Internet/DE/Content/Statistiken/BildungForschungKultur/Hochschulen/Aktuell.psml>.

Great Britain, this distinction does not seem to be as relevant.[10] All in all, the British model implies institutional separation and considerable powers for the State or the religious communities within their respective institutions, whereas the German model amounts to organisational separation of competence within the state institution. This principle can be illustrated by provisions ensuring the presence of religious topics in the media – another field where religion or religious communities may participate in public life: German law allocates broadcasting time to the Christian churches and to other major religious communities so that religious services and other religious programmes can be broadcast on public television and radio stations.[11] Again, the public institution provides the setting for religious contents and messages which are accounted for by religious communities – whereas religious broadcasts by the British public stations do not need to be attributed to a religious community[12].

Both the British and the German model are still dominated by the Christian majority (i.e. the Anglican Church and the Presbyterian Church in Great Britain; the Protestant Church and the Catholic Church in Germany). In Great Britain, most of the state maintained faith schools belong to the established Churches or the Catholic Church. School prayers in state schools are meant to be generally of »broadly Christian character«[13], whereas religious education reflects the fact »that the religious traditions in Great Britain are in the main Christian«[14]. Christian colleges and Christian theology in public universities demonstrate the Christian imprint in the field of tertiary education. In Germany, the State mainly cooperates with the Christian Churches in order to organise religious instruction in state schools and theology in state universities. Religious pluralisation, however, challenges these two models of religious participation in public life. Are the two systems capable of adequately responding to the growing demands of religious minorities, and in particular to the demands of Muslim communities? In legal terms, this raises two questions: From the religious minority's point of view, it has to be asked whether rights and other privileges accorded to the Christian churches (i.e. the right to public funding of faith schools, the right to have religious instruction introduced in state schools, the right to broadcast religious pro-

10 See, however, *Rex Ahdar/Ian Leigh*, Religious Freedom in the Liberal State, Oxford 2005, 244 seqq.

11 See, for instance, § 11 (3) ZDF-Staatsvertrag, cf. *Axel Freiherr von Campenhausen/Heinrich de Wall*, Staatskirchenrecht, 4th ed. Munich 2006, 301.

12 *McClean*, n 3, 618 seq.; see also *David McClean/Susan Howdle*, New Liberties and Church-State Relationships in the United Kingdom, in: European Consortium for Church-State Research, »New Liberties« and Church and State Relationships in Europe, Milan 1998, 389 (418 seqq.).

13 School Standards and Framework Act 1998 (c 31), s. 70; sch. 20, para 3 (2).

14 S. 8 (3) Education Act 1988 (c 42).

grammes) are equally accessible to the religious minorities. From the State's point of view it has to be assessed whether and to what extent it may provide for religious life within its institutions. Both questions will be addressed in the next two sections, before I attempt to draw a conclusion.

3. The religious minority's perspective: equal access to privileges

If a State grants certain rights to established religious communities or if it has developed special links with them, the question arises whether newcomer minority religions can claim those privileges as well. As a matter of principle, this question can be answered in the affirmative: The principle of religious non-discrimination is enshrined in German as well as in British law. In German law, one speaks of religious »parity«, a principle derived from several constitutional provisions prohibiting unequal treatment of individuals or of religious communities on religious grounds.[15] In the United Kingdom, the Human Rights Act 1998 has incorporated art. 14 of the European Convention on Human Rights according to which the enjoyment of Convention rights shall be secured without discrimination on religious grounds.[16] By contrast to the guarantee of non-discrimination in respect to any right as established in art. 1 of Additional Protocol n° 12 (which the United Kingdom has not signed and Germany has not ratified yet), art. 14 of the Convention refers solely to the enjoyment of Convention Rights. However, the European Court of Human Rights only demands that the unequal treatment falls within the ambit of a Convention right.[17] Whenever privileges accorded to religious communities facilitate religious life, this falls within the ambit of the freedom of religion guaranteed by art. 9 of the European Convention on Human Rights.[18] Thus, newcomer minority religions have the right to be treated equally, i.e. they can call for equal access to privileges.

15 The constitutional provisions with regard to religious communities are art. 4 (1) and (2), 3 (1), 140 Basic Law read in conjunction with art. 137 (1), (3), (5) Weimar Constitution; see *von Campenhausen/de Wall* (n 11), 91 seq.; *Bernd Jeand'Heur/Stefan Korioth*, Grundzüge des Staatskirchenrechts, Stuttgart 2000, §§ 168 seqq.; *Peter Unruh*, Religionsverfassungsrecht, Baden-Baden 2009, § 106.

16 Art. 1 (1) (a), 2 (a), 3 (a) Human Rights Act 1998 (c 42).

17 *Christoph Grabenwarter*, Europäische Menschenrechtskonvention, 4th ed., Munich 2009, 446 seq.; *Clare Ovey/Robin White*, Jacobs & White: The European Convention on Human Rights, 4th ed., Oxford 2006, 419; for a different perspective (infringement of art. 26 of the International Covenant on Civil and Political rights, but not of the ECHR), see *Peter Cumper*, Religious Liberty in the United Kingdom, in: Johan Witte/Johan van der Vyver: Religious Human Rights in Global Perspective, The Hague 1996, 205 (235 seqq.).

18 See, for example, ECHR (Grand Chamber), *Cha'are Shalom ve Tsedek/France*, No. 27417/95, Judgment of 27 June 2000, Rep. 2000-VII, §§ 58 seqq.

(a) Factual impediments: state funding for faith schools (Great Britain)

In reality, however, factual or legal obstacles may prevent that privileges are extended to minority religions. Let me give an example for a *factual* obstacle first. As mentioned before, there are state schools and faith schools in the English and Welsh school system. Faith schools may be financed privately (»independent schools«) or by the state (state maintained »voluntary schools«). Traditionally, the overwhelming majority of the state maintained faith schools are run by the Church of England and by the Catholic Church. Still today, the former accounts for 68 percent, the latter for 30 percent of all maintained schools in England.[19] From the 1970s onwards, Muslim parents also became interested in sending their children to faith schools. A variety of factors contributed to this development, in particular the desire to provide for Muslim education and to accommodate particular Muslim needs, such as single-sex education, dietary requirements, or Friday prayers, in school life.[20] As a consequence, private Muslim schools were founded. Nowadays, they number around 120.[21] These independent Muslim schools tried, from the 1980s onwards, to get into the state maintained sector. But initially, the attempts to obtain government funding failed. It was not until 1998 that the first faith school was approved as a state maintained school and – as of 2011 – there are only eleven state maintained Muslim schools altogether.[22]

Legally speaking, the Muslim schools had to fulfil the same requirements under the relevant school legislation as any other independent school in order to qualify for state funding. However, the Muslim demands were denied, so it seems, due to political concerns which were hidden behind »neutral« reasons such as the quality of the accommodation and empty places in the neighbourhood, but also the financial burden to the local authority's budget or its adopted multicultural policy.[23] The perspective of a growing number of Muslim schools had raised fears about segregation and religious fundamentalism and had revived

19 See <http://www.education.gov.uk/schools/leadership/typesofschools/b0066996/faith-schools/maintained>.

20 'Muslims push for state aid schools', The Times, 25th August 1985.

21 <http://www.education.gov.uk/schools/leadership/typesofschools/b0066996/faith-schools/faith>.

22 Ibid.; on this struggle in general, see *Cumper* (n 17); *Marie Parker-Jenkins*, Equality before the Law: An Exploration of the Pursuit of Government Funding by Muslim Schools in Britain, Brigham Young University Education and Law Journal 1999, 1 seqq.; *Jan Rath et al.*, Western Europe and its Islam, Leiden 2001, 240 seqq.; *Chris Hewer*, Schools for Muslims, Oxford Review of Education 27 (2001), 151 seqq.; *Urfan Khaliq*, The accommodation and regulation of Islam and Muslim practices in English law, Ecc.L.J. 6 (2002), 332 (348 seq.); *Marie Parker-Jenkins*, Equal Access to State Funding: the case of Muslim schools in Britain, Race, Ethnicity and Education 5 (2002), 273 (276 seqq.).

23 *Parker-Jenkins*, Equal Access (ibid.), 279; *Rath et al.* (ibid.), 245 seq.

general objections against private schools. The High Court ruled, in 1992, that the refusal was »manifestly unfair« and thus prepared the way for the first state maintained Muslim school. Besides, the 1993 Education Act – which was influenced by evangelical Christians whose faith schools had also been denied the status of a state maintained school – facilitates the direct public funding of faith schools.[24] Nevertheless, it remains an open question whether minority religions are effectively treated equally with regard to the financing of faith schools.

(b) Legal impediments: organisational requirements for religious communities (Germany)

My second example is meant to show that *legal* impediments may also very effectively bar religious communities from accessing certain privileges. In Germany, many religious privileges depend on a particular status, namely the status of a »religious community« according to art. 7 (3) Basic Law or the status of a »corporation under public law« according to art.137 (5) Weimar Constitution[25]. These types of organisational status have to be distinguished. The latter public law status is a necessary prerequisite for public law privileges, for instance the power to levy taxes and to employ public servants (i.e. to opt for a public employment law), and also entails other benefits, for instance tax reductions.[26] The public law status is open to any law abiding religious community whose constitution and whose number of members guarantee its permanency.[27]

In our context, the status of a »religious community« under art. 7 (3) Basic Law is of particular interest, since it implies the religious community's right to offer religious instruction in public schools.[28] However, the German Muslim associations which try to enforce this right are experiencing that is rather difficult

24 *Geoffrey Walford*, The New Religious Grant-Maintained Schools, Educational Management and Administration, 22 (1994), 123 seqq.

25 According to art. 140 Basic Law, most of the articles of the Weimar Constitution regarding Church and State relations form part of the Basic Law.

26 *Hans Michael Heinig*, Öffentlich-rechtliche Religionsgesellschaften, Berlin 2003, 281 seqq.; *von Campenhausen/de Wall* (n 11), 251 seqq.; *Unruh* (n 15), §§ 296 seqq.

27 Art. 137 (5) (2) Weimar Constitution; BVerfGE 102, 370 (Jehova's Witnesses); *von Campenhausen/de Wall* (n 11), 134 seqq.; *Unruh* (n 15), §§ 280 seqq.; *Hermann Weber*, Der öffentlich-rechtliche Körperschaftsstatus der Religionsgemeinschaften nach Art. 137 Abs. 5 WRV, in: Hans Michael Heinig/Christian Walter, Staatskirchenrecht oder Religionsverfassungsrecht?, Tübingen 2007, 229 seqq.

28 BVerwGE 123, 49; *ChristophLink*, Religionsunterricht, in: Joseph Listl/Dietrich Person, Handbuch des Staatskirchenrechts der Bundesrepublik Deutschland (HbStKR), 2nd ed. Berlin 1995, II, 439 (496 seq.); *von Campenhausen/de Wall* (n 11), 216; *Unruh* (n 15), §§ 415 seq.; §§ 449 seqq.

to qualify as a »religious community«.[29] There are two main reasons for this. On the one hand, German law makes a clear distinction between religious education (i.e. Islamic education) and religious instruction (i.e. Islamic instruction). The former – religious education – presents facts about a particular religion from the outside; thus, the State does not need to cooperate with religious communities in order to organise it. The latter – religious instruction –, however, does not only provide facts about a religion, but teaches religion from the inside, i.e. religious doctrines and beliefs are presented as true, and pupils are invited to adopt and to follow them.[30] As a consequence of state neutrality, the State by itself cannot provide religious instruction; it has to cooperate with a religious community responsible for the content and – to a certain degree – the teachers of religious instruction. Art. 7 (3) (2) Basic Law specifically states that religious instruction shall be given »in accordance with the tenets of the religious community concerned«. Thus, it makes sense that the term »religious community« under art. 7 (3) Basic Law implies a religious competence and a certain degree of organisational viability: The State needs a reliable religious counterpart. On the other hand, Muslim communities – unlike the Christian Churches – do not have a tradition of formal organisation. Some scholars even expressly object to a tendency of organising the Muslim community according to the Church model. Despite the establishment of several Muslim associations in Germany, this remains an open question: It is true that the four Muslim associations created at the national level[31] would not be disinclined to speak on behalf of all Muslims living in Germany, but most of the non-organised Muslims would object to that.

In 2005, the requests by two Muslim associations for religious instruction in North-Rhine Westphalia, which had been refused by the Administrative Court and the Higher Administrative Court, enabled the Federal Administrative Court to specify the organisational requirements for religious communities under art. 7 (3) Basic Law:[32]According to the Federal Administrative Court, the term »religious community« under art. 7 (3) Basic Law and the term »religious society« used in the Weimar provisions (art. 136, 137, 138, 141 Weimar Constitution) have a similar meaning: The religious community or society constitutes an or-

29 On the attempts to introduce Islamic education or Islamic instruction, see *Myrian Dietrich*, Islamischer Religionsunterricht, Frankfurt a.M., 88 seqq.; *Michael Ott*, Ausbildung islamischer Religionslehrer und staatliches Recht, Berlin 2009, 86 seqq.

30 BVerfGE 74, 244 (252) (Religious Instruction); *von Campenhausen/de Wall* (n 11), 215 seq.; *Unruh* (n 15), §§ 417 seq.; §§ 449 seqq.

31 The 'Coordination Council of Muslims in Germany', formed at the federal level, is composed of DITIB, the German-Turkish Union for the Institution of Religion, the Islamic Council for the Federal Republic of Germany, the Central Council of the Muslims in Germany and the Union of Islamic Cultural Centres.

32 BVerwGE 123, 49 (54 seqq.).

ganisation uniting the members of one creed or several related creeds for the purpose of fulfilling *all* the tasks assigned by the common belief. The organisation need not have legal personality; besides, it need not comprise all members of one creed or the members of one creed exclusively. However, by contrast to religious associations dedicated to *partial* aspects of religious life (charity, for example), the tasks of the religious community have to be all-embracing. The Federal Administrative Court furthermore acknowledged that umbrella organisations might also qualify as religious communities provided that the member organisations are composed of believers, i.e. natural persons, at the local level, provided that all levels are sufficiently united organisationally, provided that the umbrella level fulfils tasks relevant for the community's identity, and provided that the umbrella organisation is dominated not by associations dedicated to partial – charitable, cultural, professional, academic – aspects of religious life, but by associations dedicated to religious life in general. The two last requirements were considered doubtful with respect to the applicants. The requirements concerning organisational viability and identifiable affiliation, however, were met by the applicants.

The applicants, hoping for a political settlement of their demands, have not resumed their proceedings before the Higher Administrative Court. As a consequence, Muslim organisations have not yet been recognized as constituting »religious communities« under art. 7 (3) Basic Law and are not yet in charge of religious instruction. Thus, are Muslim organisations denied equal access to religious privileges? There is no direct discrimination of Muslim organisations, because the same requirements apply to all religious groups. However, there is a duty to accommodate religious minorities as far as possible if a legal system designed for Christian churches effectively leads to difficulties for those minorities. This claim might be based on the principle of factual or indirect non-discrimination, or – the more preferable solution – on the principle of – collective – religious liberty which comprises the right to self-determination and self-organisation (art. 7 [3] read with art. 4 [1], [2] Basic Law and art. 137 [2], [3] Weimar Constitution). It leads to a broad construction of the term »religious community« under art. 7 (3) Basic Law, leaving only those organisational requirements which are necessary for the provision of religious instruction. In this respect, the Federal Administrative Court ruling has gone into the right direction by accepting that umbrella organisations might, in principle, qualify as religious communities, and by accepting forms of religious affiliation other than formal membership. But considering the conditions set up for umbrella organisations, the Court has not gone far enough: Given that the state needs a religiously competent counterpart who accounts for the content of religious instruction, it should normally be irrelevant whether the religious identity of the corresponding Muslim organisation is formed at the local or at the national level and whether or not it is accompanied by partially religious activities.[33]

4. The State's perspective: neutrality

If a State fosters religion in public institutions by organising religious education in schools, religious studies in universities, or debates on religious issues in the media, this also raises the question of state neutrality. But what does religious neutrality mean? It can imply *subjective* rights, for example parental rights or freedom of religion prohibiting religious indoctrination in school, but it can also amount to an *objective* principle outlawing state run religious activities per se. The following section will look at both questions with regard to religious education and religious studies in Great Britain and Germany.

(a) Neutrality and objectors

It is undisputed in national law as well as in European Convention law that state schools may not religiously indoctrinate pupils. At the Convention level, this is part and parcel of the parental right under art. 2 of Additional Protocol n° 2;[34] in the German Constitution, the prohibition results from the parental rights of art. 6 (2) Basic Law and from the so called »negative« freedom of religion of the parents and the children under art. 4 (1) and (2) Basic Law [35]. As a consequence, the State must either provide opting-out clauses or construe compulsory education in a non-indoctrinating manner. This is effectively the case in Germany as well as in Great Britain. The British School legislation contains opting-out clauses for the daily act of worship (if it is still being performed at all[36]) and for

33 For a similar assessment, see *Heinrich de Wall*, Der religionsrechtliche Rahmen für die Einführung des Fachs »Islamische Studien« und für Beiräte für islamische Studien, in: Christian Walter et al., Die Einrichtung von Beiräten für Islamische Studien, Baden-Baden 2011, 15 seqq.; see also *Dietrich* (n 29), 199 seqq.

34 ECHR (Grand Chamber), *Folgerø v. Norway*, No. 15472/02, Judgment of 29 June 2007, §§ 88 seqq.; on art. 2 Additional Protocol n° 2 see *Malcolm D. Evans*, Religious liberty and international law in Europe, Cambridge 1997, 342 seqq.; *Grabenwarter* (n 17), 243 seqq.; *Jacobs & White* (n 17), 376 seqq.

35 BVerfGE 47, 46 (74) (Sex Education); 52, 223 (235) (School Prayer); 93, 1 (17) (Crucifix in the Classroom); BVerfG, Decision of 29th April 2003, Neue Zeitschrift für Verwaltungsrecht (NVwZ) 2003, 1113 (Compulsory Schooling II); Decision of 15th March 2007, NVwZ 2008, 72 (74) (Ethics Lessons Berlin).

36 Apparently, the duty to perform such a daily act of worship is widely ignored. According to a figure provided by the Chief Inspector of Schools in 2004, 76 % of the secondary schools did not hold daily acts of worship, see *Ahdar/Leigh* (n 10), 238.

religious education.[37] In German state schools, school prayers have disappeared. Besides, it has always been clear that attendance at services, prayers and other acts of worship is entirely voluntary.[38] The right to opt out of religious instruction is granted to the parents under art. 7 (2) Basic Law and to the children under art.4 (1) and (2) Basic Law.[39] If the German federal States provide for compulsory ethics lessons, the syllabus does not contain religious instruction, but information about different religions and ethical concepts.[40] Besides from being designed to provide information from the »outside perspective«, Islamic education, which is offered in an increasing number of schools particularly in areas with a high Muslim population, also operates on a voluntary basis.[41] With regard to opting-out clauses, only minor issues are in dispute, for instance the question whether children have a say in choosing religious education or religious instruction[42] or whether the opting-out conditions cause undue hardship to the pupils concerned[43].

(b) Neutrality and religious communities

At least from a German perspective, whether the State is generally barred from religious involvement by an objective neutrality principle or by subjective rights of the religious communities concerned is less clear.

Apparently and admittedly, state schools organising religious education and school prayers – the latter »wholly or mainly of broadly Christian character«[44] – or public universities running religious studies do not seem to pose a legal problem of state neutrality in the *British* system. An objective neutrality principle

37 S. 71 School Standards and Framework Act 1998 (c 31).

38 BVerfGE 52, 223 (239) (School Prayer).

39 *Hans D. Jarass/Bodo Pieroth*, Grundgesetz Kommentar, 10th ed. Munich 2009, art. 7, §§ 12a seq.

40 *Unruh* (n 15), §§ 430 seqq.

41 *Dietrich* (n 29); *Ott* (n 29).

42 In Germany, § 5 Religious Education of Children Act 1921 (»Gesetz über religiöse Kindererziehung«) specifies that a child speaks for itself from the age of 14 and cannot be forced to be taught religious instruction against its wishes from the age of 12. This statutory provision is seen to correctly fix the limits of the constitutional rights of the child on the one hand and his parents' rights on the other hand, *Pieroth/Schlink* (n 39), art. 7, no. 12b. As to Great Britain, this question has only been resolved for pupils over the age of 16 years; see Joint Committee on Human Rights, 28th Report, para 2.2. <http://www.publications.parliament.uk/pa/jt200506/jtselect/jtrights/247/24702.htm>.

43 *Peter Cumper*, School worship: praying for guidance, E.H.R.L.R. 1998, 45 (48 seqq.); *Carolyn Evans*, Religious education in public schools: an international human rights perspective, H.R.L.Rev. 8 (2008), 449 (466 seqq.).

44 S. 7 (1) Education Act 1988 (c 40).

does not exist, neither at the national level with its long history of established churches, nor at the European Convention level[45] which is only concerned with subjective rights. Furthermore, state-run religious education and religious studies do not infringe upon the subjective rights of religious communities: They can freely exercise the right to spread their religious belief, granted by the freedom of religion, by relying on religious institutions, in particular faith schools and universities. Besides, it was held by the European Court of Human Rights that the collective side of religious freedom also bars the state from interfering into infra-religious disputes concerning religious tenets or organisational questions.[46] However, as long as the State aims at providing pupils and students with an opportunity to be informed or taught about important religious subjects and does not take sides, for example by unduly favouring a particular religious group or doctrine over another, this does not violate the Convention. In practice, the question of religious education is approached in a pragmatic manner: The syllabus for religious instruction, according to statutory requirements, shall »reflect the fact that the religious traditions in Great Britain are in the main Christian whilst taking account of the teaching and practices of the other principal religions represented in Great Britain«.[47] This means that the Local Education Authorities (LEA) may be asked by the Standing Advisory Committees on Religious Education (SACRE) to review the syllabus for Religious Education with respect to the religious composition of the pupils. Besides, in many state schools with a substantial amount of Muslim pupils, «Islamic Studies« lessons have been introduced with the assistance of Muslim bodies such as the Muslim Educational Trust.[48] Similar mechanisms permit that school prayers of broadly Christian character are dropped or replaced by prayers reflecting the Muslim background of the pupils.[49]

The situation in *Germany* is much stricter. The State may unilaterally introduce school and university subjects engaging with religion from the outside, i.e. in the German terminology »religious education« and »religious studies«, or – more specifically – »Islamic education« and «Islamic studies«. But it may not unilaterally introduce school and university subjects teaching religion from inside, i.e. »religious instruction« and »theology«, or – more specifically – »Is-

45 The European Commission on Human Rights has held that the system of State Churches does not contravene the Convention: *Darby v. Sweden*, No. 11581/85, Judgement of 23 October 1990, A 187, § 45; cf. *Christian Walter*, in: Rainer Grote/Thilo Marauhn, EMRK/GG Konkordanzkommentar, Tübingen 2006, Chap. 17, § 72.

46 ECHR (Grand Chamber), *Hasan and Chaush v. Bulgaria*, No. 30985/96, 26 October 2000, Rep. 2000-XI, § 78; *Grabenwarter* (n 17), 258.

47 S. 8 (3) Education Act 1988 (c 40).

48 *Ahdar/Leigh* (n 10), 241; *Khaliq* (n 22), 350.

49 *Khaliq* (n 22), 350.

lamic instruction« and »Islamic theology«. With respect to school education, this crucial difference between the two perspectives rests upon art. 7 (3) Basic Law, which requires that religious instruction is provided in accordance with the tenets of the religious community concerned. This necessarily implies the consent of a religious community which will also be in charge of approving the syllabus and the teachers.[50]

If the State introduces and organises theology within a state university, the need to cooperate with religious communities derives from the religious community's right of self-determination, enshrined in art. 137 (3) Weimar Constitution[51] and from the objective principle of religious neutrality[52]. The established practice of cooperation between the federal States – responsible for universities – and the Christian churches is typically[53] based on formal agreements, such as concordats and state-church treaties, and entails the right of the churches to veto the appointment of theology lecturers and to co-determine the curriculum. The so-called »*Nihil obstat*« procedure allows that the churches either approve of or object to the appointment of a university lecturer on religious grounds, i.e. on grounds of his or her teachings or conduct of life.[54]By the same token, the churches have the opportunity to veto curricula and examination regulations.[55] However, it is far from clear to what extent the State's duty to cooperate, as specifically spelt out in some state-church treaties and some of the federal States' legal systems, is also constitutionally entrenched by the Basic Law – a pertinent question regarding the plans to introduce Islamic studies.

Let me suggest three points on that issue. *First*, as already indicated, it is not only the subjective right of self-determination under art. 137 (3) Weimar Consti-

50 *Jeand'Heur/Korioth* (n 15), § 308; *Link* (n 28), 488 seqq.

51 BVerfGE 122, 89 (112); *Katrin Janke*, Institutionalisierter Islam an staatlichen Hochschulen, Frankfurt a.M. 2005, 128 seq.; *Jakob Julius Nolte*, Islamische Theologie an deutschen Hochschulen?, Die Öffentliche Verwaltung 2008, 129 (133); cf. the argument based on customary law put forward by *Alexander Hollerbach*,Theologische Fakultäten und staatliche Pädagogische Hochschulen, HbStKR II (n 28), 549 (565 seqq.).

52 *Ott* (n 29), 121 seqq.

53 Some examples for informal agreements are given by *Hollerbach* (n 51) 557 seqq., 591 seqq.

54 The procedure applies during the tenure procedure; but the churches also have the power to revoke their »*Nihil obstat*« retroactively. The corresponding rights are spelled out in the concordats and state-church treaties, but also in some of the States' constitutions, cf. *Janke* (n 51), 147 seq.; *Hollerbach* (n 51) 571 seqq.; *Ott* (n 29), 40 seqq.

55 Cf., for example, Art. 5 des Vertrags zwischen dem Land Nordrhein-Westfalen mit dem Heiligen Stuhl of 18th August 1984, GVBl. NRW, 582; Art. IV des Vertrags zwischen dem Land Nordrhein-Westfalen und der Evangelischen Kirche im Rheinland, der Evangelischen Kirche von Westfalen und der Lippischen Landeskirche of 29th March 1984, GVBl. NRW, 593; § 80 s. 4 para. 2 Hochschulgesetz NRW.

tution, but also an objective neutrality principle which prevents the State from unilaterally organising theological studies. So far, German case law and scholarly writings have concentrated on the right of self-determination, which may be explained by the fact that the principle of neutrality is nowhere stated explicitly in the Constitution, that German legal tradition favours subjective rights over mere objective principles and that the Christian churches had invoked their rights (to withdraw their »*Nihil obstat*«[56] or to veto the introduction of theological studies[57]) before the courts. But the Basic Law also contains an objective principle of neutrality implying that the State is incompetent to fulfil religious tasks.[58] Thus, the State may not unilaterally introduce theological studies even if it is unclear whether Muslim societies holding rights under art. 137 (3) Weimar Constitution exist. *Second*, the scope of the right of self-determination depends on the religious community's theological conceptions. It comprises, in any event, the power to define the community's teachings and – as the case may be – to determine whether the teachers qualify from a religious (not an academic or pedagogical) point of view.[59] As a consequence, they also have to be granted if the State introduces Islamic theology.[60]

Third, pragmatic solutions can and must be found with regard to Islamic theology which may differ from the existing models of cooperation. The German Council of Science and Humanities, in its recommendations of January 2010, suggested to set up advisory committees, composed of representatives of Muslim religious communities and of non-organised Muslims, and to entrust them which the decisions on religious issues.[61] A more detailed model of how such an advisory committee could look like has been worked out at the University of Münster.[62] This model allows for both the Muslims belonging to one of the four major national Muslim organisations (representing, by membership, less than 10% of a population of around 4 million Muslims)[63] as well as the majority of non-

56 BVerfGE 122, 89 (105 seqq.) (Lüdemann).

57 BVerwGE 101, 309 (311 seqq.).

58 *Ott* (n 29), 125 seq.

59 See *Martin Heckel*, Die theologischen Fakultäten im weltlichen Verfassungsstaat, Tübingen 1986, 94 seqq., 220 seqq.; *Hollerbach* (n 51) 568 seqq.; *Ott* (n 29), 49, 55, 181 seq.

60 *Martin Heckel*, Religionsunterricht für Muslime? Juristenzeitung 1999, 741 (755); *Janke* (n 51), 151; *Nolte* (n 51), 136.

61 Empfehlungen zur Weiterentwicklung von Theologien und religionsbezogenen Wissenschaften an deutschen Hochschulen, Berlin, 29. Januar 2010, Drs. 9678-10, 80 seqq. (<http://www.wissenschaftsrat.de/veroeffentlichungen/veroeffentlichungen-ab-1980/>).

62 *Christian Walter/Janbernd Oebbecke/Antje von Ungern-Sternberg/Moritz Indenhuck*, Ursprünglicher Entwurf für eine Ordnung zur Organisation eines Beirates für Islamische Theologie, in: Walter et al. (n 33).

63 The four umbrella organisations composing the 'Coordination Council of Muslims in Germany' (n 31) claim to have 280,000 members. Recent estimates on the total amount of the Muslim population in Germany amount to 3.8 to 4.3 million, for this figure cf.

organised Muslims, to be represented. Furthermore, it would not matter whether the four national Muslim organisations joined in the »Coordination Council of Muslims living in Germany«, which cooperate with the State, effectively constitute religious societies under art. 137 (3) Weimar Constitution or whether they represent the many local mosque communities which certainly qualify as religious societies. The advisory committee model rests on the assumption that the cooperation between State and religious communities does not imply direct or exclusive cooperation with one religious community only. Instead, for the purpose of organising Muslim theology, several religious communities unite and delegate certain aspects of their respective right of self-determination to the advisory committee, whose members are elected by the religious communities. They thereby exercise their right to religious self-determination under to art. 137 (3) Weimar Constitution which includes the choice to opt for this form of cooperation. The objective principle of neutrality is upheld as well since the decisions concerning religious teachings do not have to be accounted for by the State, but can be attributed to religious communities.[64] It is true, however, that the proposal has met political resistance from the churches.[65] They probably fear that taking into account organised members and non-organised believers alike might, one day, also affect their claim to speak for all believers.

5. Conclusion

Religious pluralisation, above all the growing presence of Muslim communities in Great Britain and Germany, poses a challenge to the existing models of state-religion relations. From a *legal* point of view, newcomer and minority religions are to be treated on an equal footing. Thus, Muslims should have the same right to enjoy and to provide for religious education and instruction as the established religious communities have. From a *political* point of view, this necessity for

Bundesamt für Migration und Flüchtlinge, *Sonja Haug/Stephanie Müssig/Anja Stichs*, Muslimisches Leben in Deutschland. Im Auftrag der Deutschen Islam Konferenz, 321, <http://www.bamf.de/SharedDocs/Anlagen/DE/Publikationen/Forschungsberichte/ fb06-muslimisches-leben.html>.

64 According to *Ott* (n 29), 162 seqq., the unilateral decision by the State on how to organise such an advisory committee already infringes upon the principle of neutrality and the right to religious self-determination. However, the advisory committee might be created by a formal agreement between the State and the religious communities. Furthermore, even if the advisory committee is set up unilaterally, the religious communities *consent* to cooperate with the State, thereby exercising their religious self-determination and preserving state neutrality.

65 *Hans Michael Heinig*, Ein Staatsislam wäre grundgesetzwidrig, Frankfurter Allgemeine Zeitung of 30th March 2010, 29; *Michael Indenhuck/Antje von Ungern-Sternberg*, Dokumentation der Diskussion, in: Walter et al. (n 33) 61 seqq.

equal treatment might result in a challenge for traditional forms of state-religion cooperation, leaving essentially two options: On the one hand, scepticism about close state-religion cooperation in general and mistrust of Muslim communities in particular might lead to an overall *reduction* of this form of cooperation: In Great Britain, faith schools and universities of all religions could lose their state funding. In Germany, all forms of religious instruction and theology could lose their place within state institutions. On the other hand, the existing models of state-religion cooperation could be *extended* to newcomer and minority religions whose particularities would have to be accommodated for. It seems that the latter solution better reflects the advantages and opportunities of religious pluralisation and of a wide understanding of freedom of religion.

VIII. THE LEGAL STATUS OF MUSLIM COMMUNITIES IN ENGLISH LAW – Julian Rivers

1. Assimilation to a Church-State Model

The first, and perhaps the most important, point to make about the legal status of Muslim communities in English law is that the law itself does not use these categories.

English law does not have an equivalent to the German concept of *Körperschaft des öffentlichen Rechts*, still less the Austrian distinction between *Religionsgesellschaften* and *Bekenntnisgemeinschaften*. There are no concordats with the Holy See to give rise to differential legal positions as in Spain or Italy. The idea of »status« in the sense of a distinctive bundle of related rights which may be enjoyed by different religious groups through a single entry point, such as registration or agreement, is alien to Anglo-American legal cultures. Rather, the law of organized religions developed first by way of private law analogy to internal ecclesiastical law using doctrines of trusts (1689-1831), and then a gradual and piecemeal separating out of secular governmental functions from ecclesiastical ones (1832-1870).[1] In the course of this largely mid-19th century development, the registration of places of worship stopped being a compulsory requirement to avoid the criminal penalties otherwise imposed on non-established religions. Instead, it became an optional access point to a small set of public religious functions (e.g. conduct of marriage and relief from local taxation) now available on a plural basis to all religions. The only other possible candidate for »public status« is the distinction between charitable and non-charitable religion.[2] The most significant consequence of this lies in tax law.

Secondly, and apart from some very rare exceptions, the law does not use the category of »Muslim« or »Islamic. It uses much broader terms, most commonly now »religion«, but in earlier times and in other contexts, terms such as »worship« and »ritual« or broader categories such as »charity«. These terms were well fixed long before Islam had anything more than a tiny presence in the country.

Thirdly, the law does not relate to communities as such. Rather, legal persons, both natural and artificial, are present within communities. There are mosques, with mosque committees to run them and imams appointed to teach in them. There are *halal* butchers and *hajj* travel agencies. There are representative bodies

1 Julian Rivers, *The Law of Organized Religions: between establishment and secularism* (Oxford: OUP, 2010), ch. 1.
2 *Ibid.*, ch. 5.

such as the Muslim Council of Britain. But religious communities as such do not have a law that is recognized by the law of the state, nor do they have any personality. And there is substantial public opposition to any suggestion in this direction. The use of the term »Muslim Parliament« to describe a 1992 initiative by Dr. Kalim Siddiqui to establish a formal consultative body after the Salman Rushdie affair was deliberately provocative and arguably a public relations mistake. As the response to the Archbishop of Canterbury's 2008 lecture showed, there is even greater hostility to any suggestion that there should be Islamic courts of compulsory jurisdiction.[3]Thus community life may be continued as a matter of social reality, but the legal system reconstructs this according to its own conceptual scheme.

Underlying this conceptual scheme is a particular understanding of religious liberty and equality. We can see quite clearly a total rejection of anything resembling the Ottoman-style *millet* system of rule, whereby religious liberty is liberty to live in the community of your birth and religious equality is self-government for religious communities fulfilling a wide range of social and governmental functions. Ironically, elements of this *millet* model were adopted by British governments in colonial contexts such as India, particularly in matters of family and family property law.[4] Some of this colonial legacy lies behind ongoing Muslim requests for Islamic courts. But as far as the domestic situation is concerned, liberty and equality have been conceived narrowly and individualistically. Religious liberty is the right to adopt and practise a religion of one's choosing, which includes membership of a religious group, and religious equality is the right to inhabit a reasonably neutral public sphere in which religious identity is either muted or disregarded.

The elements of this conception of religious liberty and equality are connected with (1) a growing separation, or disentanglement, of church and state; (2) substantial autonomy or self-government, not for communities defined by birth or identity, but for religious organizations like churches or mosques; (3) belief in the possibility of the secular, or in other words, the possibility of transcending religious difference in the public sphere in the name of a common humanity and a

3 Rowan Williams, 'Civil and Religious Law in England: a Religious Perspective' (2008) 10 *Ecclesiastical Law Journal* 262. Academic responses include Lord Phillips of Worth Matravers, 'Equality before the Law', a speech given at the East London Muslim Centre on 3 July 2008, reproduced in various places including (2008) 161 *Law and Justice* 75; Samia Bano, 'In Pursuit of Religious and Legal Diversity: A response to the Archbishop of Canterbury and the 'Sharia Debate' in Britain' (2008) 10 *Ecclesiastical Law Journal* 283; Adam Tucker, 'The Archbishop's unsatisfactory legal pluralism' [2008] *Public Law* 463.

4 See, e.g., Asaf A.A. Fyzee, *Outlines of Muhammadan Law*, 4th edn., (New Dehli: OUP, 1974); Wael B. Hallaq, *An Introduction to Islamic Law* (Cambridge: CUP, 2009), ch. 7.

common justice. It should be noted that this idea of the secular occupies a studied ambivalence on the value of religion. An agenda of »privatization of religion« could be adopted by those who were hostile to its influence, or at least the influence of its organized forms of expression (anti-clericism), as well as by those who sought to defend the purity of its expression by protecting it from entanglement with government (anti-Erastianism). The quip that in France the separation of church and state was carried through to protect the state from the church, while in America it was carried through to protect the church from the state carries more than a grain of truth, and it is arguable that politically, as well as geographically, the United Kingdom lies between the two.

With hindsight, we can see that this distinctively »Western« conception of liberty and equality is closely connected with the historical unfolding and questioning of Christian social and political forms.[5] It emerges in an intellectual space dominated by Christianity and its rejection. And we may loosely ascribe the relatively minor public role given to churches in the Anglo-American strand of this legal tradition, as compared to continental European expressions, by its predominantly Protestant forms.

We can see the impact of this intellectual space very clearly in the institutional forms of British Judaism.[6] Judaism is the only non-Christian religion with a significant public presence before the mid-20th century. When the Board of Deputies of British Jews was formed in 1760 to contain representatives of all Jewish groups in order to promote and defend the rights of British Jews, it was modelled on an earlier precedent, the Dissenting Deputies of 1732. This likewise had as its principal task the lobbying for the repeal of discriminatory legislation against protestant non-Anglicans. Likewise the Office of the Chief Rabbi and the »United Synagogues« were the brainchild of Rabbi Nathan Adler in a deliberate attempt to strengthen the social and legal acceptability of British Jewry by adopting the institutional forms of Anglicanism.

Of course, this is not the whole story of the status of Judaism in English law. Having gained social acceptance (and indeed government gratitude for its heroic care of wave after wave of Jewish immigrants in the late 19th and early 20th centuries), British Jewry was able to win a few legal concessions, for example around animal slaughter methods and Sunday trading. Here we find little islands of community self-regulation. In addition, the formalities concerning the marriage of Jews have largely been excepted from state regulation, as they are for

5 See the classic treatment by Harold J. Berman, *Law and Revolution*, 2 vols., (Harvard: Harvard UP, 1983 and 2003).

6 Cecil Roth, *A History of the Jews in England* (Oxford: Clarendon Press, 1941); David S Katz, *The Jews in the History of England* (Oxford: OUP, 1994).

Quakers – a legacy of the days in which marriage was regulated by ecclesiastical, not state, law. And just as any parties to a contract can consent to arbitrate before a private tribunal, so one can seek a religious arbitration according to religious law.

To some extent, the same process of assimilation can be observed on the part of Islam as well.[7] From the start, mosques could form as voluntary charitable organisations, benefitting from central and local tax exemptions. There might be some practical obstacles, such as finding enough people with the knowledge to register a charity, or run a committee and so on, and some initial resistance on aesthetic (planning law) grounds, but in general there was no question of principle with a major monotheistic world religion taking the same legal form as other non-established Christian and Jewish groups. Imams and clerics too could benefit from a similar employment status as ministers of Christian churches. The courts rather assumed that they were similar.[8] And again there was no problem in principle with the recognition of Muslim chaplains in public institutions such as the armed forces, prisons and hospitals, as well as provision for special dietary and dress needs. Admittedly, the practical problems here were rather greater. It is inconvenient to arrange a chaplaincy or a special diet for a new minority. Does one really have to bother? And this did result in resistance to accommodating personal religious requirements. At the edges of this resistance were some more principled concerns about the reasons for uniformity of provision – particularly in relation to dress. If there is reason to require motorcycle riders to wear helmets, then there is reason to require all of them to do so, regardless of their faith.[9] But the boundaries had already been pushed in the 19th century by Roman Catholics in relation to chaplaincies, in the early 20th century by Jews in relation to diet and holy days, and in the mid-20th century by Sikhs in relation to dress and symbols. So to a large extent Muslims were able to fit into legal exceptions already won by other minorities. And there is clear evidence that in doing so, the character of British Islam was to some extent fashioned by its surrounding broader religious-cultural expectations.[10]

7 For an overview, see Julian Rivers, 'The Legal Status of Islam in Great Britain' [2006] *Derecho Y Religión* 144.

8 *Khan v Oxford City Mosque Society*, unreported, 23 July 1998; see generally Rivers, *op. cit.* n. 1, ch. 4.

9 Brian Barry, *Culture and Equality* (Cambridge: Polity Press, 2001) contains the most trenchant account along these lines.

10 See, in respect of prison chaplaincies, James A. Beckford and Sophie Gilliat, *Religion in Prisons: Equal rites in a multi-faith society* (Cambridge: CUP, 1998).

2. Equality, Multiculturalism and Security

The context in which we have to consider the current law is vastly more complex. From a purely sociological perspective it is no longer the case that the British population is more-or-less Christian.[11] For much of the 20th century there was a substantial English majority expressing some allegiance to the established church, and a significant active minority split roughly equally between Anglicanism, Roman Catholicism and other Protestant churches (the demography in Wales, Scotland and Northern Ireland is clearly different in each case, but still almost entirely »Christian« in some sense). Rather we have now a three-way split, with Christian identity becoming residual for many and giving way to clearer and more confident expressions of atheism or agnosticism, and on top of that, the rise of new religious minorities, by far the largest of which is Islam. One recent Government estimate puts the Muslim population at 2.4 million or 4%.[12]

Towards the end of the 1980s, Muslims started to make arguments against current legal distinctions in terms which ought to have been politically acceptable, but which were covertly or even overtly resisted. The first, and most obvious, of these was perhaps more symbolic than practical. It was the response to Salman Rushdie's publication in 1988 of Satanic Verses, not in terms of book burning and *fatwa*, but in an immediate legal action to secure a public prosecution for blasphemy. It did not take the lawyers long to work out that the ancient common law offence of blasphemous libel only protected elements common to the Christian religion, of which the special status of Muhammad is not one.[13] Perhaps more surprisingly, the enforcement organs of the European Convention on Human Rights managed to create space for a Christian law of blasphemy by finding that the state had a right to criminalise blasphemy if it wished, but no individual had a right to secure such a prosecution.[14] Where, then was religious equality? So the Muslim campaign to criminalise Satanic Verses gave new life to an old debate within the Law Commission from the mid-1980s.[15] A majority had argued on good libertarian grounds for the abolition of blasphemy as a criminal offence, and a minority had argued for its restatement as a general religious hate speech law.

11 James A. Beckford et al., *Review of the Evidence Base on Faith Communities* (Office of the Deputy Prime Minister, 2006).

12 Office for National Statistics, *Labour Force Survey*, 2008.

13 *R v Bow Street Magistrates Court ex parte Choudhury* [1991] 1 Q.B. 429.

14 *Choudhury v United Kingdom*, no. 17439/90.

15 Law Commission, *Report on Offences against Religion and Public Worship*, no. 145 (1985).

The arguments around blasphemy and religious hate speech were not the only equality-based disturbances to legal conventions. When the race relations legislation was created in the 1960s and 70s it used as one of the protected characteristics the idea of »ethnicity«. In an important case involving a Sikh schoolboy who had been expelled for failing to comply with a uniform requirement to remove his turban, the House of Lords held in 1983 that ethnicity embraced those religions with a strong racial component such as Judaism and Sikhism, but not those more universal religions such as Islam and Christianity.[16] This meant that discrimination in employment, education and the public provision of goods and services was not unlawful unless a specifically racial component (e.g. Pakistani, Bengali) could be identified. For Muslims for whom the religious component of their identity was more significant, this was perceived as an inequality. Again, this was disturbing, because underneath the resistance to this apparently plausible argument was a sense that religion *shouldn't* matter that much. It shouldn't be the subject of legal protection in the same way as race. The one place in the United Kingdom where we did have religious equality legislation was Northern Ireland, where tribal religious affiliation was exactly the problem we were trying to resolve!

Then there was the issue of faith-schools.[17] The United Kingdom has a strong tradition of independent (fee-paying) schooling, and there was never any significant legal problem with the creation of independent Islamic schools. Again, the argument was one of equality. There are also substantial numbers of church-based faith schools in the public sector, yet the Conservative government until 1997 always managed to resist cases for the recognition of new faith-based Islamic schools. Behind that resistance, was in many cases a sense that faith-based public education was a mere historical legacy of late 19th and early 20th century compromises. »Faith« in this context had largely become attenuated and dissolved in a general mildly-culturally-Christian background. In that sense a state-maintained church school was not really a faith school. In any case, it was not obvious that their number should be increased.

The landslide election of New Labour in 1997 with an agenda of social inclusion, constitutional reform, equality and multiculturalism brought about a marked change of approach towards Islam. This came to be expressed not only in the Human Rights Act 1998, with its rights of religious liberty and non-discrimination, but also in a series of legislative acts to promote equality.[18] In

16 *Mandla v Dowell Lee* [1983] 2 A.C. 548.

17 See Rivers, *op. cit.* n. 1, ch. 8.

18 The legal developments from 2003 onwards have now been codified in the (substantial) Equality Act 2010.

part, this was in response to the EU Equal Treatment Directive, passed on the basis of the new power in art. 13 Treaty of Amsterdam to take action to remove discrimination on various new grounds, including religion. No sooner had this new politics of multiculturalism started to take root, then the disaster of 9/11, and the London and Madrid bombings occurred to shake it to its core.

The legal response can be seen most dramatically in the Anti-Terrorism, Crime and Security Bill that was rapidly introduced into Parliament in late 2001. As well as new and remarkable powers to detain terrorist (i.e. Islamist) suspects, it contained new offences of incitement to religious hatred and religiously aggravated public order offences. In other words it accepted the Muslim argument that the old racial public order offences were inadequate. The hate speech law was too controversial at the time and was dropped; the religiously aggravated public order offences survived. But the religious hate speech offence was later reintroduced and has now effectively replaced the old Christian law of blasphemy.[19]

From a political perspective, 9/11 and the London and Madrid bombings, as well as the wars in Iraq and Afghanistan have brought religion generally and Islam in particular to a new level of public consciousness, but they have done something else much more radical. A generation ago, when people talked about »religion« they meant Christianity and they assumed that other religions could be more or less assimilated to its model. It was broadly a good thing, if not to everyone's taste. Today when people talk about religion one suspects they have Islam in mind, and it is not necessarily good. If anything, religion is now a problem.

From a legal perspective, new abstract rights to religious liberty and equality have raised the expectations of all groups while at the same time exposing the growing tensions between Christian, Muslim and atheist conceptions. This is the context in which we have to consider the question of the legal status of Muslim communities.

3. Developments in the »status« of organized religions

It has already been suggested that the idea of »status« is not familiar to English lawyers. Nevertheless, we can identify a set of rights available to organized religions. Here is one list:

19 Racial and Religious Hatred Act 2006; Criminal Justice and Immigration Act 2008, s. 79.

- right to private entity status: the right to legal personality, to own property, to enter into contractual relations, to employ workers;
- right of any private or commercial organisation to adopt a religious ethos;
- relief from local taxation for places of worship;
- relief from central taxation for charities, including those that advance religion;
- freedom from governmental financial regulation;
- freedom from governmental planning control for internal work to religious buildings;
- right to conduct marriages with civil effect;
- right to engage in ritual slaughter;
- right to provide chaplaincies in public institutions (armed forces, prisons, hospitals);
- right to operate schools, both insidethe state-funded system and privately;
- right to deliver public welfare services under contract with government;
- right to participate in formal public consultation bodies in government and the media.

Over the last ten years there have been two broad developments in the law. The first is a gain in formal recognition and collaboration between organized religions and the state; the second is a loss of autonomy on the part of organized religions. The question is whether these two developments are connected with each other, and whether they have any particular relationship with Islam.

(a) Gains in public sector collaboration

The last ten years have seen a substantial rise in the number of non-Christian chaplaincies in public institutions such as the armed forces, prisons and hospitals.[20] At one level there is nothing new or odd about this: the first Jewish army chaplain was appointed in 1892. Buddhist, Hindu, Muslim and Sikh chaplains have now also been appointed albeit as civil servants, not officers. In that sense there is still an Anglican dominance within the armed forces reflecting a residual establishment. What is interesting when one considers the other two contexts, prisons and hospitals, is the way in which the Anglican chaplains are being conceived less as first among equals, rather as one among equals. The focus is shifting gradually from the Prison Services Chaplaincy to the Religious Consultative Services, which is a body established on the basis of formal relationships be-

20 Full account in Rivers, *op. cit.* n. 1, ch. 7.

tween the Government and representatives of seven major religions. Similarly in 2002 the Multi-faith Group for Healthcare Chaplaincy was formed. The Prisons Religion Manual sets out in ever-greater detail what the requirements of different religions are, and in 2003 the National Health Service published its own best practice guidance, »Meeting the religious and spiritual needs of patients and staff«. Increasingly such internal documentation presents the main branches of Christianity in parallel to other religions. There is thus an equalizing of religions both at the level of structures and policy guidance.

This clearer expression of multicultural policy has been accompanied by a professionalization of chaplaincy services, according to which chaplains are seen less as representatives of religious organizations and more as appointed and employed public sector workers, subject to all the techniques of modern management.

Education is probably the most well-known and controversial example of New Labour's willingness to bring ethnic minority faith schools within the maintained sector. This has been most apparent in the case of Muslim state schools, of which there were none prior to 1997, and there are now around 10. What is less well-known are the accompanying legal changes whereby the role of religion in education has been clarified and constrained.[21] Once equality law was extended to cover religion or belief in education and employment, a series of exceptions became necessary to allow schools with a specific religious ethos to continue to preserve that ethos. This has applied to both the maintained and the independent sectors. So there is now an official designation procedure whereby schools identify their religious ethos. This requires formal consultation with sponsoring bodies within the different religions concerned. Designation »switches on« the ability to prefer staff and pupils on grounds of religion, and to structure the curriculum and religious worship accordingly.

Recent litigation concerning the admissions policy of the JFS (formerly the Jews' Free School) in London illustrates the limits of these exceptions well. Being oversubscribed, the school prefers Jewish pupils. In working out whether a potential pupil is Jewish, it defers to the judgment of the court of the Chief Rabbi. The Chief Rabbi, who is orthodox, takes the view that Jewishness is a matter of matrilineal descent, which in cases where the mother converted, raises questions about the validity of the conversion. A number of practising Jewish boys were not admitted on account of flaws in their mothers' conversions, while non-practising Jews are often admitted. That survived challenge in the High Court, but the Court of Appeal and Supreme Court both held that it represented

21 Full account in Rivers, *op. cit.* n. 1, ch. 8.

unlawful discrimination on grounds of ethnicity.[22] One may be religious, but what it means to be religious is now carefully confined. It is not allowed to have anything to do with race.

The underlying tension was exposed in 2007 when the Muslim Council of Britain published *Towards greater Understanding: meeting the needs of Muslim pupils in state schools*. It sets out what a school would need to do if it were to take social inclusion for Muslims seriously: provision for modest dress, including sportswear that covers completely, permission for beards and religious amulets, halal meals, provision for prayers including private washing facilities, special exemptions for Ramadan such as refraining from sport, sex education that respects Islamic morals, celebration of Islamic festivals, segregated sports, no communal showering, no dance, no use of religious images in art or worship, teaching of Arabic, no raffles, no alcohol and much more. The document exposes the extent to which the current law of education is still locked into a Christian paradigm, in which »religion« only affects specifically religious instruction and collective worship. That is the old division of »church« and»state« within the school: there is religious education (i.e. instruction and worship) which is voluntary and not subject to Government control and there is secular education which is compulsory and state-regulated.

The Government has also strongly encouraged more partnership and funding at the local level in welfare service.[23] 2004 and 2008 saw two major Government reports on working together with faith communities, the latter of which adopted a phrase of Lord Sacks, the Chief Rabbi.[24] It has a clear agenda of encouraging and funding welfare projects which include elements of interfaith cooperation. At the same time, the legal environment in which welfare services may be offered is narrowing down the ways in which religion can affect provision. The clearest example of this is the impact on Catholic adoption agencies. After an initial transition period, these were prevented from operating if they were unwilling to consider same-sex couples as potential adoptive parents.[25] While there is a relatively wide scope for religious pluralism in education and welfare services, there is much less scope for pluralism in sexual ethics. Or rather, just as the Supreme Court in the JFS case defined religion as different from ethnicity, so also what it means to be religious is partly defined by excluding sexual ethics from its scope.

22 *R (E) v Governing Body of JFS* [2010] 2 WLR 153.

23 Full account in Rivers, *op. cit.* n. 1, ch. 9.

24 Home Office Faith Commnities Unit, *Working Together: Co-operation between Government and Faith Communities* (Feb. 2004); Department for Communities and Local Government, *Face to Face and Side by Side: a framework for partnership in our multi faith society* (July 2008).

25 See *Catholic Care (Diocese of Leeds) v Charity Commission* [2010] EWHC 520 (Ch.).

Catholic adoption agencies can be Catholic in some sense of the word, but they cannot act on the basis of a Catholic family and sexual ethic.

Associated with the promotion of faith-based welfare, is the recent growth of multi-faith consultation bodies. Individual government departments have always maintained links with religious bodies in the rare areas of overlap between religion and the state. For example, the DTI has worked for a long time with the Board of Deputies of British Jews over policing the exemptions to Sunday trading legislation for Jews. Then in 1992, the Inner Cities Religious Council was formed to include representatives of the five largest religions in urban regeneration projects. This got honourable mention in the 2000 Urban White Paper and an indirect reference in the 2001 Labour party manifesto. In 2006 it was relaunched as the Faith Communities Consultative Council and based in the new Department for Communities and Local Government. It is chaired by a Parliamentary Under-Secretary of State and contains representatives from nine main religions. »Communities« no longer means just »local communities«, it also includes »faith communities«.

Even more significant is the rapid rise of local and regional multi faith forums, and their funding by Government.There are now ten regional multi-faith forums in England and Wales which typically have as their role the provision of information, training, consultation and input into regional governmental structures. All of these have been established since 2000. Some are supported by the Church of England and some are independent. The Faiths Forum for London and the South-East England Faith Forum are a result of recent Government initiatives, and the equivalent bodies for the West Midlands and Wales are also closely associated with Government. In the most recent listing of over 200 local inter-faith or multi-faith bodies in England and Wales, about 60% say that »advice and assistance to public bodies« and »acting as a consultation forum for local government« are two of their roles.[26] About 30% of these groups are actually funded by local authorities.

Thus the last decade has seen renewed forms of cooperation and collaboration between religions and the state. At the same time, the conditions on which such activity takes place have been tightened, and in that sense there has been an extension of a public secular ethos into areas of religious life where hitherto there was a greater degree of autonomy. That loss of autonomy may seem an inevitable price to pay for inclusion in the public sector, but it has also been accompanied by a loss of autonomy in the internal sphere of religious life as well.

26 Inter Faith Network for the UK, *Inter Faith Organisations in the UK: A Directory*, 2009.

(b) Losses of internal autonomy

The extension of equality laws in the private and commercial sphere to grounds of religion results in an immediate loss of autonomy. Previously, the law did not need to create a category of the »religious organization« or its equivalent. Rather, any group, association, company or organization could be more-or-less religious. However, duties of non-discrimination require exceptions for the obvious cases (churches, mosques etc.) and must therefore draw lines around the difficult cases. In fact, equality law is now working with three categories: organized religion, religious organization and organization with a religious ethos.[27] The effect of the new equality law is thus to transfer the right to determine the limits to how one should or may express one's religion in the collective life of the group from the group to the state.

However, even in the case of the most central expressions of organized religion, there has been a systematic loss of autonomy.

Religious bodies, including Islamic groups, are generally understood by the law to be formed on the basis of an unincorporated assocation which holds its property either by way of a trust or a related incorporated company. When such a body splits, who gets the property? The 19th and early 20th century case-law, which is substantial, is based on two principles. First, the party maintaining the historic doctrinal position of the religion is favoured over theological innovators. Secondly, the courts will defer to any decision made in accordance with proper internal processes. The leading case (which is actually Scottish but good in English law) is *Overtoun v Free Church of Scotland*.[28] It involved a head-on clash between those two principles.

Thus the courts have historically tried to decide the property dispute in accordance with the internal doctrine and government of the body in question. Complete autonomy might indicate that it should not be resolved at all, but deference to internal law is the next best thing. Two recent developments are worth noting. They are both illustrated by a recent case in the High Court involving a split in the Russian Orthodox Church in the UK.[29] That split was over whether the church should be under the oversight of the Patriarchate of Moscow or of Constantinople. First of all, the judge avoided the question of the internal order of the church – the question of who has authority to make decisions of this kind – and simply construed the most relevant clause of the trust deed. This reflects a grow-

27 See, e.g. and respectively, Equality Act 2010, sched. 9, para.2; Equality Act 2010, s. 202(4); Equality Act 2010, sched.9, para. 3.

28 [1904] A.C. 515.

29 *Dean v Burne* [2009] EWHC 1250 (Ch).

ing approach within the United States known as »neutral principles«.[30] The court refuses to take evidence on the doctrine or government of the church, but instead looks at the formal legal documents, whether they reflect the self-understanding of the church in question or not. Secondly, the judge floated the possibility of a scheme *cy-près* to divide up the property between the disputing parties. Since the Charities Act 1993 the Charity Commission and the courts have had an expanded jurisdiction to approve such schemes, and they have done so in cases of schism – most notably in the case of a dispute over ownership of a Hindu temple in *Varsani v Jesani.*[31]

Older attempts to understand and follow the internal law of the religious body derived from a certain judicial sympathy with, and understanding of, the problem of schism. There was a respect for self-government in disentangling the property affairs of a religious group. The new approach of fairness »from the outside« treats the internal law as unintelligible or inexplicable.

A loss of autonomy can also be seen in the recent treatment of the employment status of ministers of religion.[32] At common law, ministers of religion were treated as office-holders, that is they enjoyed a position to which financial and proprietory benefits were attached. They could not be deprived of that position except in accordance with the internal law of their religious body and the rules of natural justice: the duties to give a fair hearing and to avoid bias. From at least the 1860s the internal law of the body was understood to form a type of contract.

In a series of cases in the 20th century, the courts found that there was no contract with a minister of religion at all, let alone a contract of service. The Court of Appeal reached the same conclusion in the case of the Methodist Church in 1984,[33] and the House of Lords said more or less the same thing of the Presbyterian Church of Wales in 1986.[34] In the closing decade of the 20th century it became an almost irrebuttable presumption in the Employment Tribunals that ministers of religion – of any religion, including Islam – had no legal relationship with their religious body whatsoever.

That, of course, is the end-point of religious autonomy. Remedies are purely internal to the organization. It was never actually the position of English law, and the 20th century cases largely ignored the earlier law on office-holding. They were not wrong to do this, because the litigants in these more recent cases were

30 *United States v Mary Elizabeth Blue Hull Memorial Presbyterian Church* (1969) 393 US 440; *Jones v Wolf* (1979) 443 US 595.

31 [1999] Ch. 219.

32 Full account in Rivers, *op. cit.* n. 1, ch. 4.

33 *President of the Methodist Conference v Parfitt* [1984] QB 368.

34 *Davies v Presbyterian Church of Wales* [1986] 1 WLR 323.

not simply trying to enforce the internal law of their church. What they were trying to do was import the developing standards of secular employment law into their religious organizations before the organizations themselves had signed up. The courts would not let them.

Then, in 2003, the Employment Equality Regulations came into force. These extend beyond employment in the narrow sense to office-holding, and the explanatory memorandum suggests that they cover ministers of religion. In fact, the Regulations give rise to a whole host of questions as to exactly which positions within religious bodies are covered, and if they are covered whether there is any relevant exception. The point is that the relationship between a minister and his or her religious body is no longer simply a matter for the internal rules of the body in question.

In 2005, the House of Lords decided *Percy v Board of National Mission of the Church of Scotland.*[35] Helen Percy had resigned under pressure after having had an affair with a parishioner. She wanted to argue unlawful discrimination on grounds of sex. As she went up through the court system the answer came back: internal spiritual matter – nothing to do with us. And then the House of Lords decided by a 4-1 majority that an associate minister in the Church of Scotland was appointed under a contract »personally to execute any work or labour« within the scope of the Sex Discrimination Act 1975 and the jurisdiction of the Employment Tribunal. The impact of the judgments in *Percy* can be seen in the 2008 decision of the Court of Appeal in *New Testament Church of God v Stewart.*[36] In that case the court held that the claimant minister was employed by his church under a contract of service. The court accepted that the effect of *Percy* was to remove the presumption that there is no intention to create legal relations, but at the same time recognized the relevance of religious doctrinal considerations to the factual question whether there was such an intention. However, the judges' treatment of this point varied slightly. It is not at all clear how this will settle down in practice.

Thus we have moved rapidly from a position in which religious bodies were autonomous in the terms and conditions under which their ministers worked, to a position in which they are subject to the general employment law, with its growing body of standards and expectations, and its rather constrained acceptance of religious difference.

35 [2006] 2 A.C. 28.
36 [2008] I.C.R. 282.

A third major example of the loss of autonomy can be found in the regulation of charities.[37] Trusts for the advancement of religion in ways which confer a public benefit are charitable. Until recently the law reflected the assumption that any lawful religion is better than none, and that more religion is better than less. So trusts for the advancement of religion were presumed to confer a public benefit. The religion in question still needed to be demonstrably advanced: so closed monastic orders or purely private rites failed to qualify as charitable. But so long as there was some public access or contact with the religion, there was charity.

Under the Charities Act 2006, the conferment of a public benefit is no longer to be presumed. Of course, after an initial flurry of consultation, matters have settled down more or less where they were: the Charity Commission is not suddenly going to start finding large numbers of religious charities non-charitable. The point is that the direction of travel has changed. This can be seen in the 2008 statutory guidance of the Charity Commission. There is a tendency to see religions in monolithic terms. This is best captured in a careless limitation of charitable status to »recognised« religions, but is expressed in a variety of ways: hostility to distinctive individual positions within religions, suspicion of purposes based around only a few tenets of a religion, a limitation of relevant social welfare activities to those required by »specific obligations« of the religion; worry about the »abuse or misuse of religious teachings«.

Furthermore, until the reforms brought about by the Charity Act 1960, the law substantially protected religious groups from the regulatory oversight of the Charity Commissioners. The details of this are rather complex, but religious bodies were deliberately kept free to run their own affairs. In principle, this was ended by the Charities Act 1960, but not in practice, because regulations were immediately passed to except the major Christian religious denominations which had internal regulatory structures from Charity Commissioner oversight. A similar approach is still in place in respect of internal changes to buildings of historic significance (the »ecclesiastical exemption«). The major Christian denominations in possession of such buildings have internal processes of approval for works which parallel the regulatory regimes of local government.

In respect of charities, a Strategy Review Unit report recommended the staged abolition of financial self-regulation.[38] One of the reasons given was that it only applied to Christian denominations. The register was a national database of all charities and an important element of accountability. Regulatory oversight through annual monitoring was justified. In consequence, as well as clearing the

37 Full account in Rivers, *op. cit.* n. 1, ch. 5.

38 Cabinet Office Strategy Unit, *Private Action Public Benefit – A Review of Charities and the Wider Not-For-Profit Sector* (Sept. 2002).

ground for new public tests of »beneficial religion«, the Charities Act 2006 has strengthened the regulatory oversight of the Commission over all organized religions.

4. Conclusions

At first sight, these two broad developments appear to be pointing in opposite directions. On the one hand there are new forms of government regulation of religious activity, which might seem to indicate suspicion or lack of trust of religious bodies. Furthermore, some elements of religion (i.e. some forms of Islam) have appeared threatening to public order and security, while religions more generally often run counter to the full range of recent commitments to equality. On the other hand there are new forms of openness and new opportunities for consultation and collaboration. That may simply be a reflection of a modern ambivalence about religion. But it would seem that a deeper ideological change is taking place. The consensus that emerged from the mid-19th century onwards about the proper role of the church (and thus of organized religion more generally) is collapsing. When it collapses, so too does the separation of church and state. Recall that the separation of church and state means the autonomous church in the secular state. It is that distinctive combination which is changing. Historically, Islam has not tended to produce this type of political solution. Thus it is not implausible that the presence and political agency of Muslims in the United Kingdom is a significant cause of its demise.

THE LEGAL STATUS OF MUSLIM COMMUNITIES IN GERMANY – Gernot Sydow

1. Introduction: relevance of the concept of a particular »legal status« under German law

The accommodation of the various aspects of Islamic presence in Germany involves a wide range of issues and policy fields. It cannot be understood by looking at religious politics and the legal status only.[1] State policies do not only regulate Islam in the religious field, but also in many other spheres, for example education, employment, urban planning, halal slaughtering or security. Given the immigrant and social background of the great majority of Muslims in Germany, the major problems relating to their life do not concern their belief as such or their religious needs, but often a poor knowledge of the German language, a lack of higher education and a comparatively high degree of unemployment. The present discussions on integration in Germany and on deficits in this field often focus on Muslims, but not mainly or at least not only on their religion, but on the social status of many Muslims living in Germany. Accordingly, conflicts with the Muslim population will often be cultural rather than religious conflicts.[2] This paper, however, does not deal with immigration and integration, nor does it deal with Muslim communities in Germany in general; instead, it deals with their legal status.

Thus, this paper will focus on a particular concept of German law: a singe legal status which by itself confers a bundle of rights. However, the relevance of this category in German law should not be overestimated.[3] It cannot be equated with the concept of establishment in England and Scotland, and it must certainly not be confused with the Ottoman-style millet system. The fundamental provision of the German law concerning the question of a legal status of religious organisations is a negative one: The German Basic Law affirms that Germany has no state church or established church. The German concept of »*Körperschaft des öffentlichen Rechts*« is open to several Christian and non-Christian religious organisations and does not question the separation between the state and the relevant religious organisation. Furthermore, German law does not know a compul-

1 *M. Maussen*, The Governance of Islam in Western Europe (IMISCOE Working Paper No. 16), 2007, p. 5.

2 *Ch. Waldhoff*, Neue Religionskonflikte und staatliche Neutralität (Gutachten 68. DJT), 2010, p. D 36.

3 Cf. the remarks of J. Rivers that the idea of a legal status is alien to Anglo-American legal cultures: *J. Rivers*, The Legal Status of Muslim Communities in English law (in this volume, see p. 225 et seqq.).

sory system of legal recognition of religious communities. Religious communities have the right of self-organization, and this includes the right to choose the legal form of organization, be it informal and not legally recognized at all, or be it legally formal as an association under the legal provisions on civil associations under the German Civil Code. Religious communities may also, for example, establish religious foundations under private law.[4] On this basis, they become capable of holding and exercising legal rights, of owning property, of employing workers or entering into contractual relations.

But achieving a legal status is not at all compulsory for religious communities or any social community in Germany. A legal status is not a prerequisite for religious practice, for the life of the religious community, or for religious liberty. Germany has no system of compulsory registration, neither for religious communities nor for places of religious worship. Every individual and every group is free in his or her religious belief and practice without any need for registration, without any need for agreement by the state and without any need for a permit. It is only for a limited number of particular rights that a religious community must achieve a particular legal status: The rights to own property, to employ workers or to enter into contractual relations with third parties cannot be exercised by a religious community as such, but only by natural or legal persons. This raises the question of the legal capacity of religious organisations under private law.

Forms of formalized collaboration with the state, e.g. the right to provide chaplaincies in public institutions such as prisons, hospitals, or the armed forces or the right to impose taxes on members of the relevant religious organisation, are limited to religious communities with the status of a corporation under public law (*Körperschaft des öffentlichen Rechts*). The question of the extent to which Muslim communities can be included into this particular concept of the German constitution has not finally been answered so far. But it needs to be answered, both for the religious needs of Muslim communities and for the legitimacy of the law and its concept of *Körperschaft des öffentlichen Rechts*.

2. Muslim communities as representative dialogue partners

I will argue that the German concept of legal status – and in particular the status of a corporation under public law – has consequences for the character of the institutionalisation of Muslim communities in Germany. I will therefore start with a few sociological remarks on the process of institutionalisation of Islam in

4 *M. Rohe*, in: R. Aluffi/G. Zincone (eds.), The Legal Treatment of Islamic Minorities in Europe, 2004, p. 83 (87).

Germany. How do Muslim communities organize themselves, articulate their ideas and interests and become interlocutors and dialogue partners for local and national authorities? This process, the founding of representative Muslim organisations and their recognition as representative, is a crucial question, mainly for two reasons: the traditional structures of Muslim communities and the historical background of Muslim immigration to Germany.

The first point is relatively clear: Unlike the Christian churches, Islam has no tradition of centralized, hierarchical organizations. Islamic communities tend to diversify along a multiplicity of lines. Among the Muslims living in Germany, there is a majority of Sunni-orientated persons, but also an estimated number of 500,000 Alevis mostly from Turkey, and various smaller communities from different cultural, ethnical and regional backgrounds.[5] This paper therefore deals with the legal status of Muslim communities in the plural. We may of course speak of a Muslim community in Germany, comprising some 3.5 million people (in comparison to a total population of 82 million). Due to the fact that prior to 1989 there had been no Muslim immigration to Eastern Germany, the former GDR, the Muslim presence in Germany is still predominantly a phenomenon restricted to Western Germany (including Berlin) and especially to the industrialized areas and bigger cities with few Muslims living in the countryside. To be precise, we should speak of some 3.5 million people with a Muslim background in so far as the majority of these people are immigrants from countries with a predominantly Muslim population. But this Muslim community is not at all homogenous, and the degree of religious activities and identification is difficult to judge. As a result of these traditional structures of Islam, Muslim communities are ill-prepared to respond to the need for a structured representation – I will come back to this point later.

The historical background of Muslim immigration to Germany requires some explanation: The vast majority of Muslims living in Germany is of foreign, mainly Turkish, origin. Islamic life in Germany is predominantly of a Turkish character. Islam in Germany is a »transplanted religion«[6], practiced in a non-Muslim, traditionally Christian and partly secularised context. Islam in Germany is therefore often spoken of in the light of immigration, integration and emancipation. Only in recent years, a growing number of Muslim immigrants have applied for German citizenship so that the Muslim community begins to become a relevant voting factor in national elections.

5 *M. Rohe* (Fn. 4), p. 83 (84).
6 *M. Maussen* (Fn. 1), p. 12.

When a growing number of Muslim workers immigrated to Western Germany in the 1960s and the early 1970s, the notion was that these guest workers were foreigners, not immigrants, and that Germany was not a country of immigration.[7] Most of the migrant workers also believed that their stay in Germany was temporary. The religious needs of this Muslim population were therefore not regarded as a domestic political matter, but as a question of foreign affairs. Since the majority of Muslims had emigrated from Turkey, the assumption was that the Turkish government would provide for the workers' religious needs. For this aim, the Turkish government established a separate branch of the Turkish religious affairs office that monopolizes and controls religious affairs in Turkey. The German branch, DITIB, is still controlled by the Turkish religious affairs office which approves and pays the religious teachers and imams in Germany.[8]

In recent years, alternative Muslim organisations have been founded that either represent non-Turkish Muslims and cross the ethnic border between Turks and other Muslims or that oppose the laicistic ideology of DITIB and its close cooperation with the Turkish government. In sum, various groups claim to represent Muslim interests in Germany today, but in fact no single umbrella organization speaks for the whole Muslim community so far. While mosque committees at the local level were one of the earliest and most wide-spread forms of organisation of Muslim immigrants, the development of suitable institutions at the national level that are widely accepted as representative by a relevant percentage of Muslims and by state organizations still needs to be strengthened. The German government fosters this process with the aim of consolidating the legal status of Muslim institutions and of intensifying the cooperation between the state and the Muslim community for several reasons, including the fear of Muslim communities drifting towards fundamentalism.[9] For this aim, the German Home Minister has founded an Islam Conference as a permanent forum for dialogue between Muslim communities and members of the different branches of government.[10]

One crucial question is the integration of the imams into German society. DITIB imams are bound to return »home« – to Turkey – after five years. In many cases, they will therefore have a weak knowledge of German and a poor understanding of the German society. Partly in order to counter this situation, several German universities have begun to set up Islamic studies in recent years, mainly in order to train imams and teachers for Muslim religious instruction in the

7 *J. S. Fetzer/J. Ch. Soper*, Muslims and the State in Britain, France, and Germany, 2005, p. 100.

8 *J. S. Fetzer/J. Ch. Soper* (Fn. 7), p. 103.

9 *M. Maussen* (Fn. 1), p. 31.

10 For details cf. *N. O. Oermann*, in: M. Haedrich (ed.), Muslime im säkularen Staat, 2009, p. 11.

schools. These initiatives had been proposed by a renowned national academic institution (*Wissenschaftsrat*) and seem to be widely accepted in the political sphere – not least because of the fact that the students live in Germany, that they are (or become) acquainted to German culture and that the courses are taught in German.

3. Legal status and legal capacity of Muslim organisations in Germany

Dealing with the legal capacity of Muslim organisations involves a shift in the perspective: Having dealt with Muslim communities in Germany from a more sociological perspective, the following part will now focus on legal questions. This requires a change in the terminology: While Muslim *communities* was the adequate subject in the first part of this paper, questions of legal capacity can better be discussed with regard to *organisations* that emerge from the process of institutionalisation of Islam in Germany.

(a) Freedom of religion of Muslims and Muslim organisations

First of all, there is no doubt that Muslims in Germany are protected by art. 4 of the German Basic Law, the article that guarantees freedom of religion[11]. According to the unanimous judicial and academic opinion, freedom of religion is not restricted to established religions such as Christianity or Judaism, but also applies to Islam. In fact, the protection of minorities is the core aim of any protection of freedom of religion. Art. 4 of the German Basic Law recognizes that everyone has the right to manifest a religion or belief in worship, practice and observance. The Basic Law does not only protect the person's right to believe, but also his or her right to put the religious beliefs into practice.[12] Art. 4 is not limited to private religious conviction but also includes, for example, the right of Muslim pupils to wear the Muslim headscarf at school.

With the focus on Muslim communities and organisations rather than on Muslim individuals, the question is whether these guarantees also apply to Muslim organisations as such rather than to Muslim individuals only. The traditional view of the European Court of Human Rights was that freedom of religion is so deeply linked to personal beliefs that only human beings can claim protection by article 9 of the Convention. However, this understanding seems to be too narrow,

11 *S. Muckel/R. Tillmanns*, in: S. Muckel (ed.), Der Islam im öffentlichen Recht des säkularen Verfassungsstaates, 2008, p. 234.

12 See, for example, *A. von Ungern-Sternberg*, Religionsfreiheit in Europa, 2008, p. 222.

and the scope of religious freedom cannot be limited to private religious convictions. For religious communities traditionally and universally exist in the form of organised structures. As the European Court of Human Rights recognizes today, the autonomous existence of religious communities is therefore an issue that lies at the very heart of the protection which Article 9 of the Convention affords.[13] Under German law, associations with religious objects have always been regarded as being capable of exercising the rights under Article 4 of the German Basic Law.

The establishment of mosques or the right to engage in ritual slaughter, for example, are questions of article 4, and they are to be discussed independently of the legal status that the relevant Muslim community may or may not have. For example, due to the constitutional guarantees of religious freedom, the construction of places of worship is privileged under German law, especially urban planning law. Mosques do exist in Germany in various forms, from simple prayer halls to fully-fledged mosques. There are more than 2,000 mosques in Germany, often as centres of networks of migrant organisations. Newly built mosques, and their minarets in particular, can be regarded as symbols of permanent Islamic presence. From the point of view of an immigrant Muslim population, mosques do not only serve as a place of religious worship, but may be a part of the country of origin, a place of communal identity. One example is the new mosque built in Cologne in 2010/2011 by DITIB, the above-mentioned German branch of the Turkish religious affairs office, in collaboration with a German architect who is famous for his various church buildings. The impressive architecture of this mosque and especially the height of its dome and minarets have evoked controversial discussions not only in Cologne.

But judicial procedures on the question of whether the construction of minarets is to be permitted and which height would be acceptable are rare.[14] Constraints for the building of mosques may of course result out of policy concerns other than religion, for example urban planning, health and safety, especially fire regulations, hygiene and parking facilities, or questions of mosque design and prevailing standards of architecture.[15] These constraints may result in a refusal to grant building permits for mosque buildings, but these questions are all independent of any legal status and of the religious character of the building in question. In Cologne, for example, the local government, including the mayor, clearly supported the building of the new mosque and defended the right of Muslims to construct their own places of worship.

13 *G. Sydow*, JZ 2009, p. 1141.
14 *M. Rohe* (Fn. 4), p. 83 (88).
15 *M. Maussen* (Fn. 1), p. 13.

(b) Recognition of religious associations as corporations under public law

The concept of »status« in the sense of a bundle of rights on grounds of that particular status thus has a limited significance under German law, being limited to the concept of *Körperschaften des öffentlichen Rechts*. This concept can only be understood with a special cultural, historical and legal background: the churches and the state interact through dialogue and cooperation in the secular legal order under the German Basic Law. The traditional relationship between the state and the Churches is often characterized as »positive neutrality«: As a legacy left by the German history of state-church relations, the German Basic Law establishes a separation between church and state institutions, but at the same time secures various forms of cooperation. This cooperation is not compulsory but optional[16]: the state offers to cooperate, and the religious organisations may decide independently to accept this offer and to enter into a closer cooperation with the state – or to remain apart. This choice does not affect the guarantees of freedom of religion that are guaranteed to every individual and to religious organisations independently of their legal status. It is therefore doubtful whether Germany really corresponds to a »state corporatist polity model in which individuals are incorporated via corporative intermediate units«[17].

Religious organisations may be recognized as corporations under public law if they fulfil a number of basic requirements. This status as public corporations does not integrate the religious organisation into state organisations nor does it establish a state church. This status does not question the separation and autonomy of the religious organisation which is and remains a separation »at the root« (»*Scheidung in der Wurzel*«). As a natural consequence of this separation, the state guarantees autonomy of religious organisations. The status provides a number of rights, for example the right to nominate members to broadcast councils. A religious public corporation is in particular entitled to impose a tax on its members that is collected by the government's tax agencies. Furthermore, this status grants reductions or exemptions from taxes and public fees.[18] Achieving this status can also be understood as a symbolic affirmation of the relevance of a particular group by the state. The status as a religious public corporation is therefore generally regarded as attractive by religious organisations.

Far reaching rights require clear organisational structures und transparent procedures for decision-making, including a reliable body for decision-making. While there seems to be a broad consensus on this assumption *in abstracto*, the

16 *Ch. Waldhoff* (Fn. 2), p. D 57.
17 *M. Maussen* (Fn. 1), p. 49.
18 For details *Ch. Walter*, Religionsverfassungsrecht, 2006, p. 550.

crucial question is what the exact requirements that have to be fulfilled for recognition as a public corporation are and whether Muslim organisations can meet these requirements. Religious organisations that previously had this status under the German constitution of 1919 are also recognized as public corporations today – in particular the Roman-Catholic and the Protestant churches. Other religious communities shall be granted the same rights upon application if their constitution and the number of their members warrant for their permanency. A clear constitutional framework and a concept of membership are therefore basic requirements for the status as a public corporation.

In the German federal system, the decision to grant the status of a public corporation will be taken by the government of the relevant German *Land*. The procedure generally requires that the religious organisation has existed for at least thirty years and that its members comprise at least zero point one per cent of the total population of the German *Land* in question. The religious organization applying for this status has to ensure that transparent procedures for decision making and that a reliable body or bodies which authoritatively decide about doctrine and order are in place.[19] While various Christian and Jewish organisations have received this status in one or more *Länder*, no Muslim group has yet been granted this status. Their applications have been rejected, ordinarily because of insufficient or unclear numbers of members or because of the absence of any natural person as a member in the case of various Muslim umbrella organisations – a situation that can be perceived as unequal treatment while other commentators argue that this does not contradict the notion of religious neutrality as long as the status remains open to other, non-Christian organisations.[20] However, it cannot be denied that the structure of Christian churches was the model for this concept.

4. Future developments: creating a new legal status for religious communities?

Muslims are religious newcomers. They can reasonably argue that the state should accommodate their religious needs in the same way as the state does in regard to the Christian churches. Generally speaking, this is no problem with respect to the exercise of freedom of religion and the legal capacity of Muslim organisations under private law. But it is a problem with respect to the status of *Körperschaft des öffentlichen Rechts* and the single entry point to the bundle of rights related to this status. The requirements – clear definitions of membership,

19 *W. Hennig*, Muslimische Gemeinschaften im Religionsverfassungsrecht, 2010, p. 101.
20 *Ch. Waldhoff* (Fn. 2), p. D 80.

procedures for decision making and bodies which authentically decide about doctrine and order – are easily met by the churches, but difficult to fulfil by Muslim communities due to their traditional structures. While it is relatively clear that no Muslim organisation meets the requirements to become a *Körperschaft des öffentlichen Rechts* at present, there is no consensus at all on how the German legal order should react to this situation. No doubt equality is a fundamental and indispensable concept of the German Basic Law – in general and with respect to religious communities. But what are the consequences of this concept?

One possible answer could be that the law may remain unchanged. The attractiveness of the status as a *Körperschaft des öffentlichen Rechts* could then force Muslim communities to assimilate to the model of Christian churches: a process of »churchification« (*Verkirchlichung*) in so far as it assimilates the structures – not the doctrine, of course – of Muslim organisations to the structures of the Christian churches. Certainly, Muslim organisations are under no legal obligation in this respect, but the attractiveness of the status as public corporations gives strong incentives to build up structures similar to the churches. If a Muslim organisation fulfils the requirements one day, it will certainly be entitled to the same rights as the churches. Otherwise, Muslim communities will remain organisations under private law only. The question would then be in how far the law can channel the ongoing process of institutionalization of Islam without violating the fundamental principles of religious freedom and autonomy.

Other commentators state that the law must react to the present situation: either in the way that the requirements to be granted the status of *Körperschaft des öffentlichen Rechts* have to be altered and relaxed, or in the way that a new legal status should be created. This new legal status would be open in particular for Muslim communities that do not fulfil the prerequisites for *Körperschaften des öffentlichen Rechts*, but should nevertheless include the opportunity to register in a particular form as a religious community. A model could be the »*Bekenntnisgemeinschaft*« in Austrian law. This would add a third organisational model: legal capacity under private law, corporation under public law and – somewhere in between – a new, particular status as a religious community. However, *Christian Waldhoff*, a professor of public law at the University of Bonn who has recently proposed this model, concedes that this new status would mainly be of symbolic character.[21]

21 *Ch. Waldhoff* (Fn. 2), p. D 89.

Contributors to this Volume

Peter Cumper (Leicester) – Senior Lecturer, University of Leicester

Peter Edge (Oxford) – Professor of Law, Oxford Brookes University

Lars Friedner (Uppsala) – Secretary General, Church of Sweden

Michael Germann (Halle-Wittenberg) – Professor of Public and Canon Law, Martin-Luther-Universität Halle-Wittenberg

Mark Hill QC (Cardiff) – Honorary Professor of Law, University of Cardiff

Ian Leigh (Durham) – Professor of Law, Durham University

Katharina Pabel (Linz) – Professor of Public Law, Johannes Kepler-Universität Linz

Augur Pearce (Cardiff) – Researcher, University of Cardiff

Julian Rivers (Bristol) – Professor of Jurisprudence, University of Bristol

Gernot Sydow (Limburg/Freiburg) – Extraordinary Professor, Universität Freiburg; Legal Adviser, Diocese Limburg

Lucy Vickers (Oxford) – Professor of Law, Oxford Brookes University

Antje von Ungern-Sternberg (Munich) – Senior Research Fellow, Ludwig-Maximilians-Universität München

Christian Walter (Munich) – Professor of Public and Public International Law, Ludwig-Maximilians-Universität München

Hinnerk Wißmann (Bayreuth) – Professor of Public Law, Universität Bayreuth